D1326341

THE NEW
MAIOLICA

Contemporary approaches to colour
and technique

MATTHIAS OSTERMANN

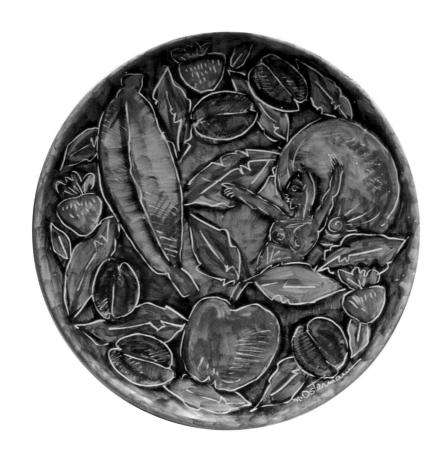

A & C Black • London
University of Pennsylvania Press • Philadelphia

First published in Great Britain 1999
A & C Black (Publishers) Limited
35 Bedford Row, London WC1R 4JH

ISBN 0-7136-4878-3

CIP catalogue record for this book is available from the British Library.

Copyright © 1999 Matthias Ostermann

Published simultaneously in the USA by
University of Pennsylvania Press
4200 Pine Street
Philadelphia, Pennsylvania 19104-4011

ISBN 0-8122-3513-4

Library of Congress Cataloging-in-Publication data
Ostermann, Matthias.
      The new maiolica: contemporary approaches to colour and technique
   / Matthias Ostermann.
          p.   cm.
      Includes bibliographical references and index.
      ISBN 0-8122-3513-4 (alk. paper)
      1. Glazes. 2. Pottery craft. 3. Majolica.   I. Title.
   TT922.088 1999
   738. 1′44--dc21   99-20674
                                                                     CIP

Cover illustrations
Front Tile detail: Dry-blended colours on tin-glaze, by Matthias Ostermann
Back Tile: Trailed saturated coloured maiolica glaze, by Matthias Ostermann

Frontispiece Platter: 'Devil in the Fruit', by Matthias Ostermann
Cover and frontispiece photographs by Jan Thijs

Cover design by Dorothy Moir

Design by Sharyn Troughton

Printed and bound in Singapore by Tien Wah Press Ltd.

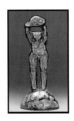

Contents

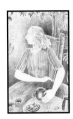

Acknowledgements

A book of this nature is above all a work of collaboration. It would not have been possible without the extensive involvement and contributions of many people, both in and outside the ceramic professions.

First and foremost I would like to thank writer and editor, Sean McCutcheon, and photographer Jan Thijs, both of Montreal. Unless explicitly credited otherwise, all the photographs in Chapters Two, Three, Four, Five, Six, and Eight are Jan's. Without these two most important collaborators this book would not have been possible. Special thanks also go to Alan Caiger-Smith in England, for his foreword, and his long-standing encouragement and support of my work.

My heartfelt thanks to the following ceramists: Linda Arbuckle, in Florida, for providing so many of my American contacts; Karen Burk, of the New Brunswick College of Art and Design, for giving me the first push towards this book; Daphne Carnegy and Emmanuel Cooper in London for advice, contacts and encouragement. For contact addresses, thanks to: Richard Zakin in Oswego, New York; Janet Mansfield in Sydney, Australia; Karl Fulle and Evelyn Klam in Berlin; Roser Fornells Oliver in Barcelona; Antonio Vivas in Madrid; Eduard Hermans and Bernard Asselbergs of the Rietveld Akademie in Amsterdam; Georgina Fine in Moustiers-Sainte-Marie, France; Thomas Stimm in Austria; Fritz Vehring in Bremen; Paul Mathieu in Vancouver; Farraday Sredl in Phoenix, Arizona; Yvonne Hutchinson-Cuff in Perth, Australia; and, finally, Daniel Kruger in Munich.

I would like to thank especially Jean-Paul van Lith and his wife Rose-Anne in Biot, France, for their contacts and wonderful introduction to Provençal ceramics and wine.

For further contacts and information, thanks go to Robert Rustermier in Rhode Island, Ina Brekelmans in Amsterdam, Alberto Bertelli in Rome, Umberto Cirrito in Montreal, Professore Gian-Carlo Bojani of the Museo Internazionale delle Ceramiche di Faenza, and very special thanks to Pieter-Jan Tichelaar in Makkum, Holland, for a memorable day spent among old tiles and wonderful pots.

For technical information, thanks to Paul Green-Armytage of Curtin University in Perth, Australia; Bruce Cochrane in Mississauga, Ontario; Eric Wong in Brampton, Ontario; and Frank Tucker of Tucker's Pottery Supplies in Toronto. Very special thanks go to ceramist Ron Roy of Scarborough, Ontario for his in-depth (out of my depth) glaze information in this book's appendix.

For proofreading and advice, thanks to the following artists and ceramists: Gabriele Schnitzenbaumer in Munich; Royce and Trudi McGlashen in New Zealand; and Roswitha Wulff in Sydney, Australia. Special thanks go as well to Timothy Wilson of the Ashmolean Museum in Oxford, England, for his kind corrections of this book's historical chapter.

The following persons and organisations have been generous in providing both information and imagery: Christie's Images in London; Galerie Ra in Amsterdam; Renate Wunderle of Galerie B-15 in Munich; Suzann Greenaway of Prime Gallery in Toronto; The Fine Arts Society in London; Koninklijke Tichelaar in Makkum, the Netherlands; Sue Jeffries and Meredith Chilton of The George R. Gardiner Museum of Ceramic Art in Toronto; Le Musée des beaux-arts in Montreal; The Offices of Instructional Resources at the University of Florida.

Thanks to all of the artists who contributed imagery to this book, and to those whose imagery I was unable to use.

For helpful production advice, thanks to Linda Lambert, my editor at A & C Black, and to James Forest of Copies Ressources in Montreal.

To Margaret Brügger in Munich, thanks for moral and financial support.

Special thanks are due to the Canada Council for the Arts and Le Conseil des Arts et des Lettres du Québec. The research for this book would not have been possible without their generous financial assistance.

To my mother Lila Ostermann, thanks for unflagging support and encouragement in all my endeavours.

This book is dedicated to the loving memory of my friend and mentor Isolde Rest.

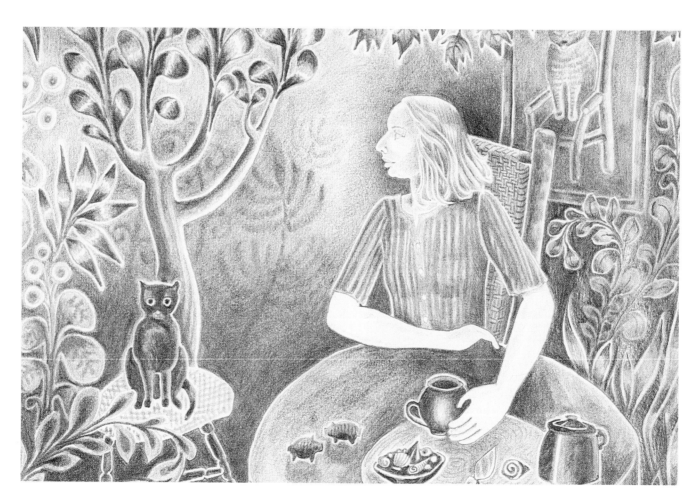

Portrait of Isolde Rest, 1978

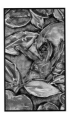

Foreword

This book is both a guide and an exploration. Explorers set their minds on reaching new and unknown places, but to make a good beginning they need a guide's intimate knowledge of the preliminary foothills and passes. With his insight into the maiolica of other ages, Matthias Ostermann can guide us expertly past the initial blind valleys and lead us to vantage points from which we can make new discoveries for ourselves. He combines the experience of a guide with the vision of an explorer; knowing what has already been done, he sees also what might come to be, and he shares the journey with us stage by stage.

Though history lies outside the scope of his book, Matthias is well aware of it. We do not begin our work as blank sheets: we are supported by methods and knowledge handed down by those who went before us – by some kind of living tradition. Traditions are not necessarily conservative: they can provide the ground for innovations which in turn shape the knowledge handed down to succeeding generations.

Maiolica techniques have always been a blend of tradition and innovation. To take just one example, the highly original *faïences fauves* of Matisse, Derain, Vlaminck, and Rouault, were made possible, in the early years of this century, by the evolution of glazes, pigments, and kilns for conventional tableware during the preceding hundred years. Without that traditional backing, the exhilarating works of these artists would not be with us today.

People of many times and places have contributed to the maiolica heritage. The white glaze was first devised a thousand years ago in an attempt to imitate Chinese porcelain. Those early potters discovered that it could be decorated in colours in ways that porcelain could not, and we today are still following up the consequences of that innovation. In Persia, the white tin glaze was used almost exclusively for reduction lustre and minai enamels – two other far-reaching innovations. The green and brown pottery of the western Mediterranean was mostly painted directly on the clay and covered with a semi-opaque tin glaze which let the colour fuse through from below, an innovation which transformed the older tradition of unglazed imagery. Italian *maiolicari*, vastly extending the palette, established the custom of painting and over-painting on the surface of the powdery glaze, using tones of colour to indicate modelling and perspective depth. They developed figurative imagery to a degree never matched before, and seldom since. The blue and white delftware of the Low Countries, inspired by the newly imported Chinese porcelain, applied these techniques to produce European forms and images that were soon being used as models by the Chinese themselves. In such ways, new vision continually regenerates established techniques. That, in a 20th-century context, is the purpose of this book.

In a sense this book began with a letter Matthias wrote to me around 1978 – a 'How do you do it?' letter, as he called it, for he was full of ideas, but did not know how to put them into effect. By luck, I was about to visit Canada to give workshops and lectures. We met, and I stayed with him on Ward's Island, in Toronto, delving into ideas and technology, answering questions and leaving some unanswered. Matthias has long since assimilated all he needed from what I had to offer, and taken it into realms I never dreamed of. Those discussions gave me the strange feeling of being part of an age-old process, seeing my knowledge regenerated by his new vision.

Tin-glaze maiolica has no body of technical literature to equal that of stoneware and porcelain, but it does possess one of the most precious books of all ceramic history - *The Three Books of the Potter's Art*, written in Casteldurante by the Cavaliere Cipriano Piccolpasso in 1557, and illustrated with detailed drawings of equipment and of potters carrying out the various stages of their work. Piccolpasso expressed the hope that, through his book, the art of maiolica would reach beyond the traditional artisan workshop and be exposed to 'lofty spirits and speculative minds'.

Matthias understands very well that technique in isolation is a blind alley; it evolves only by giving expression to new ideas, new experience. The concept and the means work together. In passing on his vision, he might well cite Piccolpasso's own generous saying: 'It is better that many should know a good thing than that a few should keep it hidden.'

Alan Caiger-Smith.

Shalford, April 1998

CIPRIANO PICCOLPASSO, DRAWING, THE FIRING OF THE KILN
From *The Three Books of the Potter's Art*, 1557.
Courtesy of the Board of Trustees of the Victoria and Albert Museum

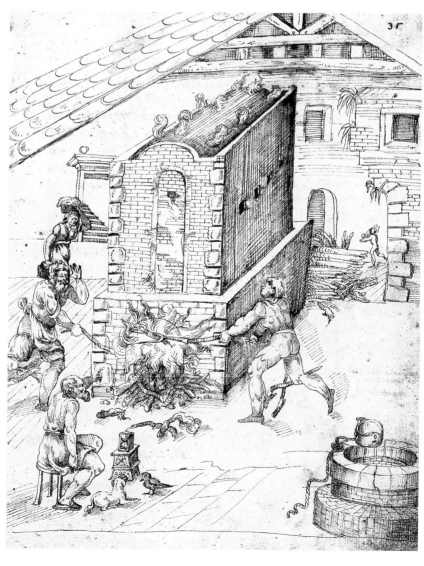

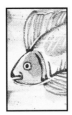

Introduction

The purpose of this book is to give the ceramist, both student and professional, an insight into the great variety of techniques to be explored within the medium of tin glaze. I hope, as well, to present as broad a spectrum as possible of contemporary maiolica expression. Though I focus on low-fire tin glaze, anyone with an interest in decoration could use these techniques at other temperatures – with minor modifications and different results.

Being slightly intimidated by technology (I have yet to drive a car, for instance) I am a kitchen-sink, hit-or-miss potter. Yet despite this, one way or another, in my own way and time, I have managed to solve technical problems in the studio. These pages provide practical approaches, based on my own experiences, to image-making and problem solving. These, I hope, will not only be useful, but will also stimulate the reader's creativity.

Some people grow up with a clear idea of what they want to do in life and, guided by appropriate education and training, move directly into their chosen profession. My involvement with ceramics, and particularly with maiolica, came about in a more roundabout way. After an injury obliged me to abandon hopes of a career as a modern dancer, I began to play with clay in a therapeutic way. I found, in time, that my involvement with pottery went far beyond therapy. There was something intriguing about the necessity of mastering the diverse skills of the potter: throwing, decorating and firing. There was a kind of mental balance involved as well: when my mind and ego

became too lofty, the daily banal mud-slinging work would bring me right back to earth.

I learned basic throwing and general studio skills during three years in Toronto as an informal apprentice and friend to Isolde Rest, a German-born and -trained potter. Her legacy to me was not just one of skills, but also a model lifestyle in which living and working are well integrated. In 1973, I was on my way to England, attracted by the prevailing Anglo-Oriental stoneware aesthetic, when I was waylaid in Ireland, seduced by its music and glorious countryside. By lucky chance, I got a job for a year as a full-time thrower at Shanagarry Pottery in County Cork. The workers there were divided in a traditional way, into throwers and glazers, both of whom executed work designed by the pottery's owner-founder. All work – throwing, trimming, and handling – was done in sets of six dozen pieces. By the time my year was up, I had become fluent at throwing but not, as yet, at glazing, decorating, or firing. More importantly, I was not yet sure whether my vocation was to be a potter. I headed on to England, and was fortunate to be introduced to Bernard Leach in St Ives. He gave me an afternoon of his time. Memorable, and decisive for me, was part of our conversation. He asked how many years I had been working in clay, and what were my intentions.

'Four years', I replied, 'and I'm not sure what I intend to do'.

'Why don't you give it another four years', he said 'and then see how you feel'.

That conversation made it clear to me that becoming a potter, like any other profession, required years of training and serious commitment. I returned to Toronto and, late in 1974, started my own modest studio. For a number of years I produced simple, decorated domestic stoneware. Though I felt somewhat on the margins of the ceramic mainstream, which was characterised by high-fired reduction glaze such as celadon or

temmokku, I continued working in oxidation with electricity.

In 1978, a grant from the Canada Council for the Arts financed a study tour of China, Korea and Japan. To my surprise, I found that some of the work I was most attracted to, such as the Tz'u-chou wares of the Chinese Sung dynasty, had deliberately favoured an oxidating atmosphere in firing. The results – the warm, creamy whites, with crisp, contrasting decoration – confirmed

CORTONA, ITALY, 1981

Photograph: Matthias Ostermann

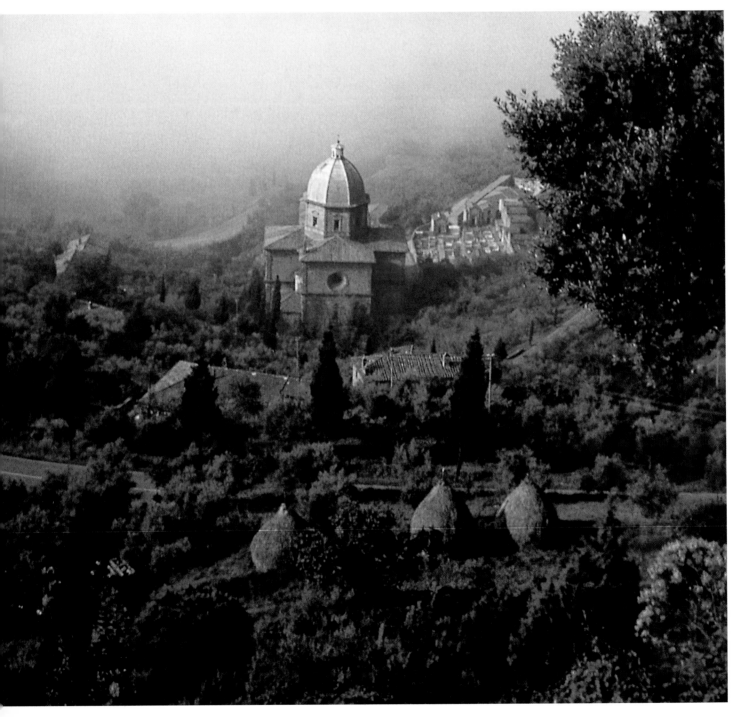

oxidation as my preferred firing medium. Though I continued to work in stoneware on returning to Canada, I began to grow frustrated with its limited colour palette. My desire to draw and paint was leading me to explore the rich colours of low-fire maiolica.

In 1981 another grant from the Canada Council sent me to Cortona, Italy, as a participant in the University of Georgia's study-abroad programme. I travelled widely, visiting traditional potteries in Deruta, Faenza and Gubbio, enjoying good Tuscan food and wine, and feeling increasingly at home in a place, and a ceramic culture, that embraces narrative and colour with gusto. Upon my return to Toronto, despite the prevailing prejudice against the use of any kind of earthenware, I was firmly committed to maiolica.

Maiolica, I believe, is a painter's medium in its own right. With its inherent and unique qualities of colour and surface luminosity, it is a versatile, demanding, frustrating and compelling medium.

Notes on terminology

The meanings of words change from place to place, and over time. When I first moved to Montreal, for example, I was confused at mealtimes. In France, breakfast is called *petit déjeuner*, lunch *déjeuner*, and supper *dîner*. But in Quebec, breakfast is *déjeuner*, lunch *dîner*, and supper *souper*. A Parisian in Montreal would do well to learn the local terminology if he does not want to be served croissants for lunch.

Similarly, the word *maiolica* has been used, and is used, to mean different things.

From the art-historian's point of view, and that of most established European practitioners, *maiolica* (or, in French, *majolique* or *maïolique*) refers primarily to tin-glazed earthenware made before and up to the 17th century, and made in the stylistic tradition of the Italian Renaissance.

Almost all North Americans (myself included), Australians, and some British tin-glaze practitioners use the word *maiolica* to designate both the technique of in-glaze painting on tin-glazed earthenware, and the resulting wares.

In North America the word is sometimes spelled 'majolica'. I feel that the latter term should be restricted to designate the range of earthenware developed in England by the Minton pottery in the 1840s. Though visually related to maiolica, this work is not true tin glaze.

In continental Europe, notably in France and Germany, tin glaze is called *faïence* or *fayence*. In the south of France, in the old production centre of Moustiers-Sainte-Marie, the tin-glaze practitioner is still known as a *faïencier*.

I have also heard the medium of earthenware in general described as *faïence* in France. In Quebec, this term can simply describe either earthenware technique or any earthenware clay body. (In Quebec, tin glaze is referred to specifically as *majolique*.)

The use of the term *tin glaze* in a contemporary context can be misleading, since most ceramists have replaced expensive tin oxide as the opacifier in the glaze with more reasonably priced, and equally effective, zirconium silicate. I cannot write or talk enthusiastically about 'contemporary trends in the use of zircon-opacified glazes'. In this book, aimed at English-speaking readers, I use the terms *maiolica* and *tin glaze* interchangeably to refer both to the techniques and to the products of low-fired, tin- or zircon-opacified glazed earthenware.

How the book is organised

Chapter One sketches the history of maiolica. **Chapter Two** discusses the aesthetics and planning concepts that inform any work. **Chapter Three** deals with materials, glazing and firing. **Chapter Four** discusses theory of how colour is perceived, and the practical steps of mixing and testing by which a colour palette is developed. **Chapter Five** discusses brushes and brushwork. **Chapter Six**, 'The Painted Fish' illustrates a full range of surface-decoration techniques, using images I have prepared specially for this book. **Chapter Seven** shows the work of other contemporary tin-glaze practitioners from around the world. **Chapter Eight** tackles typical problems encountered in tin-glaze production, and suggests solutions. The book ends with food for historical, technical and philosophical thought in the form of a list of recommended reading

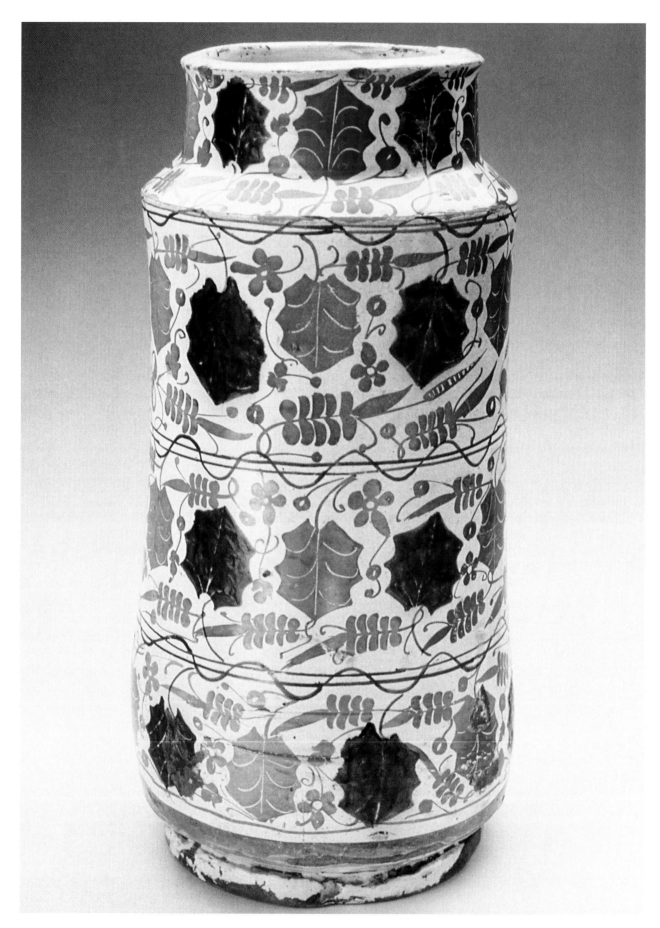

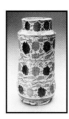

A Brief History of Maiolica

MUSEUM VASE

It contains nothing.
We ask it
To contain nothing.

Having transcended use
It is endlessly
Content to be.

Still it broods
On old burdens -
Wheat, oil, wine

ROBERT FRANCIS

The history of tin glaze spans more than a thousand years. The evolution of maiolica, and what different cultures have expressed through this medium, make a complex and fascinating study. What follows is a brief sketch. (For the full historical picture, I highly recommend the works of Alan Caiger-Smith, Daphne Carnegy and Timothy Wilson.)

Tin-glazed wares originated in 9th century Mesopotamia (present-day Iraq), most likely from a desire to imitate the white T'ang Chinese wares that had been carried across the trade routes and found such favour at the Middle Eastern courts. Since the techniques of porcelain clays and high-

HISPANO-MORESQUE DRUG JAR, h. 38 CM, MANISES, C.1450–1500.

Tin glaze with incised cobalt and gold lustre.
Courtesy of Le Musée des beaux-arts de Montréal

temperature firing were then unknown in Mesopotamia, Islamic potters created a semblance of the white surface by opacifying their transparent alkaline glazes with tin oxide, effectively masking the buff-coloured earthenware clay body. Seduced by the white surface, artisans began to decorate it with oxides. In time, distinctive patterns emerged, becoming more sophisticated and changing with shifts of locale, patronage and prevailing taste. The other important development was that of the use of reduced-pigment lustres on tin glaze in a third firing, a carry-over from pre-Islamic Egyptian glassware.

With the spread of Islam through North Africa and into the Iberian peninsula, lustreware and in-glaze painting techniques – on-surface decoration that fuses into the glaze in the second firing – became well established in Spain, possibly as early as the 11th century. Throughout the 13th century these Hispano-Moresque wares, produced in such important centres as Malaga and, later, Manises (Valencia) gave visual evidence, both in technique and iconography, of the successful fusion of eastern and western cultures. (See picture opposite.)

During the 14th and 15th centuries the Moresque lustrewares found an active market in Italy via such trading ports as Majorca. The term *maiolica* by which such wares are now known may come from the name Majorca; it may also derive from the Spanish phrase – *obra de Málequa* – applied to work produced at the famous potteries of Malaga.

Until the mid-16th century *maiolica* referred exclusively to lustrewares of Spanish and Islamic

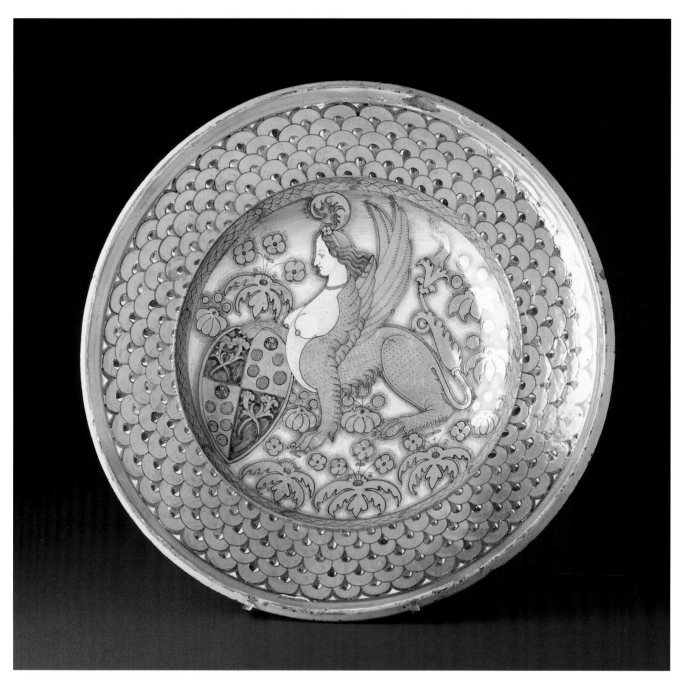

CHARGER, d. 43 CM, DERUTA, ITALY, C. 1520.

Tin glaze with cobalt and gold lustre.

Courtesy of The George R. Gardiner Museum
of Ceramic Art, Toronto

origin. By the second half of the 16th century the term was being used in Italy to refer to tin-glaze wares being made there. These, usually in the form of dishes, large chargers, and *albarello* jars, were valued as both useful and decorative objects. (See above.) Often the image side of the piece consisted of a poor tin glaze, highly deco-

rated, and then enriched with a thin lead-glaze *coperta* (covering), to give brilliance of colour, and gloss. The backs were sometimes just glazed with transparent lead glaze.

Italian maiolica and lustreware, although initially heavily influenced by the Moresque wares, developed a distinct visual style characterised by complex, painted narratives. The themes were drawn from allegorical, classical and Biblical sources, and expressed the humanistic values of the Renaissance, and its fascination with the past. This was one of the rare moments in history when

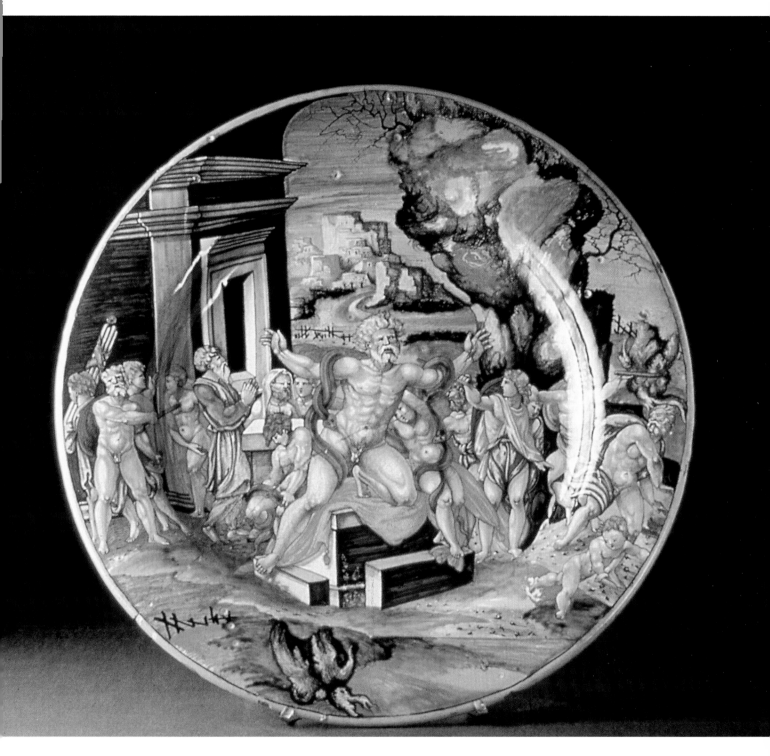

PLATE: 'LAOCOON AND HIS SONS', d. 43 CM, URBINO, ITALY, C. 1535-1540.

Tin-glazed earthenware.

Courtesy of The George R. Gardiner Museum of Ceramic Art, Toronto

ceramics – notably the highly elaborate paintings of the *istoriato* wares of the *cinquecento* – were ele-vated to the realm of fine art. (See above.) The works of such 15th-century artists as Martin Schongauer and Albrecht Dürer often served as stylistic and thematic models for these wares.

By the mid-1500s, maiolica was spreading to France, and to central Europe. As techniques changed, in some places the *coperta* was replaced by the all-in-one tin glaze. This favoured the sim-

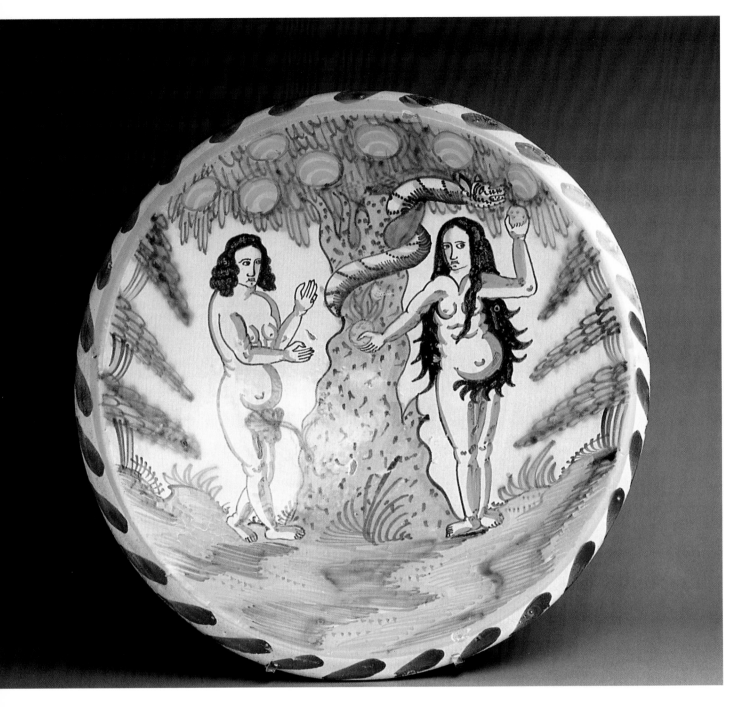

pler process of in-glaze painting. These kinds of wares came to be known as *faïence*, from the name of the city of Faenza, in Italy – the near-dominant producer and exporter of fine tableware in the later 16th century.

As maiolica production spread, each part of Europe produced stylistic innovations. Antwerp, in Flanders, became an important tin-glaze production centre, and from here tin glaze found its way to Holland and England in the late 1500s. In the Netherlands, the passion for Chinese blue-

CHARGER: 'ADAM AND EVE', d. 45.5 CM, LAMBETH, ENGLAND, C. 1685.

Tin-glazed earthenware.

Courtesy of The George R. Gardiner Museum of Ceramic Art, Toronto

and-white porcelain imported by Dutch traders led to the immensely popular imitative blue-and-white delftware (named after the Dutch city of Delft). (See photograph on p. 21.) Both in Holland and later in England, delftware became the general appellation for tin glaze. In sea-faring Portugal,

16

which already had a long-standing affinity with tin glaze through its historical Moorish connections, the Chinese and Delft blue-and-white influence made itself felt, particularly in the realm of architectural wall tiles. In England, London, Bristol and Liverpool became active production centres, exploiting tin from Cornwall, Europe's major source (see picture opposite).

Around 1800, the traditional European *faïence* potteries were supplanted by the new and thriving industrialised porcelain factories such as Wedgwood in England. Using the newly-discovered European porcelain clays – hitherto only found in China – and more sophisticated casting and production techniques, these factories catered to a broad and growing market. New popular attitudes and tastes, allied to mass production, changed the face of European ceramics. However, in the mid-18th century, notably in southern Europe, traditional tin glaze was still in demand, and local production continued alongside porcelain, though at a lower level in the market. In such places as Gubbio and Deruta in Italy, traditional maiolica is still being produced.

The Arts and Crafts Movement in England in the 1880s, led by artists and critics such as William Morris and John Ruskin, was a rebellion against the massive proliferation of impersonal, machine-made objects. Their purifying ideals – re-establishing direct links between maker and user, and rehumanizing the applied arts – stimulated a revival of handcrafts. This did not always entail a total rejection of industrial process. The great Catalonian architect Antonio Gaudí, for instance, encouraged numerous potters, sculptors and blacksmiths, and, by incorporating their works into his structures, managed to integrate handcraft with industry.

For the contemporary ceramic maker, times and social structures have changed. Not always willing to have his or her skills absorbed by industry, and unable to return to the traditional role of village potter working in a communal context, the ceramist has established a new working context: that of the individual studio-potter. Since the beginning of the 20th century, most ceramic makers have fitted into this category.

For the first half of the 20th century, the prevailing ceramic aesthetic in northern Europe and the English-speaking world revolved around high-fired stoneware and porcelain. Dominant in England, and exported from there to other English-speaking countries, was the aesthetic imported from Japan by Bernard Leach and Shoji Hamada in the 1920s. Its concepts of visual harmony were founded on integrating truth to materials with simple hand-making processes. Another important influence in continental northern Europe was the Bauhaus school, with its industry-influenced ideal of form following function. Neither of these ideologies left much room for any development in tin glaze, with its inherent – and possibly frivolous – affinity for colourful surface treatments and narrative. Change came after the 1950s for a number of reasons: a reaction against austerity; a *rapprochement*, in vision and venue, between the fine and the applied arts; and a desire for more eclectic expression that included more colour and narrative. By the 1980s, colourful earthenware in all possible contexts had made a major comeback. It can now be found alongside stoneware and porcelain. Maiolica, once again, is thriving.

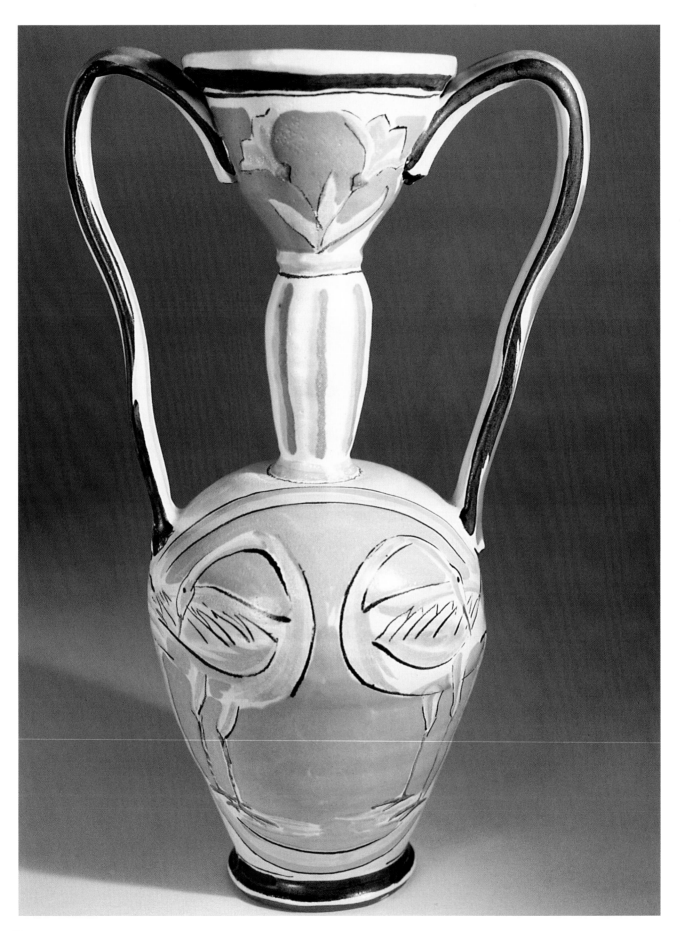

Object and Image

'The best way to impart character and personality to pots is to turn your attention to other matters; to make them with as much concentration as you are capable of, to enlarge your skill over as wide a range as possible, to get to know your materials by living with them, trying to understand them, and finding out little by little – not with your head but with your body – how they want to be treated; in fact, to treat them with proper respect as we would a friend. Then, nothing can stop your personality from appearing in your pots. They will be as individual and unmistakable as your handwriting. But the handwriting has to be legible; if it isn't, the message – the meaning – will not be communicated.'

MICHAEL CARDEW

Our impulse to make and to build, to draw and to decorate, like our need to express ourselves in dance and in music, is old and universal. Most children will draw without inhibition or analysis, interpreting the world as they perceive it. The urge is strong enough in some of us to make us artists. We painters, sculptors, illustrators and potters, whether simply making useful objects or striving to convey a message, are expressing, in our chosen medium, a particular vision of the world.

Almost everybody is curious and wants to learn, and so can become a viewer or participant in the works of artists and makers. To succeed, any form of artistic expression requires such a viewer or participant. The dialogue between artist and viewer requires a common aesthetic language. This language can be shared concepts of visual beauty, of pleasing harmony. It can involve a shared sense of humour, mystery, satire or even confrontation – whatever stimulates curiosity and emotional involvement. If the artist's language is too complex, too self-centered, the viewer may shy away from participating, unable to make the leap into learning. If the language is too simple, the viewer is not invited to linger and explore the art object. The result, in both cases, is no engagement, no dialogue. If the intention of the maker is clear and steady, however, and the viewer is receptive, then the resulting dialogue can be compelling and exciting, and both participants discover new territories of thought and appreciation.

Aesthetics and appreciation

The process of perception, appreciation and identification with a work of art is highly individual.

OPPOSITE: DALE PEREIRA (CANADA)

VASE WITH BIRDS, h. 34 cm, 1988.
The form is assembled from composed elements with painted decoration and wax resist on gas-fired tin glaze.
Photograph: Dale Pereira

'I consider the decoration very traditional ... with the banding reinforcing the structure erased by the white glaze. I chose to use the image of the two birds because their awkward elongated forms seemed to have something in common with the shape of the pot.'
Dale Pereira

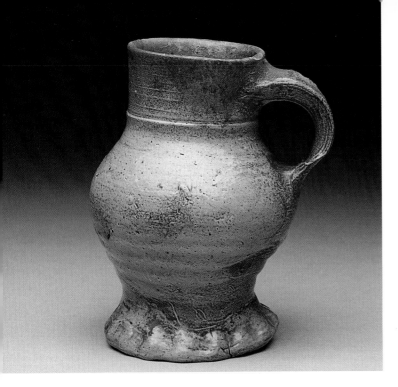

Profound art and craft works for me on more than one level. To illustrate this, I will discuss a pot that I own – a small medieval, German, salt-glazed drinking cup (see above). The intention of the potter was, no doubt, to create a simple vessel for use. Most of the potter's aesthetic choices were probably based on functional and economic considerations – this pot is a quick, no-fuss production item. At the basic level, my response to this piece is an emotional one, a gut reaction. As both drinker and potter, I recognise its function straight away, and appreciate the economy and freshness of its maker's gestures, still apparent in the fired clay. Particularly endearing is a wipe-mark left by the maker's thumb on the bottom of the pot.

Pots can be like people. It is no accident that their parts – foot, lip, belly, handle and so on resemble, and are named after, the parts of our bodies. Pots, like us, are containers – which can make them potent symbols of, amongst other things, fertility, femininity, the inner life and the soul.

My little pot rocks wildly on its crooked base, is dented and its foot is split, yet these flaws are irrelevant in the context of the freshness and spontaneity of its execution. To me, this pot is endearing and no more flawed than is a freckled face. Its proportions are noble, its belly fulsome, and its finger-held handle just right. Its personal-ity is as clear to me as an old friend's. It is uncomplicated and cheerful, and reminds me of a cheeky London sparrow.

I respond to this piece at another level when I contemplate its history. I have seen its like in Breughel paintings and, cup in hand, can imagine myself in the scene on the canvas, joining with the peasants at the wedding. Through this pot I join in the dialogue with its maker, one that has been going on for some five hundred years with its former owners and users.

Object and image

Decorated pots, whatever their intended use, have always been both object and image. The earliest Mesopotamian wares, dating as far back as 4000 BC; the enormously sophisticated red and black Greek amphorae of the 6th century BC; the ancient Mimbres pottery of New Mexico; the great maiolica *istoriato* wares of the 16th century – all show potters' desires to bring together object and image in meaningful ways. Some of the images on these decorated wares, and the integration of such images with objects, give us our only glimpse into the lives and rituals of long-lost cultures.

The impulse to decorate pots, to create ceramic images, is still active today. Contemporary makers, however, do not necessarily draw on religion, culture, ritual or folklore for their images in the way their predecessors did. What motivates ceramists today? What are our purposes? Where do our images come from? How do we express ourselves in distinct, relevant and personal ways?

The process of image-making is mysterious and highly individual. What comes first, perhaps, is the artist's need to express something in a specific form – in line and colour, say, rather than in movement or sound. He or she is motivated to express something particular: a feeling of devotion, say, or curiosity about how something works, or the desire to teach and inform. Inspired by sources as varied as nature, works of art, current cultural icons, personal experience, and fantasy, the artist then begins to explore an image. Some artists begin with abstractions: lines, patterns, shape relationships, colours or textures. I tend to be a narrative artist. I begin with a story

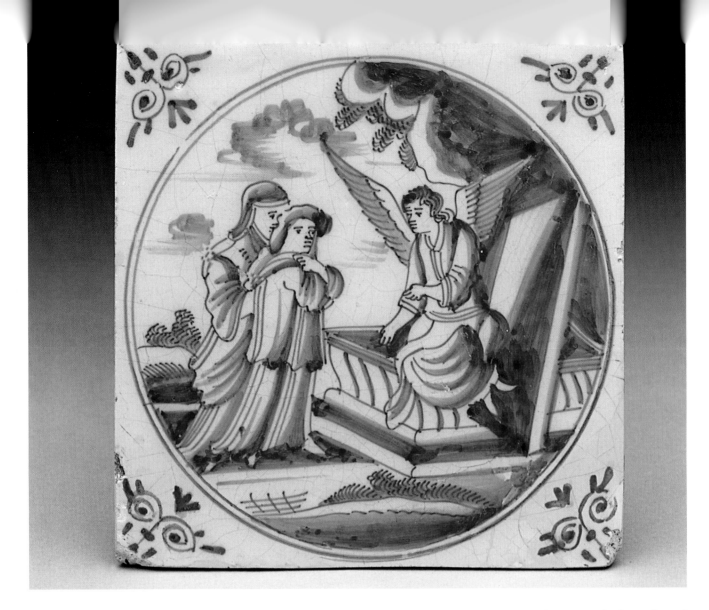

TILE, 13 CM X 13 CM, AMSTERDAM, THE NETHERLANDS, C. 1750.

Tin glaze with cobalt decoration.

that stimulates me to visualise characters and to explore themes figuratively, usually within the framework of a particular ceramic object.

When it comes to the actual creation of the image a number of concrete choices have to be made. How can object and image best be combined? What is the most fitting scale, the most appropriate and clear visual language, the best technique to convey the idea? Those of us who draw and paint and decorate have, by repeated practice, found our own practical answers to such questions, our own ways of entering into dialogue with viewers.

To illustrate some of the steps involved in successful image-making, I would like to discuss another object from my own collection – a small tin-glazed tile from Amsterdam, circa 1750 (see above).

It depicts Mary Magdalene and Joseph of Arimathea by the empty tomb in which Christ had been buried, hearing from an angel of His resurrection.

What motivated the maker was a desire to share a devotional experience. What inspired him was the story of the resurrection. To tell this story he chose a clear language; he drew a picture. The dialogue occurs with viewers who recognise the story, identify with its characters, respond to its drama, and are moved to contemplation. (I am assuming the maker was a man; it is unlikely, at that time, that women were employed as professional tile decorators.)

It is important to note some of the concrete devices the artist has used to focus this image and make it credible. He chose to work on a tile, an ideal flat surface for decoration. Conceived for mounting among many others on a hallway or kitchen wall, this tile is both decorative and func-

21

tional. The technique he used is simple: cobalt line and wash on low-fired tin glaze. The main focusing device of his composition is a strong circular frame to contain the story within the square of the tile. The eye is always brought back to the central action. The severity of the circle is mitigated by four charming ox-head corner motifs which lighten the mood – and also, very likely, link surrounding tiles.

A further focusing device is the use of symmetry. Left and right are clearly delineated in the tableau by the equidistant placement of the figures around a central space. This creates a sense of stillness which, allied with the posed stance of the figures, makes for a mood of calm and reverence. An overall harmony is created through the use of balanced positive and negative spaces in the form of an equal measure of light (white) and shadow (blue) within the circular frame. The character of the drawing itself is another inducement to linger with the image. It is precise, if not a little stilted, yet stylistically a little naive, and hence charming. Repeated parallel strokes (the wings, robes, clouds) remind us that it still is a humble decorative piece made among many, drawn economically, without undue self-consciousness and elaboration.

Most good figurative drawing is based on observation, research and practice, with the ability to render a thing seen, remembered or imagined with an economy of gesture and a fitting use of materials. Here, the artist's observation is apparent in the lifelike drawing of the figures, with well-defined areas of light and shadow created through simple line drawing and wash shading. Credibility is enhanced by the characters' expressions of solemnity, suitable to the occasion. The realistic interpretation of perspective, of foreground and background, allow the viewer to place the figures in a believable landscape. All in all, this one small Dutch tile has managed to work satisfyingly on a number of levels, presenting an image of lasting impact and engagement.

Style and originality

I would like to discuss personal style and originality in an image, and the kinds of pitfalls too often encountered in image-making: plagiarism and pastiche.

Style is the immediately identifiable and individual mark of the artist. Style is not achieved by volition. Rather, it comes from much practice and much problem-solving in honing techniques, materials and process into fluid expression.

Originality of style is a function both of practice, and of depth of research.

We are always absorbing imagery, and storing it for future reference. Explicit copying is a valid way of studying or learning to visualise more clearly. Life- and still-life-drawing are long-accepted standard disciplines. However, both work and time are needed to go beyond copying, to create. Plagiarism occurs when, rather than creating an image through practice and research, someone takes an image made by another person, perhaps modifies it slightly, and presents it as his or her own. I believe that original work is only produced when artists develop the ability to examine their subjects, allowing what they see to percolate through their own experiences and feel

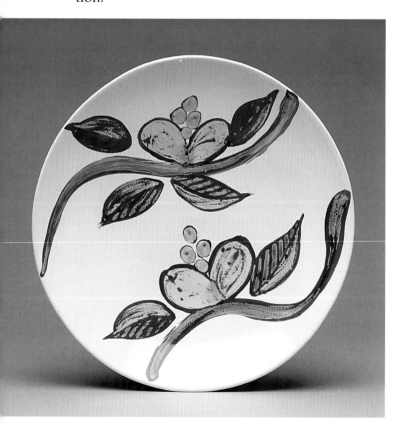

WARREN TIPPET (NEW ZEALAND)

BOWL, d. 29 CM, c. 1980–1990.

Porcelain with overglaze enamel decoration.

ings, thus producing a unique image, a personal interpretation.

How we synthesise information matters. To illustrate, let me choose a maple leaf as my subject. Having unconsciously absorbed the image of such leaves on Canadian flags, endless baseball caps, and a million ashtrays, I am aware of the pitfalls of recreating a pastiche – of reproducing an image seen so often that its conventions are taken for granted. Were I to pick up a leaf, lay it on a plate, spray some colour over the top, and remove the leaf, I could naively say, 'Image of a leaf on a plate'. No research, no percolation, no interpretation – and no great plate. The visual language is too simple. The viewer's eye is not invited to linger.

On the other hand, I might spend some time looking at leaves: at their structure, shape, at colour, at their movements in a breeze. I might examine my own attraction to them, and spend some time in sketching and colour studies. I might then choose a technique suitable to the mood or idea I wish to convey, practice away, and come up with an original image.

Some kinds of work are best done only once – the vision and energy expended may need to culminate in just one image, one telling. On the other hand, the repeated gesture leads to familiar and easy technique, and in turn to fluid variations on a theme with which the artist continually deepens her or his identification. My own training as a production potter has convinced me of the value of repeatedly tackling the same image. As Alan Caiger-Smith has said, 'there is a difference between inattentive repetition, which leads eventually to something pretty vacant and facile, and repetition done with attention, which is really a growing thing, giving rise to the process of maturing that you only see long afterwards'.

My immediate response to a ceramic object is based on its visible character and not necessarily on my appreciation of its maker's technical achievement. Such achievement is implicit in most good work, but it is not, for me, the be-all and end-all. Ceramics being an art that involves solutions to demanding technical problems, there is, perhaps, a temptation to produce pieces that are technically accomplished but lack emotional expression; pieces in which much has been solved, but little said. The converse can also be true; inadequate technique can stunt the expression of a valid idea.

I would like to note some of the elements that determine the style and character of a piece by New Zealand artist Warren Tippet that I consider an example of well-resolved work. This is a simple shallow-footed bowl with an opaque white glaze, and overglaze enamel decoration applied in a third firing (see picture opposite).

What strikes me immediately is the vigour and ease of brushwork which gives this piece its great strength and liveliness. The wave-like shapes promote a continuing sense of movement, even beyond the natural frame of the bowl. Rhythm is created by their easy parallel placing into a loosely partnered dance. The freely interpreted plant motif, hovering between figurative and abstract, creates a slight sense of mystery. The strong contrast between the framed, contained colours and the stark white background creates drama, and the image floating above the white creates a sense of depth.

In the play and balance of a minimal colour palette, predominantly cool greens give sudden focus to the two central areas of warm yellow. The division into three unequal spaces adds spice. The attachment of some leaves and detachment of others adds variety, and allows the image to breathe. The simple unflanged bowl itself, without interfering throwing marks, freely supports the exuberant, almost over-large pattern, containing but not restraining it in a gentle and controlled curve.

I will conclude with a quote from Bernard Leach:

> 'It is also important to remember that, although pottery is made to be used, this fact in no wise simplifies the problem of artistic expression; there can be no fullness or complete realization of utility without beauty, refinement and charm, for the simple reason that their absence must in the long run be intolerable to both maker and consumer. We desire not only food but also the enjoyment and zest of eating. The continued production of utilities without delight in making and using is bound to produce only boredom and to end in sterility.'

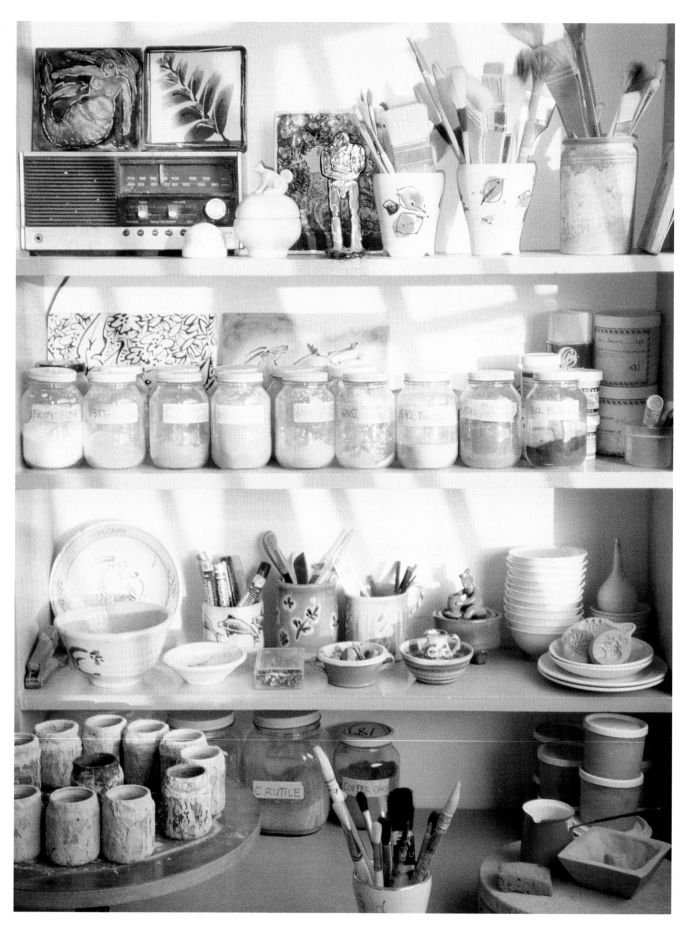

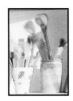

Materials and Procedures

'I have had to work hard. Anyone who works just as hard will get just as far.'

J.S. BACH

'Habit begins as a spider's thread and ends as a steel cable.'

CHINESE PROVERB

You are what you eat, I've heard it said. I assume this means that our state of health and mind are directly connected to the quality of food, physical and mental, that we choose to ingest. Perhaps this saying can also apply to our work, the visible product of specifically chosen materials and procedures.

The question of specialisation in one particular area as regards materials and firing methods is one that is addressed fairly early on in most ceramists' careers. Depending on our education, we may have the option of experimenting for a period of time before making a specific commitment, or over time, one kind of work may simply lead to another. Few ceramists are so eclectic as to juggle several different kinds of clay, firing methods and temperatures at the same time.

In my own case, my choices of materials have always been clearly dictated by my own particular talents and proclivities. That is to say, clay, glazes and firing need to enable my drawing and colour work. The subtle changes in glaze surface induced by accidental wood- or salt-fired effects

MY MONTREAL STUDIO, COLOUR MIXING AREA

Photograph: Matthias Ostermann

have never really been within my range of interest as a maker, although I admire them enormously. In fact, a wood-firing potter visiting my home and expecting wall-to-wall maiolica colour, found a large collection of traditional and contemporary reduction-fired pots. Perhaps because my studio is so filled with colour, there is something restful about coming home to quiet temmokkus and celadons, away from my own particular colour preoccupations.

Nonetheless, these preoccupations have led me to make specific choices in the clays and glazes that I use. Even when working in the stoneware and porcelain firing range, I've always looked for light, discreetly coloured clay bodies and glazes that were smooth, temperature-stable, with the ability to both absorb and reflect light, as well as promoting brilliance of colour. These criteria in mind have led to the gradual development of the glazes I now use. These were created through the combining of materials and testing rather than through molecular formulation.

Clay

My clay body is a light, cream-coloured commercial earthenware that vitrifies well at my chosen glaze temperature of 1046°C (Orton large cone 05). It is fine-grained, to avoid the endemic maiolica white-spotting problems that a fire-clay body can induce. Since most of my work is thrown or slabbed on a reasonably domestic scale, a grittier body is not required as it might be for larger-scale constructions. Since I'm a city boy, I do not dig or mix my own, but buy it neatly packaged from my supplier, like nicely de-boned fish fillets. I prefer a cream colour to terracotta red, since I rarely desire to contrast the red body colour with the white tin glaze for effect. I do keep another red terracotta body on hand, however, for occasional red-clay decoration, or other kinds of slip work. Since I do a lot of throwing, the body must be smooth and elastic. The choice of clay body is important not just for colour and workability, but also for fit-compatibility with the chosen glaze. Since many ceramists like myself choose to buy rather than invent their own clay body, but in fact use highly individual glaze recipes, the clay-glaze fit needs to be addressed and resolved through testing at the chosen temperature. Chapter Eight will address some solutions to fit problems that might occur. Other important considerations in choosing a clay body are the function of the ware itself, and its resistance to shocks and heat with use. Today, ceramic suppliers can offer a large variety of clay bodies to suit most aesthetic and functional needs at any specific temperature.

Glaze

As mentioned earlier, the following glaze recipes reflect above all my need for a temperature-stable glaze that will clearly hold drawing and brushwork, promote bright colours, and provide a good functional surface. All recipes have worked well when mixed up from substitute raw materials in other countries. (I have, in the appendix, provided formulae, analyses and ratios for my glazes and for some other materials, so that equivalent glazes – glazes with the same function, but made from substitute raw materials – can be prepared.)

The following raw materials provide specific functions, as listed, to the glazes I use.

Frits Ferro frit 3124 and ferro frit 3195 are lead-free boron frits. These are basically almost complete glazes in themselves, providing calcium, sodium, boron, silica and alumina to a mixture that has been fired and reground to a very fine mesh. They can be seen as man-made low-temperature feldspars, supplying the necessary melters to the glaze in relatively insoluble form.

Feldspars Nepheline syenite and Kona F4 Spar are both naturally occurring feldspars. They are included in many glaze recipes because they supply sodium and potassium in a soluble form along with silica and alumina. They can be seen as 'cooked' materials – that is to say, already combined, and therefore requiring less heat to melt than if they were supplied in purer form.

Clays Ball clay (Bell dark) and kaolin (EPK) are clays that also provide alumina and silica, as well as helping to keep the glaze in suspension and providing a smooth, workable, raw-glaze surface. For better glaze whiteness I prefer the lightest colour of ball clay possible.

Silica (flint) Silica is the basic glass-former in glazes and usually occurs in smaller amounts on its own in low-fire glazes. Due to its refractoriness the flint also helps to keep the glaze from over-fluxing.

Whiting (calcium carbonate) Whiting provides calcium oxide to the glaze. It is not a flux at low temperatures, but does contribute to colour-response and opacity, and can contribute to surface hardness.

Zirconium silicate Zircopax, Superpax, Opax, etc. are brand names for zirconium silicate. They all have roughly the same amount of silica and zirconium in combination, with the main difference between them being particle size. I use Zircopax as the primary opacifier or 'whitener' in the glaze, as opposed to tin oxide, the traditional opacifier. Apart from the fact that tin oxide is more than twice the price of any zircon opacifier, there are also some surface qualities associated with tin of which I'm not so fond: it gives a dense, very opaque white, with little light penetration, and a tendency to promote pastel-like surface colour, especially in the blue range. If the white achieved in the glaze is too cold, then, regardless of the opacifier used, the base glaze colour can be brought into a warmer, cream range by the addition of up to two percent of rutile (ceramic, not granular).

The following are the glaze recipes I currently use:

Maiolica Glaze no.1 / Orton large cone 05 (1046 °C)

This is my standard glaze. It has a good, non-powdery surface for brushwork, and keeps decoration stable over several cones of temperature. It also keeps well, and does not settle, even for months on end, and does not run and drip, even when slightly overfired. I do not use kiln wash on my shelves (one less thing to worry about) since the necessity of preventing pots from sticking does not occur. The ingredients are generally reliable, available and not too expensive.

Maiolica Glaze no 1

Ferro frit 3124	60.0
Ferro frit 3195	10.0
Ball clay (Bell dark)	6.5
Kaolin (EPK)	6.5
Silica	4.0
Whiting	2.0
Zircopax	11.0
Total	100.0

Maiolica Glaze no. 2 / Orton large cone 1-2 (1154 °C -1162 °C)

This is a modification of the first glaze for slightly higher temperatures, which I developed for use for working in Australia and New Zealand, where it seems that earthenware bodies in general tend to vitrify at slightly higher temperatures.

Maiolica Glaze no 2

Ferro frit 3124	62.0
Ball clay (Bell dark)	9.0
Kaolin (EPK)	9.0
Silica	6.0
Whiting	3.0
Zircopax	11.0
Total	100.0

Matt Maiolica Glaze no. 3 / Orton large cone 05 (1046 °C)

This glaze has a sugary matt surface which allows colour work and lustre to appear matt as well. Relative to glazes no. 1 and no. 2, this glaze has a fairly powdery surface when dry, and requires more careful application and handling.

Maiolica Glaze no 3

Ferro frit 3124	60.0
Nepheline syenite	5.0
Kona F4 Spar	5.0
Kaolin (EPK)	6.0
Silica	12.0
Whiting	4.0
Zircopax	8.0
Total	100.0

Glazing

In my working procedures I try to aim for some kind of conscious economy of gesture. It could be laziness, and not wanting to do more than is absolutely necessary, or just an unwillingness to fiddle, but I think it really has more to do with trying to create good work with the least amount of fuss, in order to actually get paid for my time. Since most of my income comes from my work, and I am addicted to eating and travelling, this becomes a not inconsiderable factor. My production training in Ireland, where efficient routine of work was necessary for commercial viability, no doubt has contributed to my approach. There is also something to be said about work that is gesturally fresh and not overworked. A good cook once told me: 'Use the best ingredients you can find, and stir as little as possible.' Since I dislike mushy food, I have taken this advice to heart in the studio as well as the kitchen. I have learned to throw plates without bats, simply lifting, placing, trimming, and drying them in such a way that there is no distortion or warping. This means one less object to find, handle, scrape clean, and stack. I believe you can train your eye and body to do almost anything, and be as efficient as possible with a minimum of gesture. Glazing is no exception to this. It is perhaps one of the most difficult of tasks to learn to do confidently and well, particularly since any miscalculations or errors in handling are less apparent immediately than would be errors of construction or decoration which leap out to the eye at once.

To begin with, the above mentioned basic ingredients are weighed out dry and then screened wet through an 80s mesh sieve (North American measure, or metric aperture 180 microns), with no gum or binding agents added. The amount of water in the mixture determines the consistency – in this case, a little thicker than milk. This may need to vary according to the way in which the piece is being glazed. I glaze mostly by pouring and dipping. If the bisque happens to be very high-fired and less absorbent, a thicker mixture might be needed and a longer drying time expected. If, on the other hand, the bisque is fairly porous, and/or the piece is large or com-

MY MONTREAL STUDIO, PAINTING AREA

Photograph: Jan Thijs

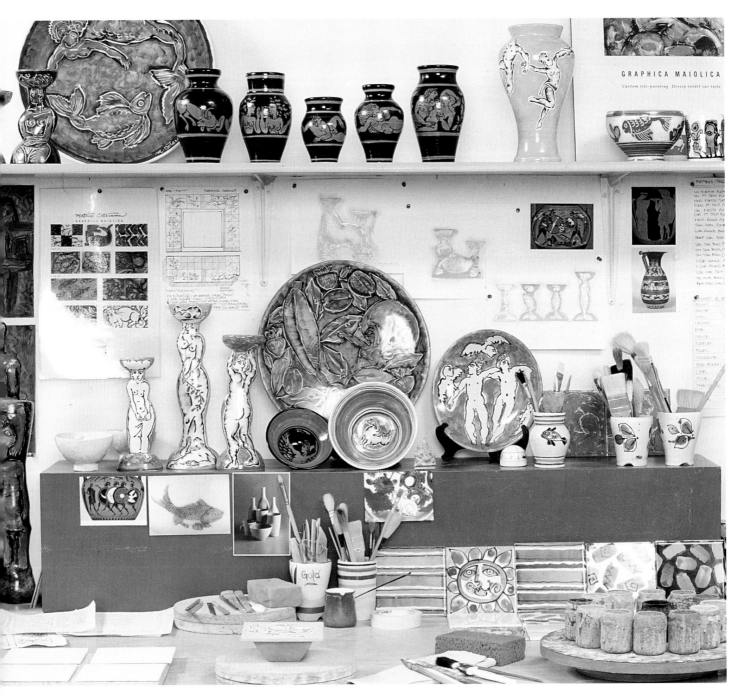

plex, requiring slower, more careful handling, then a thinner mixture might be advisable. What is important is to keep the glaze stirred well at all times during use. All glazing has to be done with great attention to overlapping glaze marks or drips, since these will stay very visible (and usually unwanted) under any colour work. The knack with glazing, having established the correct glaze consistency, is to develop a confident and repeatable movement strategy that allows the piece to be covered quickly and evenly without annoying drips or undue glaze build-up on the edges, where it might shear off after firing. This strategy includes large enough pails and pans, and more than ample glaze quantities for dipping. Spray glazing is also an option, although one which I have not explored.

For taller vessels or deep bowls, I tend to pour glaze inside, roll it around, pour it out quickly and evenly while rotating the piece, and then immediately turn the piece upside-down, and dip to glaze just the rim. Alternatively, I might immediately immerse the entire piece (still upside-down) as far down as the foot ring or base. Once the glaze has dried enough for handling, the unglazed portion of the piece can be dunked, right side up. Since tin glaze is so very susceptible to any surface irregularities, the idea is to give those areas to be decorated the smoothest possible coating, and to relegate any overlap marks to the bottom of the piece where they will be least noticeable. Any wet finger marks or mistakes should be touched up only when the piece is completely dry. Large shallow bowls, plates and platters, I will swoop and dip into large, well-filled pans, holding them with two spread fingers of both hands. Glazing tongs are an option here, but for some reason I have never used them. Important here, when lifting out the piece to shed drips, is to work quickly, shaking and rotating the piece in such a way as to avoid too much build-up of glaze on the lower edge. Once the piece has dried somewhat (half an hour or so) I will then take it up, lightly rub over, and touch up finger marks with a brush and glaze, and then scrape and wipe the bottom. Usually, I'm doing several dozen pieces at a time, so there is an orderly routine developed. Once the last of the series is glazed, the first one is ready for touching up and cleaning. The advantage of doing this very soon,

as opposed to the next day, is that the glaze is easier to scrape, and the slightly damp piece can be repeatedly handled at this point without roughing up the surface unduly, which does happen when the piece is handled dry. A rough surface, of course, will impede later brushwork. Sometimes a light, fine spray of gum and water, or a few dabs with a well-squeezed, damp sponge, can make a roughed-up surface workable again.

For cleaning up the bottoms of pieces, I prefer scraping and sponging to waxing, mainly because a watery glaze mixture is rubbed into the clay. This helps to seal the body, but is not thick enough to stick to kiln shelves during firing. With practice, scraping and sponging is as quick a method as any waxing procedure, all steps considered.

For any further work to follow – waxing of borders, decoration resists, as well as any on-surface colour work – I allow the glazed piece to dry fully overnight to ensure maximum adhesion and clarity of fired colour later.

Colour stains

To achieve my colour work I use low-fire commercial ceramic stains mixed with frit and water. I will sometimes combine these with metallic oxides and carbonates such as cobalt and copper, or with rutile. I will address in depth the whole process of colour blending, mixing and testing in the next chapter, but to begin with, it is important to check with the supplier that what you buy is in fact suitable for 'in-glaze' painting at your particular firing temperature. Most stains are usually multipurpose for under- and overglaze work, and have a reasonably wide firing range. However some, such as body stains, are intended for other purposes, such as colouring clay bodies, and these may be far too refractory to be of any use on a glaze, and will remain dry upon the surface after firing.

One of the things I have found important in the handling of ceramic materials, especially colour stains, is the necessity of being reasonably orderly and systematic. This appeases not only my compulsive German tidiness and need for visual order, but also makes me part of a comfortable known process, a ritual if you like, in which there are few unwelcome surprises that could affect the work adversely later. Colours are easily polluted through carelessness, and poorly labelled bags and jars can lead to composition mistakes and wrong colours.

Preparation procedures can be a warm-up for the work that is to follow later. The mixing-up of the colours is the small ritual that puts me into the proper frame of mind conducive to the relaxed concentration colour brushwork requires. For example, when preparing my colour mixtures, I tend to mix up small quantities, enough for each session, rather than stocking up for weeks ahead. Not only does this train my eye afresh each day to maintain my established colour palette, but it also provides a pleasant meditative precursor to the work to follow: in much the same way, the simple physical gesture of kneading clay prepares the mind for the thrown shapes to follow. Since I dabble back and forth quite a bit between my colours, the pollution problem is avoided by repeated fresh mixings.

Spatial organisation of the actual work area needs to be considered as well. My work to be painted is kept on a banding wheel for constant rotation, either high up at eye level for outside decoration, or low down and flat, for platters and tiles. The rotation keeps me in visual control of the entire piece, and avoids excessive handling. My colours I keep to the right, usually low down since I've already encountered 'tennis elbow', the inflammation of the elbow joint due to prolonged suspension of the arm in one position during decoration. Colours lower down encourage brush movements from the scapula, rather than the elbow. I mention this because so many of the ceramist's long-term physical habits can lead to problems (lower back, elbows, wrists, etc.). I think some kind of awareness of posture and habits needs to be developed to avoid long-term problems. The colours themselves I keep on a large rotating disc in 'rainbow' order, from light to dark. This means colours are quickly and easily identified in a spectrum, and a right-handed mistaken dip from yellow into orange is less dramatic than from blue into yellow. I rinse brushes well between colour changes, keeping them flat and ready on an absorbent surface. This prevents them from becoming soggy, and helps to preserve their shape. I also keep myself supplied with a large pail of rinse water, and all non-essential clutter is cleared away to give me lots of elbow room, and the space to accommodate generous brush gesture. Work is lit from above and both sides. Chapter Five discusses the choice, use and maintenance of brushes.

Firing

Firing with electricity is probably the least complicated (and perhaps least exciting) of all firing methods. The use of actual fuel and flames, the controlling of an oxidation or reduction atmosphere for specific glaze effects – all of these add extra spice (and work) to an exciting procedure that perhaps tickles the subliminal pyromaniac in all of us. City bylaws usually impose strictures that prohibit the use of fuel-fired kilns in residential areas by imposing industrial standards of ventilation. In North America, most fuel-fired potters tend to locate in rural areas. For myself, being city-born-and-bred, and mildly terrified of fire, I am more than happy to fire in an electric kiln (not so very different from my kitchen stove) and to have a short and uncomplicated firing cycle that permits me to come and go freely and spend some spare time in local cafés. More to the point is the fact that most ceramists choose their firing methods according to the effects they seek in their finished work. Celadons and copper reds demand a reducing fire; tin glaze does not. In fact, I prefer the warm, creamy whites of oxidation to the more cool, bluish tones more common to reduction whites. Important for me is the total stability and dependability of the electric fire, where the detailed painted surface is all-important, and accidental flashing or unpredictable colour changes will be problems, not attributes.

I use two seven-cubic-foot (two-cubic-metre) top-loading kilns which, when running at full capacity, can each be fired almost every second day. My approach to bisquing and glaze firing is almost identical. For bisquing, I always ensure that the wares are entirely dry, so that I don't have to linger about with a slow preheating process. Pre-heating occurs during the night, with the kiln lid fully down, bung holes open, and all switches at one-third power. Over 12 hours or more, any moisture has had time to escape, as well as any unpleasant bisque odours. My studio is in an industrial warehouse, and an extractor fan in a window next to the kiln ensures good cross-ventilation to the outside. At any point during the following day, I turn all switches to their maximum and keep all spy holes open. From that point on, my firing time is between three to four hours to reach my bisque temperature of 999°C (Orton large cone 06). The fact that not all levels of the kiln come to temperature at the same time, with the lower third taking at least an hour longer, means that the largest part of the kiln is subjected to a soaking of heat at its peak temperature for at least an hour. Since white spots and pinholes due to insufficiently cleared bisque are a standard maiolica problem (see Chapter Eight), the prolonged soak at the end of the bisque firing is essential, as is keeping the kiln well ventilated, especially if the stack is tight.

For glaze firing, the process is virtually identical, except that I fire one cone higher and close all spy holes after pre-heating. Again, the built-in soak time of over an hour at the end of the firing helps to promote a smooth melt and allows time for blisters on the glaze surface to heal over.

Cooling times for both bisque and glaze firings are about 24 hours, at which time the work has cooled sufficiently to be comfortably unloaded. I try to avoid rush scenarios in which I am obliged to unload a fairly hot kiln before it has fully cooled and risk the possibility of dunting uncooled wares. To further minimise this risk, I have also double insulated my kiln lids, to help prolong the cooling process. In general, firing and cooling slowly tends to promote better glaze surfaces and to avoid problems with clay/glaze fit.

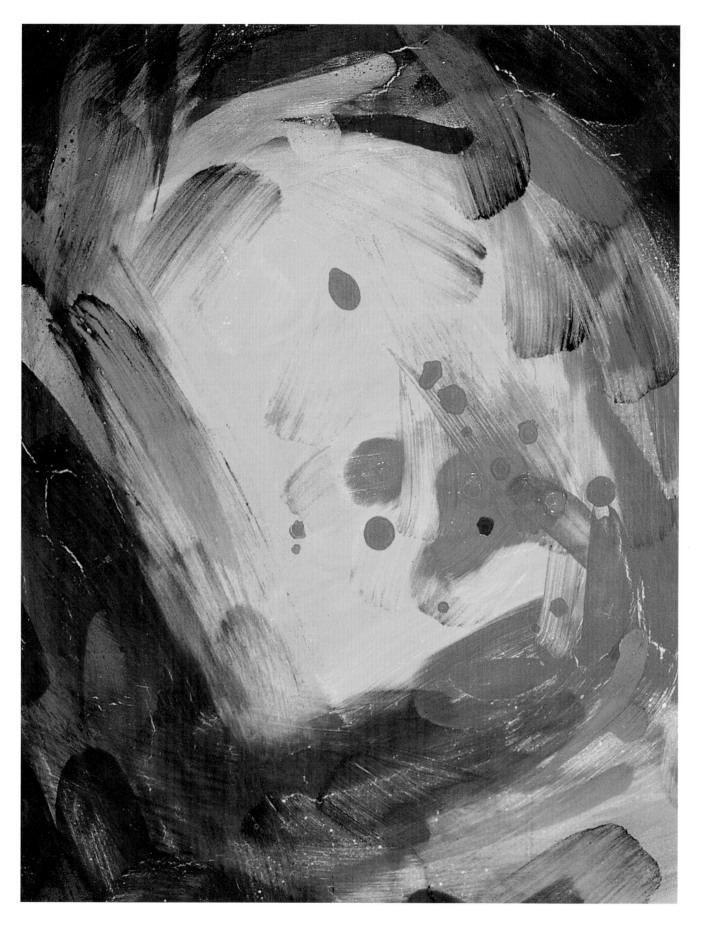

CHAPTER FOUR

Colour

'Blue is a mysterious colour, hue of illness and nobility, the rarest colour in nature. It is the colour of ambiguous depth, of the heavens and of the abyss at once . . . of the blue movie, of blue talk . . . of anode plates, royalty at Rome, smoke, distant hills, postmarks, Georgian silver, thin milk, and hardened steel.

Yellow is a colour, for all its dramatic unalterability, with a thousand meanings . . . it is the colour of cowardice, third prize, the caution flag on auto speedways, adipose tissue, scones and honey, urine, New Mexico licence plates, illness, the cheeks of penguins . . . Easter is yellow.

Red is the boldest of all the colours. It stands for charity and martyrdom, hell, love, youth, fervour, boasting, sin and atonement. It is the most popular colour, particularly with women . . . it is the colour of Christmas, blood, Irish setters, meat, exit signs, Saint John, Tabasco sauce, rubies, old theatre seats and carpets . . . and the cardinals of the Roman Catholic Church.'

ALEXANDER THEROUX The Primary Colours

ABSTRACT STUDY OF COLOUR ELEMENTS
Brushed stains on zircon-opacified maiolica glaze.

Colour theory

Alexander Theroux's *The Primary Colours* has grasped the essence of how we relate to colours. Our perception, assimilation, and subsequent use of colour is highly subjective. Our response to it is immediate and emotional and almost taken for granted, since colour is all around us, a major part of our visible world. Colour can evoke cultural and spiritual associations, and strong emotions; it can attract and repel. All of us develop some kind of innate colour sense, as is evidenced by the colours we wear and surround ourselves with. They can influence our mood, perception and even our behaviour.

For the artist wishing to use colour, that subjectivity is enormously important in establishing contact with the viewer. There are all kinds of theories regarding the physics, and psychological and physiological effects of colour. Some of these, notably Johannes Itten's major treatise *The Art of Colour*, are well worth studying, if only to obtain knowledge of objective principles that might serve in the evaluation and processing of colour in a given work. But theory alone is not enough; to use colours effectively, I think an artist must nurture the intuitive ability to visualise colours and their interaction. Our use of colour as a language is a direct reflection of our innermost sensibilities and character. Itten himself states that 'for the artist, effects are decisive, rather than agents as studied by physics and chemistry . . . Colour effects are in the eye of the beholder . . . The deepest and truest secrets of colour effect are invisible even to the eye, and are beheld by the heart alone. The essential eludes conceptual formulation.'

I suspect that most artists do in fact approach their work without too much specific theory, but are aware that certain physical laws of colour do exist and can be exploited. For example, complementary colours are opposing, contrasting colours: red and green, blue and orange, yellow and violet. The human eye for some unknown reason, automatically seeks to 'complement' a colour seen alone with an after-image of its 'opposite'. An artist can put this natural phenomenon to effective use, creating strong visual and emotional impact in an image through the immediate juxtaposition of two such colours – very useful knowledge.

Colours are perceived by contrast and comparison, and work through interaction with one another. The eye is always establishing relationships, and seeking to impose some kind of balance and order. The way in which this visual information is processed is, as mentioned earlier, highly individual. There is no rule to say that one particular viewpoint is more valid than another. But a more highly developed colour sensibility will lead to more interesting options in the artist's use of colour, and seeing and practice are necessary training elements.

My own approach to the use of colour (being more or less self-taught) has been non-theoretical and subjective. In having to articulate what I do, I find that I can in fact subject my results to some framework of theory. To help the reader develop an individual colour palette, I will make practical suggestions based on what I have learned in developing my own palette. I have corroborated some of the ideas I suggest with 'official' colour theorists. For instance, Itten's premise that we perceive colour by contrast – that is, by perceiving the differences between compared colour effects – is one I have used intuitively, and found both sensible and workable.

A working palette is created by balancing some of the following colour elements.

Primary colours (yellow, red, blue) are those which cannot be created by mixing other colours, and from which all other colours are mixed.

Secondary colours (orange, green, violet) are those which are mixed up from the primaries. For example:

YELLOW + RED = ORANGE
YELLOW + BLUE = GREEN
RED + BLUE = VIOLET

Cold or warm colours are those which we perceive as giving sensations of temperature – and hence affecting our mood. This is, of course, highly subjective. A colour may be seen and felt as either cool or warm depending on its context. Warm colours, generally, are those with a lot of yellow in them. Cool colours tend to contain more blue. Warm colours have associations of heat, nearness, dryness, opacity, density and action. Cool colours can evoke coldness, distance, moisture, transparency, depth, calm and mystery.

Complementary colours, being opposites on the colour wheel (see below), have the unique ability to dramatise each other – to vibrate when

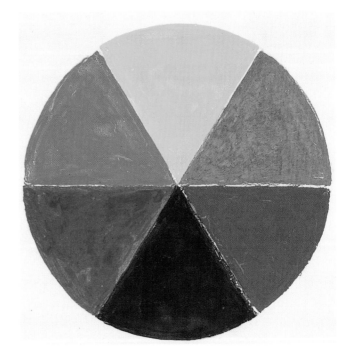

COLOUR WHEEL

These colours – like all the others in this chapter – are fired coloured stains on zircon-opacified maiolica glaze. In the colour wheel, each secondary colour is flanked by its two primaries, and each colour is pointing to its complement.

placed into juxtaposition. This fact was well known to, and used by, such French impressionists as Seurat and Cézanne, and the Dutch painter Van Gogh.

Colour contrast refers to the practice of placing two colours together that are distinctly different (they can be complementary, or not). What is useful here is that when blended on-surface, they can create intermediary shades.

Colour tone, as I see it, is the proportion of light to shadow provided by the colours in an image. If that image is converted to a black-and-white photocopy, tonal values clearly appear as black, white and intermediary gray tones. Good examples of such tonal contrast can be found in paintings by Rembrandt, in which he creates strong visual drama by using a limited number of colours and brilliant highlights in larger dark, surrounding fields. In a ceramic context, this is easily seen in some Dutch delftware (see photograph on p. 21), in which only blue and white is used, and light-dark tonal contrasts are readily visible.

By *colour intensity* I refer to the relative saturation of a given colour. In a ceramic colour mixture, the amount of water directly determines the final intensity – from pale, watercolour tones, to fully opaque, concentrated colour.

Colour composition concerns the organisation and placement of colours, their surface distribution and spatial relationships.

Colour impact, to me, is one of the most important of colour concepts, and synthesises how most of the parameters defined above interact and affect my perception. The visual impact on me of certain colours – intense reds, strong green, bright blues – is, primarily, emotional. I use them to highlight or define the most important areas of focus in an image, such as faces, hands and eyes. Sometimes I like to introduce what I call a 'mystery' colour: one that occurs in a very small area, only once, and hence becomes a curiosity.

Colours are like instruments in an orchestra: depending on the music, they have assigned roles either as principal or as supporting players. Secondary or supporting colours include the less intense yellows, mauves and light greens. There might also be some designated tertiary colours assigned to the background, or used as minimal accent and outline colours. (I often use black, dark green, khaki and white in this role.)

Theory enables objective analysis, but it cannot replace intuition and actual practice with colour. A good cook does not necessarily go by the cookbook; it is the cook's sense of taste, and ability to combine flavours to create new flavours, that makes a dish exciting. So, too, for the colourist.

Developing a colour palette

One of the major differences between painting on paper or canvas and working with ceramic colours is the latter's propensity to change in the fire. We are obliged to go through lengthy, con-

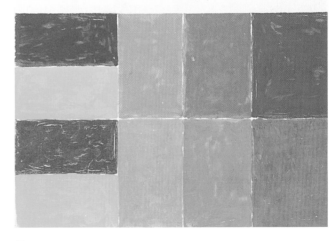

FIRED AND UNFIRED COLOURS

These two sets of colour progressions demonstrate the difference between the unfired (top) and fired (bottom) glazed surface.

35

trolled testing procedures in order to come up with final, repeatable colour recipes that become the basis of our palette. One obvious example of this colour change is cobalt carbonate. In its raw, unfired state it can be gray, pink, or mauve, yet when fired it blooms into an intense blue. In other words, while actually painting, the ceramist never sees his or her true palette. Such qualities as colour intensity, light and dark contrast, and transparency are readily visible, but most colours appear as a paler version in the unfired state (see chart on p. 35). True colours emerge, phoenix-like, only after the fire. Other influencing factors can be the kind of base glaze used, the degree of temperature, and firing conditions. We are obliged to work from our 'fired' memory, anticipating future results from observations of fired work.

The process of testing colours in order to create a personal colour palette is not necessarily complex, but does require time and a systematic approach. I believe that there is an individual colour palette lurking in each of us, waiting only to be brought into the light. One might go about the task of developing a palette from scratch in two stages. First, practice colours on paper to train the eye to recognise and create contrasts. For the purpose of this training, any water-based medium, such as watercolours or acrylics, will do. Then, still working on paper, the exercise switches to using ceramic stains in order to begin establishing a basic working palette. The colours on white paper will resemble in intensity colours applied to a white raw glaze. The second stage deals with transposing this information onto a glazed tile and firing it, as well as pursuing more individual colour research, also by way of firing.

Colour mixing

For the first stage, having perhaps already played with some watercolours, begin with:

- some basic ceramic stains
- frit (of the same kind as in the base glaze)
- water
- a supple, medium-sized square-tipped brush
- a dozen or so clear plastic or glass mixing containers
- a stirring stick

- blank paper (absorbent newsprint for brush practice, white cartridge paper for the actual palette)
- pencil and pad for note-taking
- the attitude that you are about to enjoy yourself like a child at kindergarten

In creating a colour palette blend primary colours (yellow, red, blue) to provide secondary colours (orange, green, violet). For practical, ceramic purposes, primary colours should include:

- a good lemon yellow
- a warm strong red
- a cool pink-red
- a turquoise
- perhaps a strong blue

The stains I use are commercial ones (as discussed in Chapter Three). When looking at an overall colour range, keep in mind that the more intense your initial primaries are, the stronger will be your overall palette. Pastel colours cannot produce bright, intense hues. However, one is often bound by what is locally available, and a more subdued colour palette can also be attractive.

The actual colour-mixing process is simple – combine colour, frit and water. I do not sieve my colourants, nor do I add binding agents, such as gum. I find that gum in the mixture can inhibit future surface-blending techniques, but it might be helpful in the glaze itself if the latter is very powdery and smooth brushwork is being blocked. My own glaze contains a lot of clay and has a good workable surface. The frit helps melt the colour stains, which can tend to be rather dry when fired on their own. Fritless colours can provide an interesting surface treatment for some kinds of work, but for a good shiny surface, the proportion of frit to colour should be about 50:50. This is an appropriate ratio for the temperature at which most of my work is fired, in oxidation, at 1046 °C (Orton large cone 05). If the temperature is raised, the relative amount of frit may have to be reduced. Testing in the kiln will confirm the appropriate ratio of frit to colour for any given temperature.

At this point it might be a good idea to apply your basic commercial stains to a glazed bisque tile, with and without frit, and to put them through the kiln at your chosen temperature. This should give you a good sampling of the kind of final surface and depth of colour you might expect, the warm or cool range into which the colours fall, or of any potential problems.

The following is a sample stain-frit-water mixture.

Green mixture
1 part yellow stain
½ part turquoise stain
1½ parts frit
water

For repeatable measurements of small testing quantities, I use a teaspoonful as my basic unit. Another ceramist once showed me a simple, accurate and repeatable way to subdivide this unit. Fill the teaspoon with your colour stain, and level off with a straight blade. This is now your basic 'one part'. Empty it onto a fired, glazed white tile, and pat it into a square of uniform thickness. With your blade, subdivide that square into halves, quarters, eighths or even sixteenths. I find one-eighth to be a sufficiently small subdivision, and tend to move up from there. Over time, I have learned to measure by eye. For larger quantities, the principle remains the same: you simply increase your basic unit of measure (tablespoon, cup, etc.).

As mentioned earlier, in addition to colour stains I use some standard metal oxides and carbonates: cobalt carbonate for blue, copper carbonate for smoky green, red iron oxide for gold to dark brown, manganese dioxide for purple/browns, and rutile (ceramic, not granular) for strong ochre tones. Addition of the above materials (with the exception of rutile) does not require additional frit since they are active fluxes in themselves. For example:

Colour stain and cobalt mix for purple/mauve
1 part cool pink-red
½ part turquoise
¼ part cobalt carbonate
1½ parts frit
water

Rutile, the exception, does require frit. For example:

Colour stain and rutile mix for orange/yellow
1 part yellow stain
¼ part warm, strong red
¼ part rutile
1½ parts frit
water

The amount of water added to the mixture of colour and frit determines your final colour intensity. For testing purposes, I recommend a fairly opaque mixture. To test it, I stir the mixture well and, using a medium-size, supple Chinese calligraphy brush, lay down a quick, generous, long stroke on paper. If the stroke is watery and transparent, your mixture is too dilute. If the stroke is fluid and firm, without transparency, the mixture is good. If the stroke is blocked and ragged and does not pull through, then it is likely that the mixture is too concentrated, and more water should be added.

The tendency is to start off with far too much water, which necessitates continual adding of more stains. Water is cheaper than stain, so it is best to start with little water, and add as you go. Keep in mind that colours settle quickly and need to be constantly stirred. The brush also has a tendency to push and compress colours to the bottoms of the containers. Remember also that colours are easily polluted, your mixing brush-water should be frequently changed, and your brushes should be well rinsed between colour changes.

The palette

Having established your work space, necessary materials, and a knowledge of the mixing process, you are ready to begin creating a palette on paper. Start with the primary-colour stains mentioned above. For now, omit the oxides because they change colour too radically when fired. You can explore these oxides in the second stage of testing. For now, you are developing your colour sensibility only on paper.

I think it is easier to begin with a small palette – six to nine colours, say. More colours will certainly emerge in time as your eye learns to contrast, visualise, and invent. At present I work with 12 to 14 colours.

I suggest you aim for the following:

- yellow*
- orange
- warm, strong red*
- cool pink-red (rose)*
- purple-mauve
- strong blue*
- turquoise*
- aqua green
- lime green

* These colours will serve as your primaries, and all your other colours can be mixed from them.

You might, at this point, look at your primaries and decide whether they fall into the warm or cool range. Two warm primaries give a warm secondary. Two cool primaries give a cool secondary. A combination of warm and cool primaries can give either warm or cool secondaries. For instance, if a purple is desired, then the obvious formula red + blue = purple will not work if one of the primaries is warm and the other cool. Take the example of mixing warm, strong red with cool turquoise. The orange in the red becomes the complement of the turquoise, and complementary colours, when blended, tend to become gray in tone — in this case, brown. What is needed is a cool pink-red that, when mixed with cool turquoise, should give a cool purple-mauve (see study on right). However, keep in mind that *anything* is worth testing. You might just need a brown in your palette. What may now seem unusable, may later, when your changing colour sensibilities require something else, be ideal. To this end it is important that *every* colour combination be labelled and documented for future reference. In time you can build up a veritable visual library of colour that can be used as a basis for further exploration. This will be discussed further in the second stage of colour testing.

WARM AND COOL COLOUR STUDY

Top: Warm, strong red with cool turquoise gives brown.
Bottom: Cool, pink red with turquoise gives purple.

Back to the palette itself: rather than attempting to create multiple variations of just one particular colour (this can happen at the second stage of colour testing), I find it best to modify all the colours of the palette at any one time. As I mentioned earlier, colours are perceived by contrast, and the learning occurs when each colour change is seen in relation to the entire palette.

I begin the process of developing a palette by arranging my colours in a horizontal row in rainbow order, from left to right: yellow, orange, red, rose, purple/mauve, blue, turquoise, aqua green, and lime green. I maintain this order each time I modify the palette, so that all yellows, for example, are aligned in a vertical column. Each row is a modification and improvement of its predecessor. Progressive changes are thus visible down the columns of the stack of palette rows, and the final colour palette on the bottom row ends up as the most balanced and harmonious.

In creating a balanced or harmonious palette I look for three things. First, sufficient contrast of colours, with no two resembling one another too closely. This allows for blending of new intermediary colours. Second, a balance of roughly equal warm to cool colours, and the third balancing factor, and not so easy to ascertain, is what I call a family-related colour sense. That is to say that your eye can travel along the row of colours without one discordant colour leaping out.

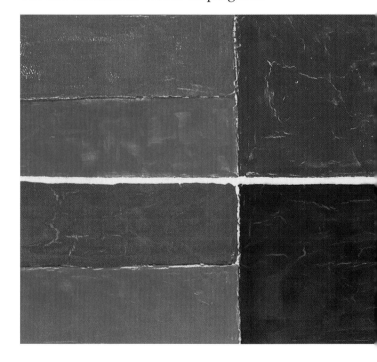

COLOURS AND SUGGESTED MIXTURES

YELLOW	ORANGE	RED	ROSE	PURPLE/ MAUVE	BLUE	TURQUOISE	AQUA GREEN	LIME GREEN
1 part yellow	1 part yellow	warm strong red (as is)	cool pink/red (as is)	1 part cool pink/red	strong blue (as is)	turquoise (as is)	1 part turquoise	1 part yellow
⅛ part warm strong red	¼ part strong red			¼ part turquoise			¼ part yellow	¼ part turquoise
frit	frit	frit	frit	frit	frit	frit	frit	frit

Before mixing up any colour stains in quantity, there are some important things to keep in mind. Strong dark colours absorb lighter ones and should be used in very small proportions. Their dominance is very easily underestimated. When starting to mix up two or more colours, begin with your basic measure (teaspoon) of the lightest colour first, then add the stronger, darker colour in very small increments (say one-eighth part). As an example, one teaspoon of strong blue might well require eight of yellow to make any kind of green. For one small colour test, this is of course very wasteful and expensive.

To start your first row, lay down your colours in rainbow order from left to right, perhaps using the suggested mixtures in the chart above.

Having now established the first line of colour on paper, you examine the colours and look for things to modify.

For example, your yellow and orange may be too much alike in colour, so you may have to darken or lighten one or the other, or both. Similarly, your yellow and lime may also be too close, and require modification for greater colour con-

trast. There are some basic rules to remember when modifying colours. Do not lighten with white or darken with black. To lighten, you can increase your lighter base primary. To darken, simply keep increasing your darker primary.

In looking at the balance between warm and cool colours, you may find too many of some and too few of others. For example, you may have too many cool greens and no warm yellow-green. Rather than trying to convert them, you might simply create a new warm green and eliminate the cool one that seems most redundant. There is no fixed rule about the proportion of warm to cool colours in a palette, but I find that a roughly equal balance gives more colour contrast options for the kind of work that I do.

The third balancing colour check might be to look for colours that are not family-related or that feel out of line with the rest. Keep in mind that colour discordance is a subjective perception, and that some colours have different chemical bases,

TWO INCREMENTAL COLOUR TESTS

Top far left: **Turquoise and yellow for aqua-green.**
Top left: One yellow plus one-quarter turquoise.
Top right: One yellow plus three-quarter turquoise.
Top far right: One yellow plus two turquoise.

Bottom far left: **Warm strong red plus yellow for orange.**
Bottom left: One yellow plus one-eighth warm strong red.
Bottom right: One yellow plus one-quarter warm strong red.
Bottom far right: One yellow plus one half warm strong red.

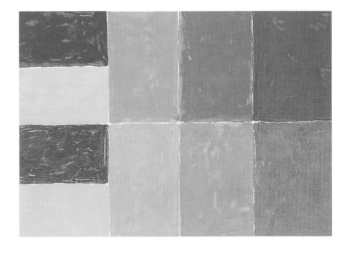

and hence different kinds of intensities. There are always one or two that I feel are clashing, and need to be toned down and brought into visual concordance with the rest.

A principle applied by Renaissance painters was that every colour in the palette should contain a very small amount of every other. This way the palette is entirely harmonious and colours are related. What I do is simply add a tiny amount (one sixteenth part, more or less) of the colour's complement – this seems to bring it into line. This is also another way of slightly darkening a colour, or of swinging it from warm to cool (or vice versa).

Having made some changes, lay down your second row, including both modified and unmodified colours. Look again for any modifications that might be needed, and incorporate them in your next colour row. It may take three, or more, colour rows to reach your final palette (see p. 41).

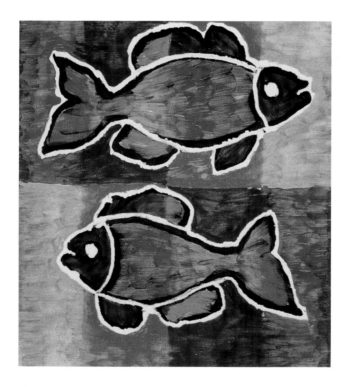

Having made some changes... (see p. 41).

Complementary colour study

Wet-blended colour stains on matt maiolica glaze. The brush strokes within the fish were laid down in the opposite direction to the background for added visual tension. The foreground (fish) colours are hovering over their complementary colours in the background for extra colour contrast.

Colour testing

The second stage of colour testing happens by applying the colours to glazed bisque tiles, and firing them. All the colour rows worked out on paper can now be fired. The fired palette is the one you will actually be working from. It gives leads as to directions and idiosyncrasies you might wish to pursue, indications of aesthetic and technical problems needing solution, and experi-

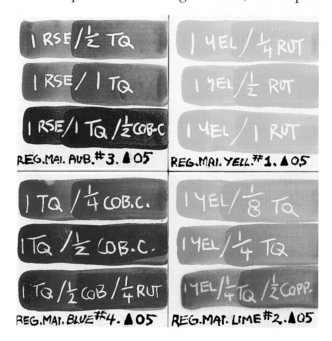

Sample fired colour tests at cone 05 (1046°C): regular maiolica glaze no. 1

Some of these have succeeded, others require still more testing. Note how the juxtaposition of the tiles can show colour interaction. The observations that follow can lead to further testing and to the development of a final colour palette (see p. 41).

Top left: **Test for aubergine purple**. The cobalt carbonate is obviously too dominant in the third row, and needs to be radically cut-back if not left out, to bring the colour back to a redder and lighter colour range.

Bottom left: **Test for strong blue**. The rutile has the effect of greying and subduing the blue in the third row. The second row is the strong, not too garish blue I'm looking for.

Top right: **Test for strong yellow**. The third row finally has sufficient rutile to create the strong yellow I want.

Bottom right: **Test for lime green**. The copper carbonate addition to the third row darkens the lime too much, but gives an interesting smoky effect. The second row is the colour I'm aiming for.

ence with the actual, final colour. All future changes are based on fired information.

This is where more detailed colour research leads to a gradual accumulation of colour samples, which will serve as a concrete reference. Here is where you focus on such things as:

- creating graded warm and cool tones
- complementary colour studies (see palette below)
- combining with black and white
- testing to determine how surface is affected by the amount of frit
- testing for degrees of transparency and opacity
- blending of stains with compatible oxides and carbonates
- testing for results at varied temperatures

My basic format for such testing is a small commercial bisque tile (11.5 x 11.5 cm). I like this size because each tile can take three or four graded colours and, when a number of colours have been tested, the tiles can be laid down and slid along-

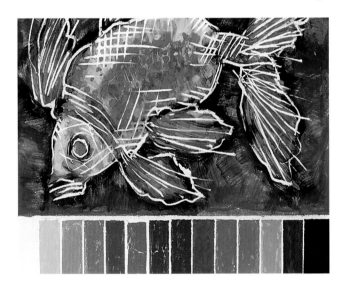

THE FINAL COLOUR PALETTE

All the colours aligned in 'rainbow' order were used to create the fish image. Some of the previously discussed colour elements (such as the use of contrasting and complementary colours) are at work here. To give further impact to the image, the fish was painted in predominantly warm colours, while the background recedes in cool tones.

side one another to exhibit colour interaction. They are also easy to store (see p. 40).

If one were testing for colour over a vertical surface, with thick/thin glaze contrasts or underlying texture then, obviously, those surfaces would have to be constructed.

The actual work on-tile proceeds as follows. What I usually do, having given the tile an even, poured, medium-thick coating of glaze, is to wait or to force-dry the tile, so that it is absolutely dry before any colour work is done. If the glaze coating is still damp, then the wet, applied colour can drag up opacified glaze into the colour itself, resulting in a muddy, subdued look after the firing. If the tile and glaze are fully dry, then water from the brush can be absorbed, and the colour stays on the surface. Using a square-tipped, fairly soft brush (mixture well stirred, of course), I will pass a controlled stroke across the entire width of the tile, and overlap another stroke from the halfway mark. This allows me to see transparency and opacity effects. I write the actual mixture-recipe on the tile by scratching right through the colour (*sgraffito*), so that this information is immediately visible. With fine-line black stain I might also identify the tile's code, glaze and temperature along the bottom. Most results will end up in a notebook, along with any pertinent observations.

Stage two is the longest of the two phases of testing; it goes on for the rest of your working life. When I am not engrossed with production work, it is a great luxury to sit down quietly, to play and experiment with colours, to know that this is the time for pleasurable dabbling, and for getting back in touch with the basics.

'Colour is life, for a world without colours appears to us dead. Colours are primordial ideas, children of the aboriginal colourless light and its counterpart, colourless darkness. As flame begets light, so light engenders colours. Colours are the children of light, and light is their mother. Light, that first phenomenon of the world, reveals to us the spirit and living soul of the world through colours.'

J. ITTEN *The Art of Colour*

41

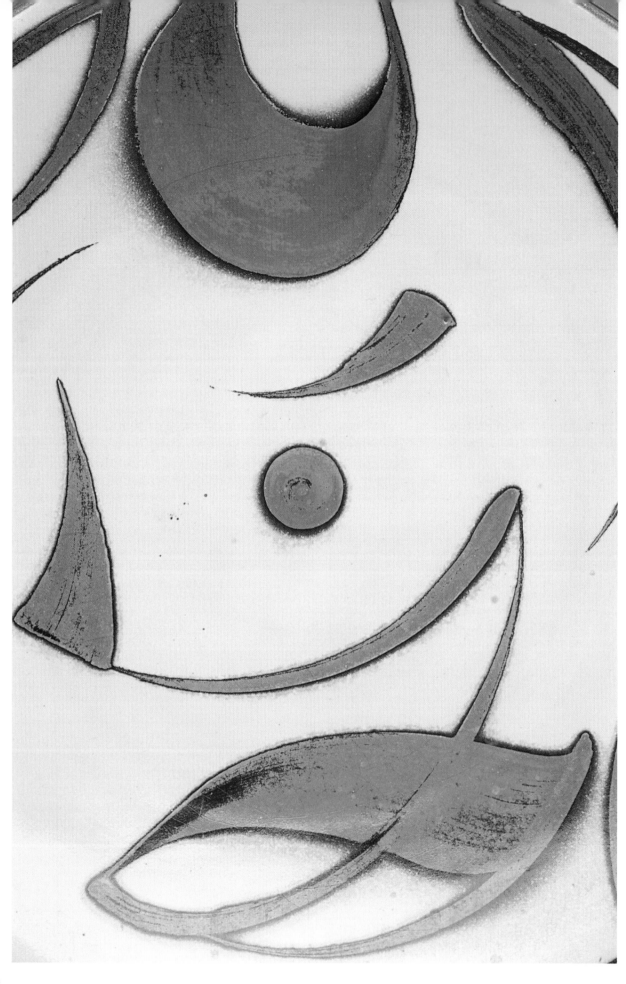

Brushes and Brushwork

'Il faut croire à ce qu'on fait pour bien le faire, et à trop voir les ficelles de son métier, on perd cette qualité de spontanéité, d'émotion, d'inspiration qui fait toute la différence entre l'artifice et l'art, et donne à ce dernier sa saveur d'authenticité.'

ROMAIN GARY

Brushes

A brush is one of the most intimate and gestural of all tools – it becomes an extension of our own body. Brushwork reflects not only the artist's intent in presenting an image, but also her or his ability to meld fluid and controlled gesture into concrete expression, be it line, wash or colour blending.

A comfortable brush to me is much like an old pair of shoes, working best when it is worn out and soft, and just about to fall apart. Like new shoes, brushes need to be broken in. I'm always a bit anxious when I have to discard the old for the new. I will wire and tape up a disintegrating brush handle to the point of ugliness, until the bristles fall out and the thing is no longer workable. I feel more possessive about my brushes than about my clothes or toothbrush. They are, as mentioned earlier, an extension of my body, the direct link between the mind and the surface to be painted, important enough to justify a tiny bit of possessive neurosis.

ALAN CAIGER-SMITH (UK)

PLATE WITH BRUSHWORK (DETAIL), 1994.
Red-gold reduction lustre on tin glaze.

I tend to divide my own brushes into four basic use-categories: fine line and outline brushes; colour fill-in brushes; graded wash brushes, and on-surface blending brushes. Each of these types is chosen to convey a particular characteristic to the image, such as crispness, softness, movement, or a focus on linearity or tonality of colour. The success of these effects, and hence the success of the image, depends on a number of control factors which occur simultaneously and need to be well rehearsed. These factors include the type, shape and size of brush, the load of water and colour mixture, the length, width and speed of the stroke, and the degree of applied pressure. In-glaze painting on tin glaze demands a fair degree of brush control, since every nuance of each stroke remains visible after firing. A successful gestural stroke will remain clear and bold; a sloppy or vacillating one, painfully incomplete. Most brush strokes can be laid down once only. There is little room for hesitation, correction, or overwork. The assurance needed to lay down a stroke with ease and fluidity comes from continued practice.

It is the character of the brush stroke and its impact on the image that determines the choice of brush used. For very fine line- and outline-drawing, I use point-tipped Chinese calligraphy (*sumi*) or sable brushes. The brush must be long enough, with a well-defined tip, flexible yet resistant, and able to hold a reasonable amount of water. The darker Chinese brushes (usually a mixture of soft squirrel hair and stiff horse hair) are best for long, drawn-out strokes and fluctuating lines. Sable and sable/synthetic mix brushes will serve here as well, but retain a little less water. Full-tipped sable brushes can also be cut to create a fine, long tip emerging from a larger reservoir head, for very fine line drawing requiring an extended stroke.

The white Chinese calligraphy brushes (rabbit hair if fine, goat hair if coarse) have good water-holding capacity. I use the larger round- and point-tipped brushes for colour fill-in and creating brush shapes. For this purpose I might also use some softer round- and square-tipped sable and synthetic brushes. For larger wash areas I will use soft, white, square-tipped Chinese brushes. These have a good capacity for holding water and maintaining a long stroke. Finally, for on-surface blending, I use stiff-bristled synthetic brushes, which can range from very fine-detail brushes to large house-painters' brushes, depending on the scale of the image.

There is certainly no rule for the number or type of brushes to be used in any given project – the choice is totally personal. Some determining factors in brush choice might include the character and effect of the stroke desired, the resistance of the glaze surface (unfired or fired), and the size and scale of the work.

Brushwork

To my mind, there are some other important elements to be considered in the promotion of successful brushwork. These are both the mental and physical stance of preparedness and comfort necessary for easy and fluid gesture, as well as a reasonably well-organized work space. From the mental point of view, I need to be relaxed enough to give myself easily to the gestures required; I need to be in a rather unpressured and meditative state of mind. I find that mentally I can categorise most of my ceramic-related activities as 'energetic' or 'plodding but necessary' or 'meditative', etc. Throwing, the pulling of handles, and brushwork fall into the latter category.

To get into a meditative state of mind I will spend time doing minor preparatory tasks such as mixing colours, fussing over my workspace, or choosing the right music. If I find I'm just procrastinating, or cannot relax, then I will postpone the brushwork, and do something less contemplative. Since brushwork is one of my favourite

work activities, I can slip into the required gear fairly quickly. Posture and the spatial organisation of the work area is important not only for maintaining physical comfort over a prolonged period of work time, but also for providing enough breadth of space to accommodate a generous stroke. Often the stroke's gesture is larger than the painted stroke itself, and needs room to move and breathe. Smaller, more precise work may need close eye-to-object distance, and a more compact gesture. I find that usually any physical discomfort or mental malaise will reflect upon the stroke, and inhibit its ease and spontaneity. As mentioned in Chapter Four, practice on paper, with plenty of elbow room and a relaxed stance will in time give a good sense of what is required in terms of choosing and using a brush for a given effect. As in the throwing process, brushwork is very much an activity where the forceful domination of materials and tools is not the key to control. Rather it is the giving over of oneself to the physical process with relaxed concentration, partnering rather than dominating, that engenders fluid and expressive work.

A final word, on the care and maintenance of brushes. I have had even the most inexpensive of Chinese brushes last for years with proper care. I rinse my brushes well in water after use and dry them lightly on a towel. I might twirl them between my finger tips with a bit of spittle, which makes them keep their points. I dry them overnight on their side, point down a little, so water cannot soak into the handle. Bamboo-handled brushes are particularly susceptible to filling up with water and splitting. Finally, I do not stir up colours with brushes, nor ever leave them standing point down in water for any time at all – that is the quickest way of shortening their life span.

In the following images I would like to illustrate some specific brushwork. There are, no doubt, far more ways to use a brush than shown here, but these are some of the ones with which I am most familiar. I have used the fish on tin-glazed tile as a standard image for simplicity of illustration. It occurs again in the next chapter in a greater variety of configurations and techniques. Here, the brushes and tools used are displayed below the image in the order in which they are used, from top to bottom.

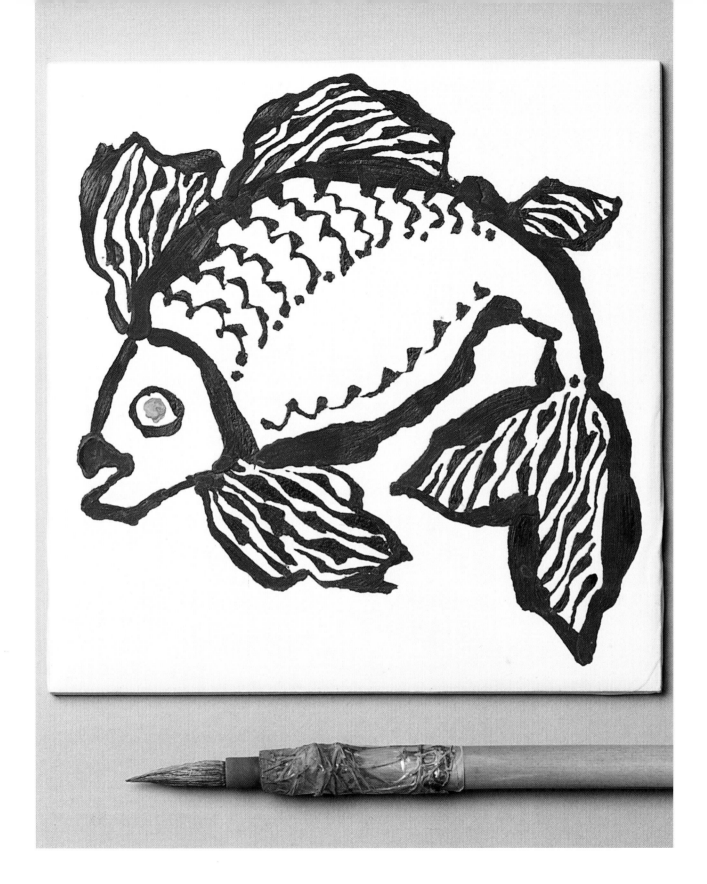

BRUSH LINE AND SHAPE

In this image a Chinese mixed-hair calligraphy brush (much abused) has been used to create a black outline and details. The degree of pressure of brush to surface with a heavy water/stain mixture creates a controlled line that also has a defined, fluctuating shape. The matt surface of the glaze and the dry, fritless mixture add an element of surface texture.

45

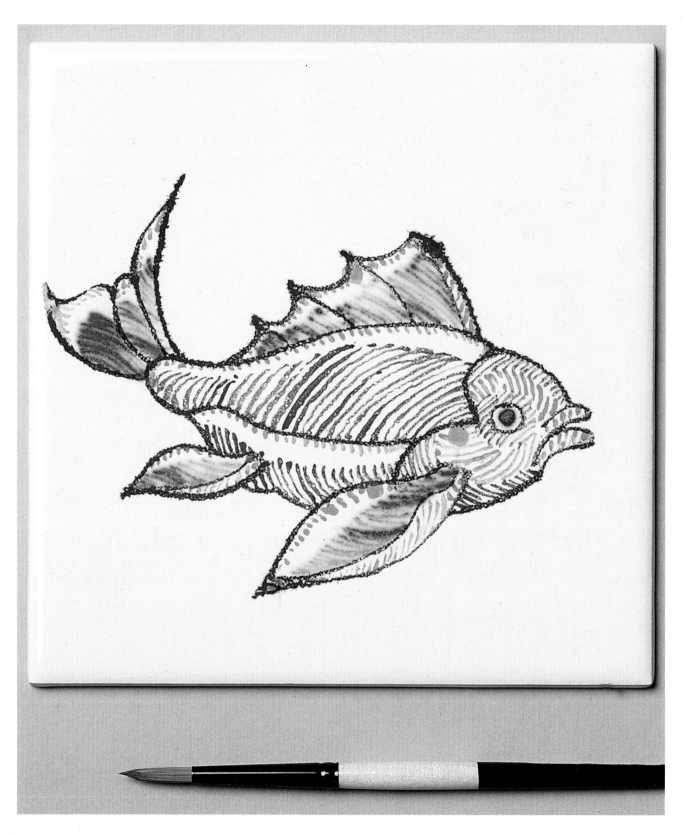

BRUSH OUTLINE AND DETAIL

I've treated this image very much like a fine-line drawing, using a fine-tipped narrow sable/synthetic brush and the traditional four colours: cobalt-blue, copper-green, ochre and manganese-brown. The fine contour lines and shading details create an effect very much like that of a woodcut.

46

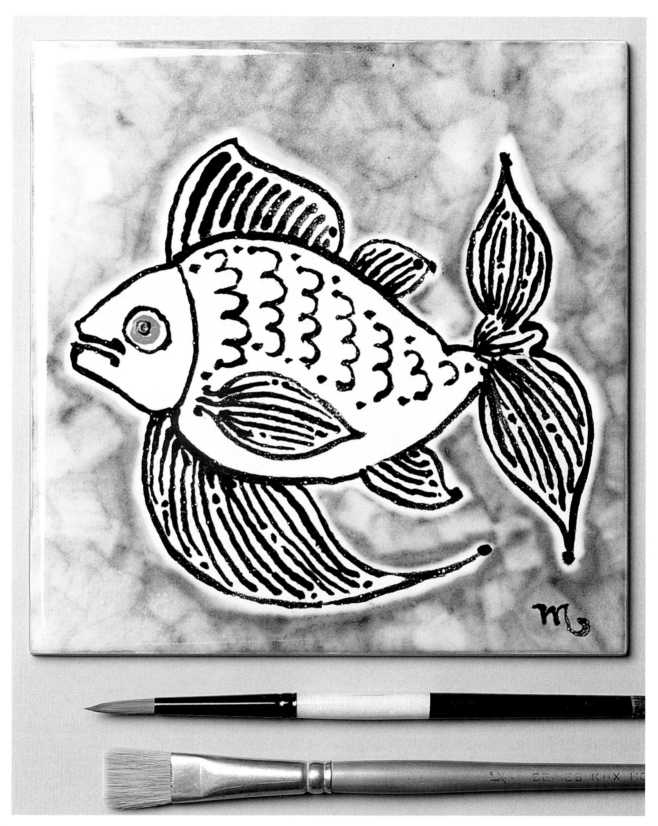

BRUSH OUTLINE AND BACKGROUND FILL-IN

The fine brush has been used for outlines and details in black. The white area within the fish is dramatised through a texture-like application of copper carbonate and water over the background, using a small, square-tipped sable brush. Note the smoky transparent quality of the fired copper.

47

BRUSH OUTLINE AND COLOUR FILL-IN

The fine brush has been used again to create a black stain outline. A rounded synthetic brush fills in the colours of the fish in graded strokes. The same brush creates the shapes for the leaf pattern, which is then outlined in fine black. The

minimal *sgraffito* detail around the eye is lightly scratched in through the colour into the glaze with a sharpened bamboo tool.

48

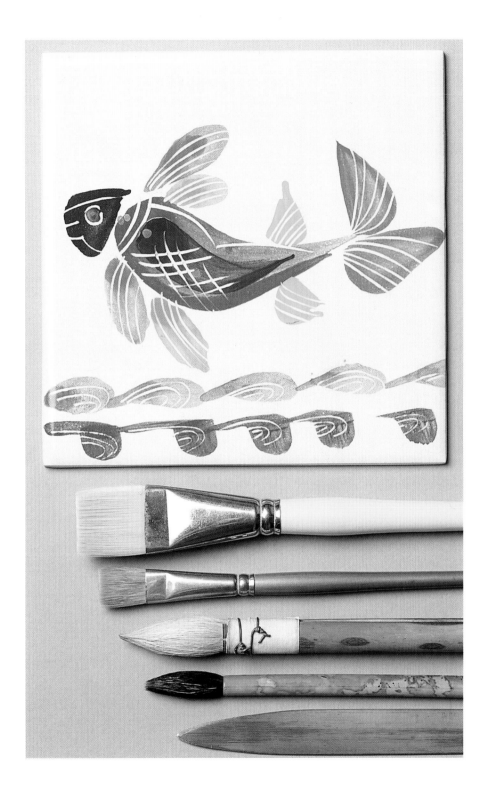

BRUSH SHAPE

The shape of the brush itself can be used to create distinctive patterns. In this image, the body of the fish has been rendered with a wide, square-tipped synthetic brush, laid down from left to right, and lifted off with a twist to end in a pointed shape. The darker inner colour detail has been done in the same way, using the smaller square brush. This same brush, dragged sideways and pressed down, creates the lower wave pattern. The large point-tipped Chinese calligraphy brush flicked sideways creates the head and tail shapes and, laid down point first, the green fin shapes. The smaller dark, pointed mixed-hair calligraphy brush, again flicked sideways, creates the small yellow fins and, laid down point-first from left to right, the upper wave pattern. *Sgraffito* line detail is added with the bamboo tool.

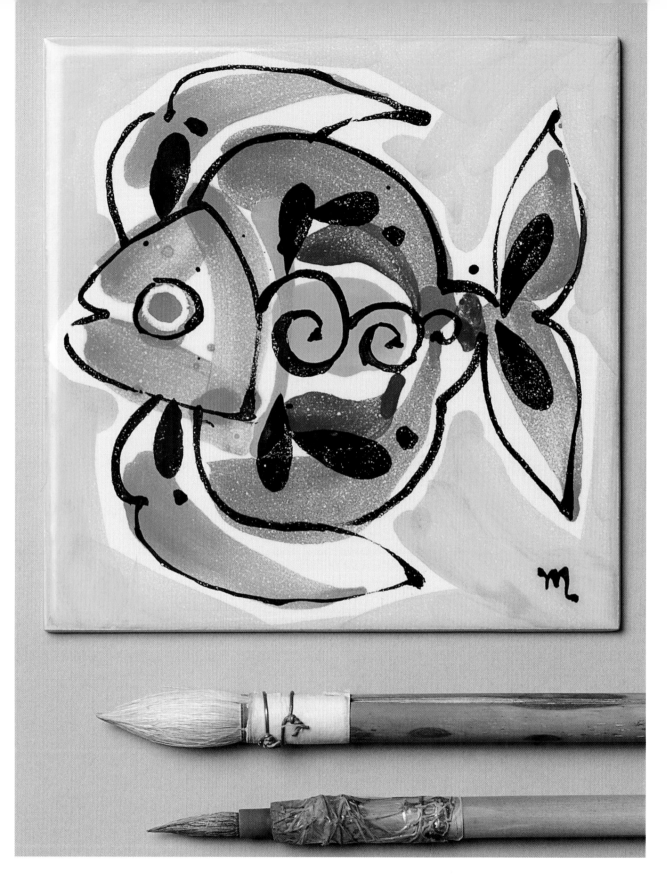

BRUSH SHAPE, BRUSH OUTLINE AND BACKGROUND FILL-IN

The large brush has been used to lay down the various coloured shapes that make up the fish's body. The small brush defines the black outline and black detail shapes. The larger brush is used again, heavily loaded, to fill in the solid yellow background. The white is left by omission.

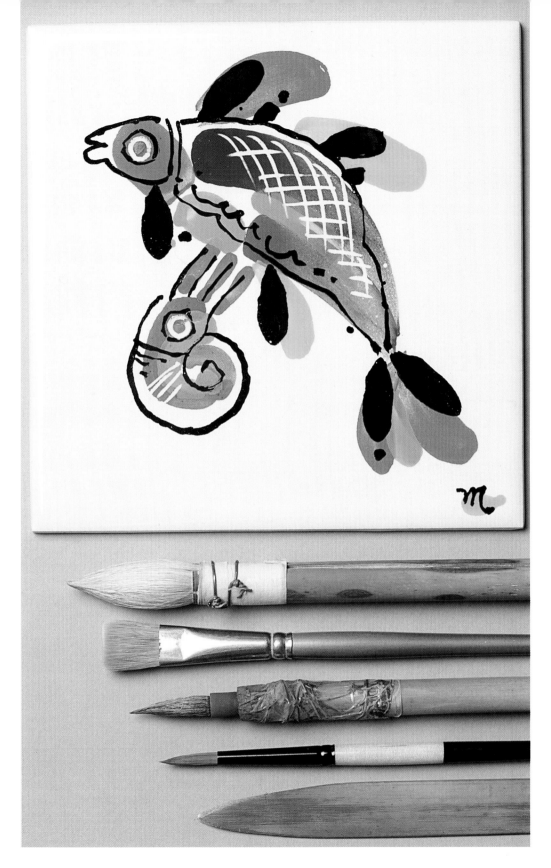

BRUSH SHAPE, OUTLINE AND *SGRAFFITO*

The basic colour areas are laid down first using the large calligraphy brush for the fish fins and tail and for the body of the nautilus. The square-tipped brush provides the brush shapes for the head and body of the fish. The smaller calligraphy brush lays down the black fin details, and the very fine sable brush superimposes the outline drawing. *Sgraffito* detail is added with the bamboo tool.

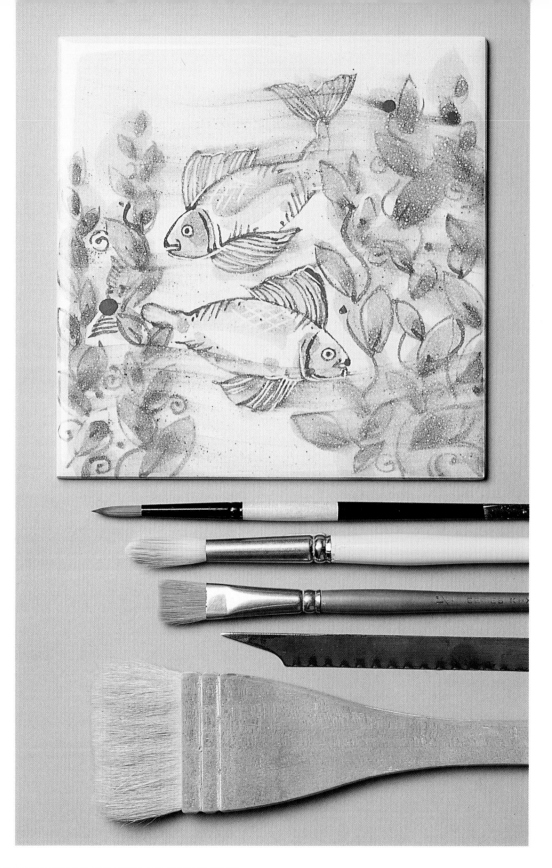

BRUSH SHAPE, BRUSH OUTLINE, *SGRAFFITO* AND SURFACE WASH

Here I've stayed in the monochrome blue colour range, using a diluted mixture of cobalt carbonate and water. First, a line drawing is done using the fine brush, with outlines filled in lightly using the round- and square-tipped brushes.

Very fine *sgraffito* highlights are added using a sharp metal tool (a filed-off hacksaw blade). Lastly, a wide, soft Chinese brush dipped in water is used to blur lightly over the entire image, for a soft, underwater effect.

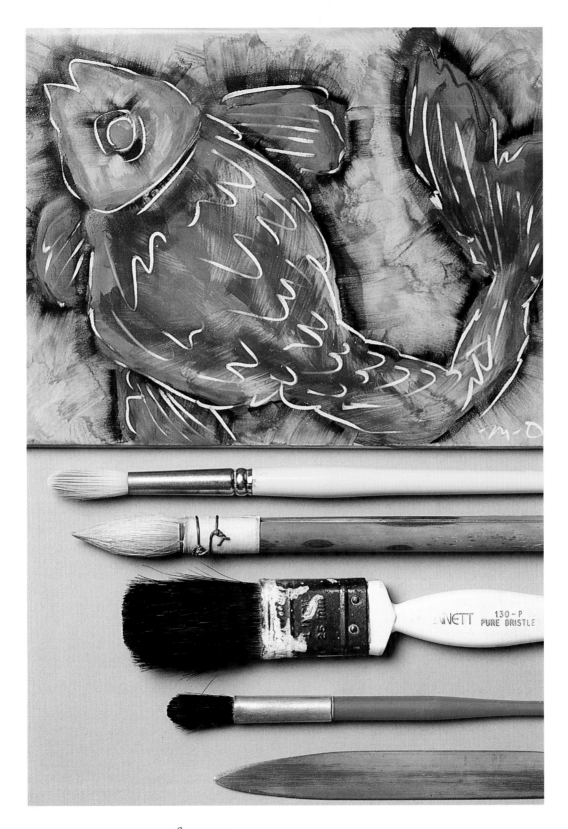

BRUSH OUTLINE, ON-SURFACE BLENDING AND *SGRAFFITO*

In this image the colour mixture is used in its full intensity. Using the small round-tipped brush, a dark green general outline is laid down. All other colours are loosely and generously applied inside and outside the outline with the large calligraphy brush. The two stiff, dark synthetic brushes, not too wet and frequently rinsed, are used to blend all the colours on-surface in directionally controlled strokes. A loose *sgraffito* sketch over the initial outline completes the image. Note how in some areas (the left fin, for instance) the scratched line can cut lightly through one colour to another, without reaching the white glaze below.

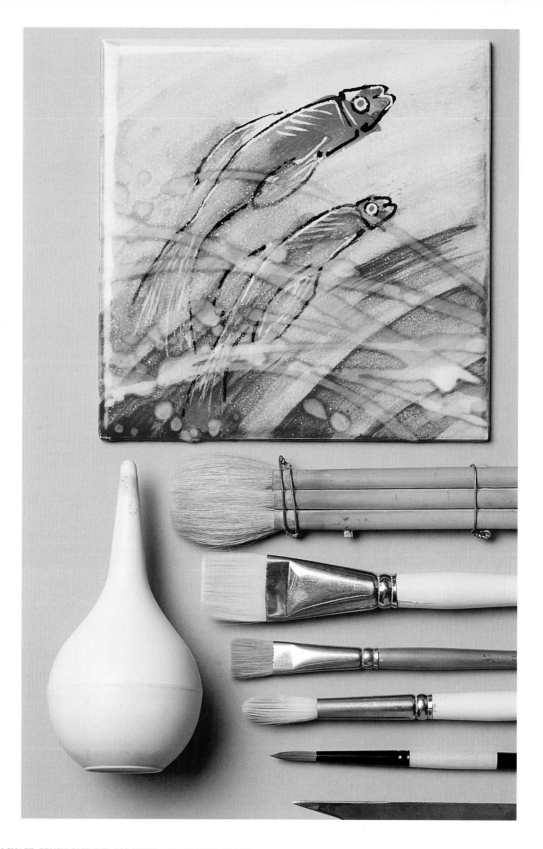

WASH, BRUSH SHAPE, BRUSH OUTLINE, *SGRAFFITO* AND TRAILED GLAZE

This image is one that requires a little more planning. A soft wide Chinese brush (broken off from a wider one to create different widths) has been used to lay down a light, graded cobalt wash, intensifying toward the bottom. Square brushes create the fish-body shapes, and the round tipped brush is used for head and fins. The fine sable brush adds the black outline, and the metal tool is used for white *sgraffito* detail. Matt maiolica glaze is loosely trailed over the image with a rubber bulb syringe to create an overlapping wave effect.

54

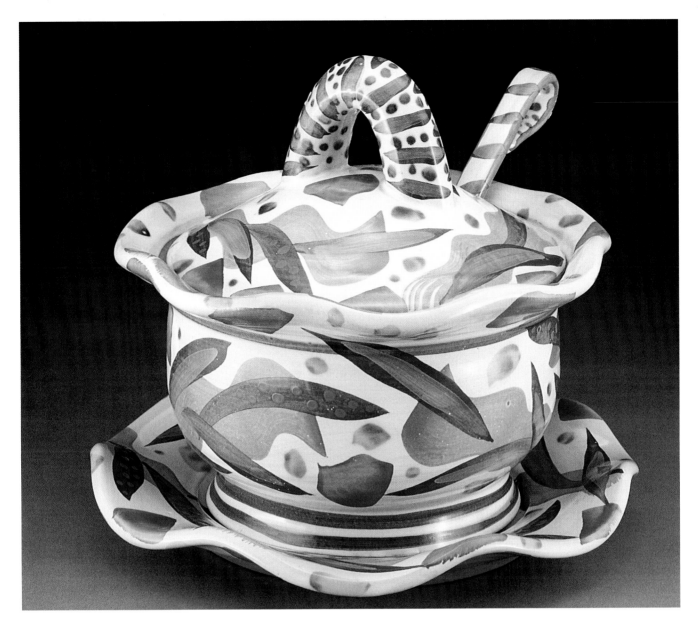

STANLEY MACE ANDERSEN (USA)

TUREEN, d. 27 cm, 1997.

This tureen set comprises a supporting plate and ladle. The work was wheel-thrown and altered. After glazing the raw-glaze surface was quickly and directly painted (with a commercial stain/frit mixture), using brush shapes and without preparatory underdrawing. Thick white slip below the surface (on larger pieces) adds surface texture beneath the glaze. The work was fired to 1115°C.

Photograph: Tom Mills

'Among the inspirations and influences I am aware of are my wildly overgrown vegetable and flower gardens; my daily association with nature; my mothers love of dinnerware; my travels to lands of vibrant colour (the Mediterranean, Spain, Morocco); and the exuberance of common pots of the past.I am concerned with line, colour and patterns, and their relationship to pottery forms. Maiolica allows me to create the liquid flowing lines, splashes of colour, and overlapping brush strokes that produce the sense of casual, playful spontaneity that I wan to express with my decoration.I want my utilitarian table and kitchen ware to become part of the daily flow of an individual's domestic life, enhancing the enjoyment of preparing, serving and presenting food.'

Stanley Mace Andersen

CHAPTER SIX

The Painted Fish

'Technique alone has no depth of meaning: as in poetry, where the most perfect technique in rhyme and verse, without a valuable thought and emotion behind it, would not make a poem of any significance, so too with pottery.'

MARGUERITE WILDENHAIN

'Technique and skills must be absorbed and wrapped up and put away to become such an integral part of yourself that they will be revealed in your work without your thought.'

SHOJI HAMADA

I am often asked why the painted fish is such a recurring theme in my work. Tongue-in-cheek I reply that it's easier to draw a fish than a moose. Upon reflection, I would say that there is a real and long-term fascination here. The fish represents colour, movement and flowing line, all elements that through gesture and materials translate readily into an image. As a swimmer, I can envy the fish's ease of motion through water; as a thinker, I can contemplate the difference between its habitat and mine, and enjoy its exoticism. As a painter I can emulate its fluid movement in a swift brush stroke.

USING COLOURED GLAZES

Colour-saturated maiolica glazes have been trailed over a yellow base glaze. The black fish is carefully painted in around the trail lines, and accented with *sgraffito*.

While fish imagery has been one fascination – and indeed, a recurring theme in many ceramic cultures – the medium of tin-glaze maiolica has been another. It fulfils my need for painting, narrative, and exploration of colour more than any other ceramic medium. It offers up enough variety of expression to satisfy even the most demanding ceramic gourmet.

Techniques and approaches

By technique I mean the sequence of steps, the use of gesture and materials that create a specific image. Approach refers to the strategy, the point of view, the discriminating eye that uses technique to give individuality to the image and bring it home to the viewer.

The learning of a technique is a tangible and concretely definable process, and as such is more quickly understood. Much less so is the development of a personal approach (as discussed in Chapter Two) which requires long-term research, allied to a particular vision. Through continued discipline and work practice, one learns to anticipate the visual results that any chosen technique will produce, and technique and approach begin to inform each other in an active manner. That is when the work becomes involving and exciting. Just as a technically perfect voice can fail to interpret a song, leaving me admiring the sound, but unmoved, so virtuoso technique without a personal approach leads to cold work – work that lacks character, that fails to communicate, that fails to touch the heart. However, if the two – technique and approach – have worked together, then a statement has been made that involves me in an active dialogue with the maker. This is the crux of what image-making is about.

Ideally, technique and approach should go hand in hand, but this is not always so. In reality, I find I often lack technique to express a certain vision, or have developed techniques without a particular focus. This produces an elastic tension, which leads not to frustration, but rather to new research: my vision expands, as do my techniques, as does the vision again, and so, finally,

STAMPS

The stamps used here have been moulded from clay, impressed when soft, and refined and smoothed in the leatherhard stage, prior to bisquing. I prefer bisqued clay stamps to plaster for durability. The stamps are impressed into soft red clay. In this image a thinner coating of the tin glaze allows the red clay colour to shimmer through.

new work is created. All work, no matter how good or complete, is still a work-in-progress. That is to say that for the maker it represents the culminating point of a period of learning, and is the stepping stone for the development of future work.

In this chapter I have attempted to illustrate as many techniques and approaches as can be squeezed together under the generously ample umbrella of maiolica. I have included techniques that are squarely in the maiolica tradition, others that are borrowed from other ceramic traditions, and others again that are entirely contemporary, or newly invented. I use the fish as an illustration of an image being renewed in a great variety of configurations, to show the widest spectrum of techniques and approaches. Almost all the imagery in this chapter is of work that is electric-fired in oxidation at 1046 °C (Orton large cone 05). In creating this imagery, I have stayed within my

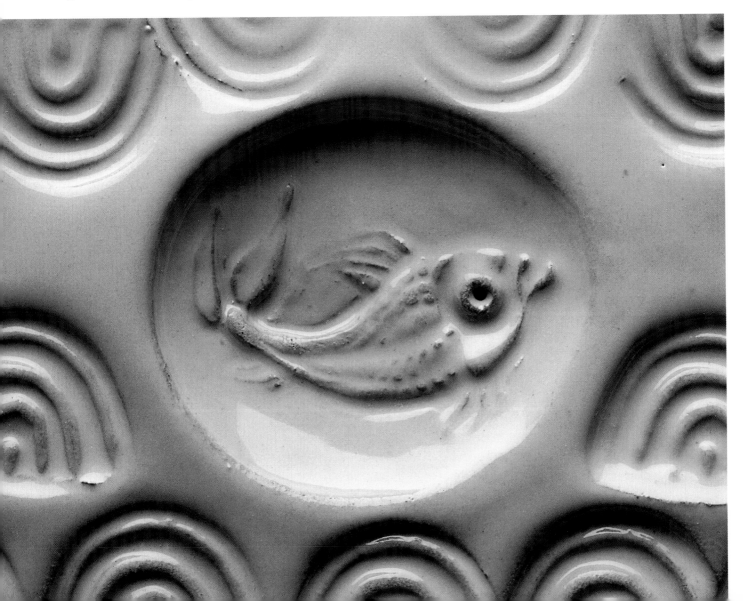

own range of interests and limited expertise. I do not include such viable and interesting techniques as reduction-fired effects, spray-glazing, *cloisonné*, sintering for a harder surface, underglaze slips, overglaze enamels, photo-transfer prints, decals, etc. Some of these will occur in the next chapter, which features the works of international contemporary maiolica artists. The techniques I do explore are drawn from my own repertoire. Most of them involve in-glaze painting, in all its variations, and use the brush as the primary vehicle of expression.

1. Using clay relief

There have been some historical maiolica precedents for the incorporation of clay relief, with or without the use of colour. Two notable examples would be the large segmented painted wall reliefs of the Della Robbia workshop in Italy in the early 16th century, and the later *Bianchi di Faenza* wares of the mid-16th century.

SPRIG AND COMBING

A sprig is a stamp (again, bisqued clay) where care has been taken to create sufficient depth and smooth edges so that the sprig shape lifts out in one piece without catching or separating. Malleable clay is pressed firmly into the negative stamp shape, excess clay smoothed off the edges, and the shape lifted out gently with a fine blade edge once a visible shrink line appears. The flat surface of the sprig is wetted slightly, and pressed onto the moistened leatherhard surface of the object to be decorated. Combing is also done at this stage, using a coarse wooden comb section.

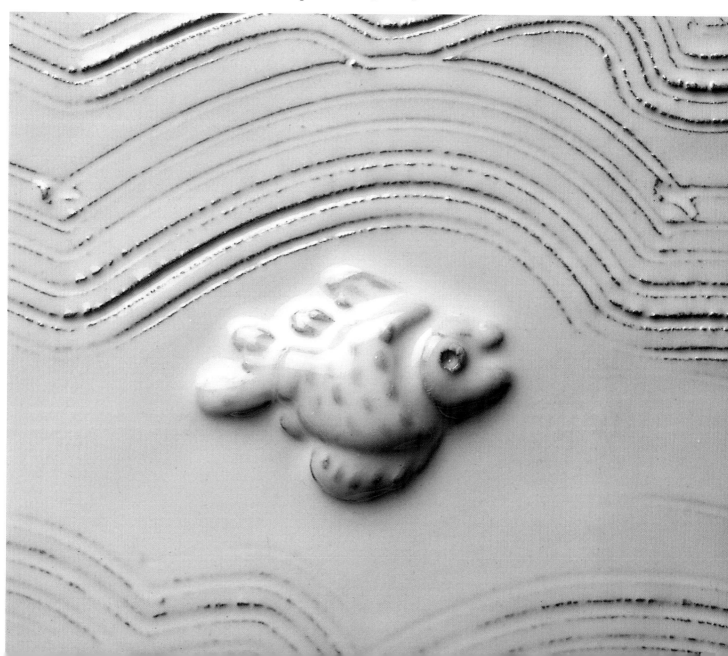

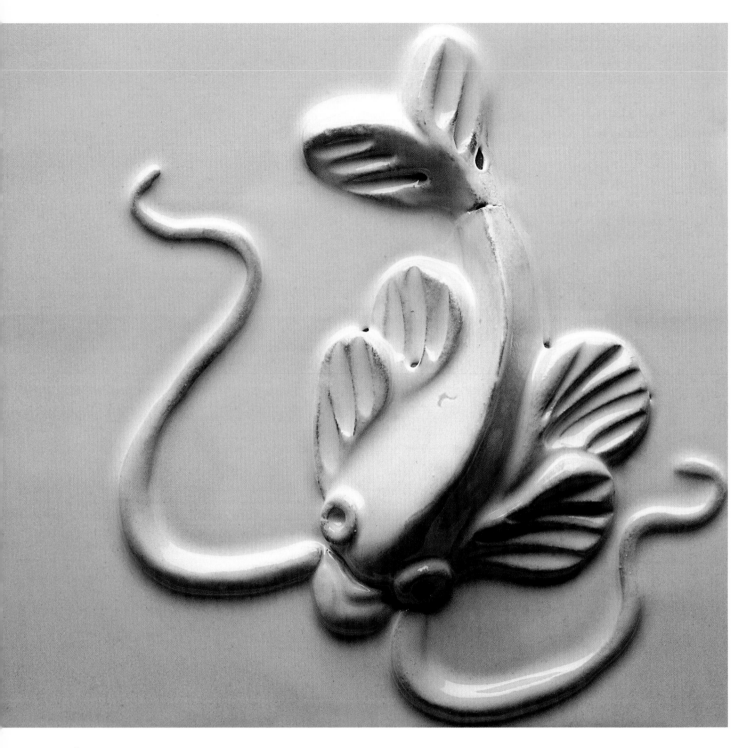

COIL RELIEF

Balls of clay of varying sizes are rolled into tear-drop shapes and pressed into position
onto dampened leatherhard clay. Small coils and balls are added, and texturing
is impressed with varying wooden modelling tools.

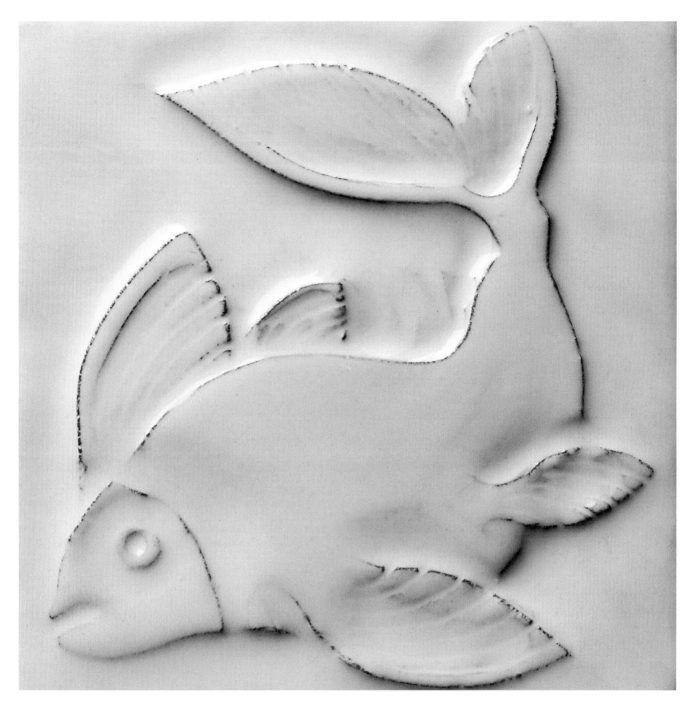

LOW RELIEF

An image is sketched onto leatherhard red clay, and the background pared away
to a lower level with a sharp metal loop tool. The fish image then appears raised
in low relief. Small accent details can be cut in or impressed. Clay colour will show
through at the edges if the glaze is not too thickly applied.

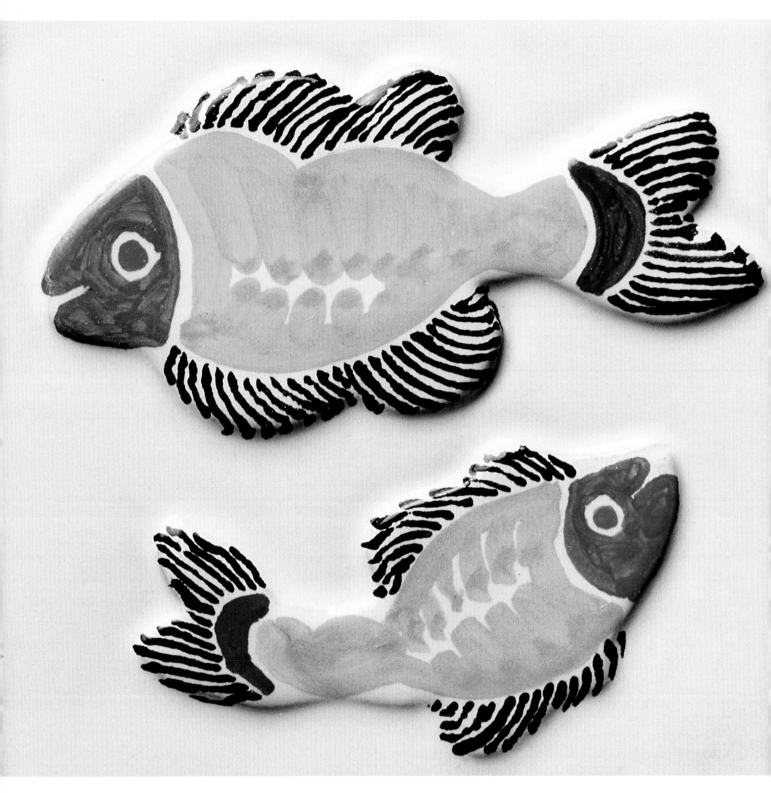

Small slabs of damp clay are rolled out and cut into required shapes, much like cookies.
They are moistened and firmly tamped down onto the leather-hard clay surface,
taking care not to trap air underneath. They appear as relief below an image of brushed coloured
stains on glaze. I have used an off-white rather than a red clay body here, under a
medium-thick glaze coating, to avoid any interference of clay colour with surface colour.

2. *Using clay/glaze contrast*

These techniques work best with a red terracotta body, since the clay itself is deliberately exposed to contrast with the white tin glaze.

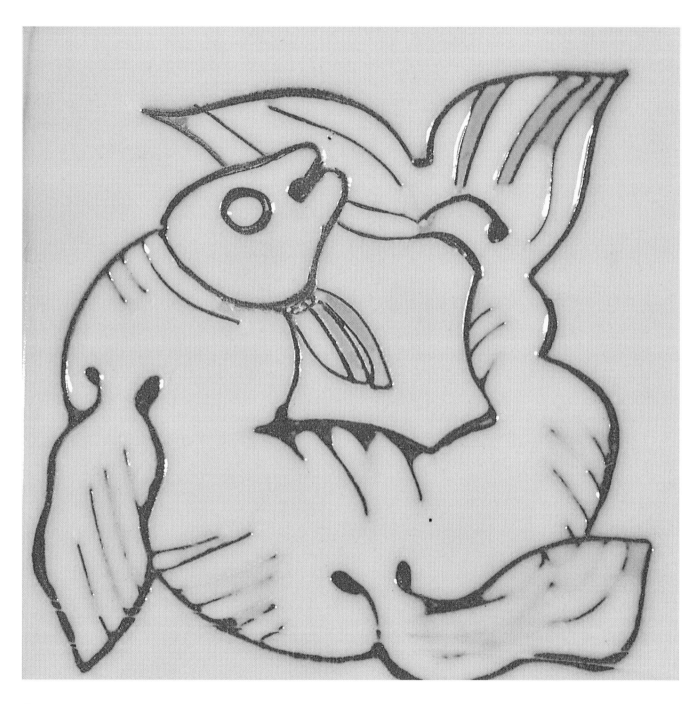

GLAZE *SGRAFFITO*

Here a flat bamboo tool with two sizes of point is used to scratch a pattern through the white glaze to the red bisque body below. If the glaze is well-dried, and this is done cleanly, the melting glaze will leave smooth, round-edged lines on, and give a faint gloss to, the exposed red surface.

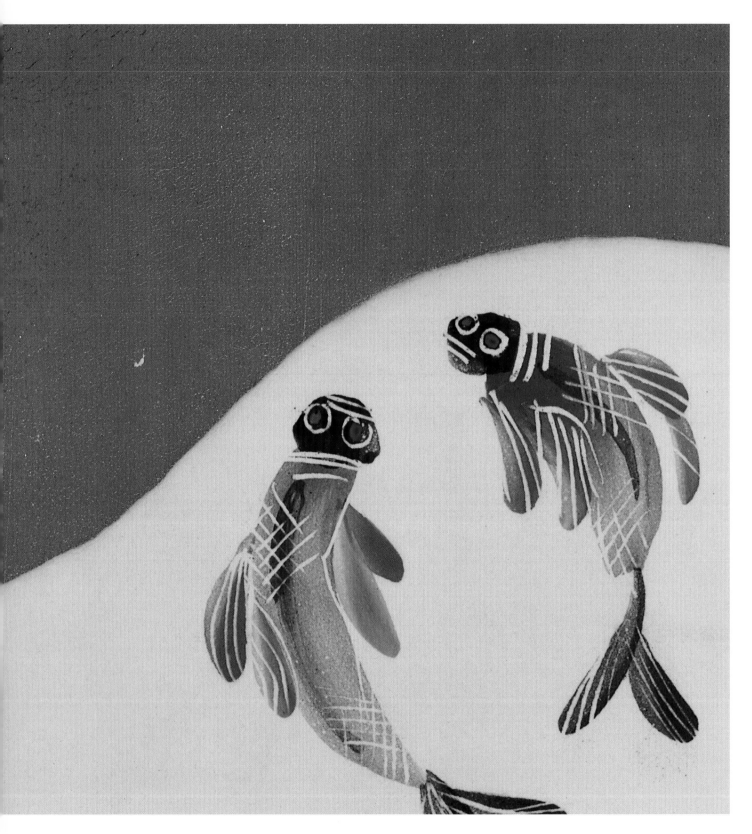

CLAY/GLAZE CONTRAST

Glaze is poured in a controlled wave over the red bisque surface to create a clean line of contrast.
Fishes are brushed on quickly with coloured stains, using brush shapes, and details are
lightly defined with *sgraffito* through the colours into the glaze, but not through to the clay body.

64

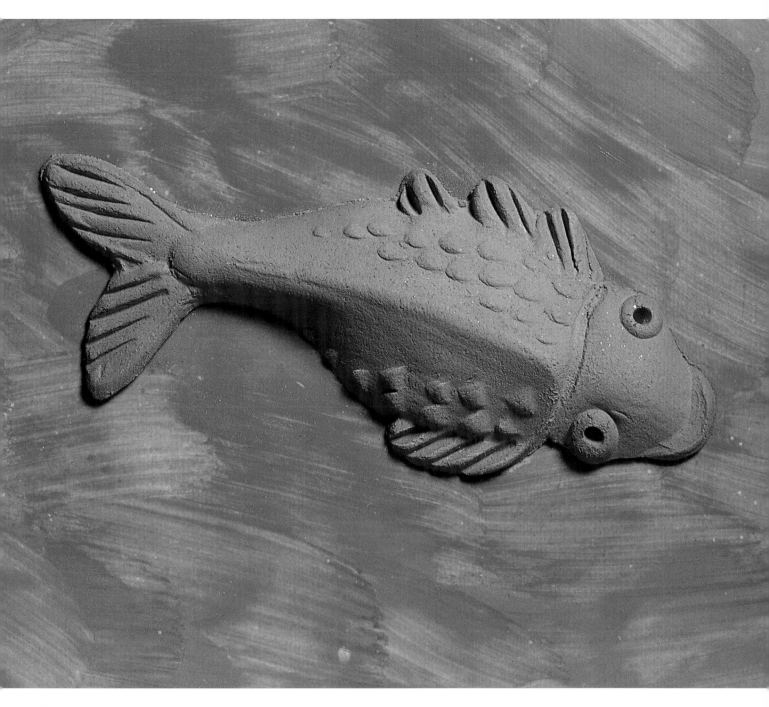

CLAY SPRIG ON COLOUR

A fresh red terracotta sprig is moistened, laid directly on the flat, glazed, and green-painted surface, and fired through in the second firing. It will fuse to the glaze below. For a vertical surface, it is best to attach the sprig in the leatherhard phase, bisque normally, and wax the sprig to resist the glaze and colour.

3. Using a limited palette

Some of the best known tin-glaze wares are the traditional blue and white delftwares of Holland (see p. 21). The use of the cobalt carbonate for fine-line drawings and wash effects of varying intensities allows for a large range of expression using only one basic colour: in this case, blue.

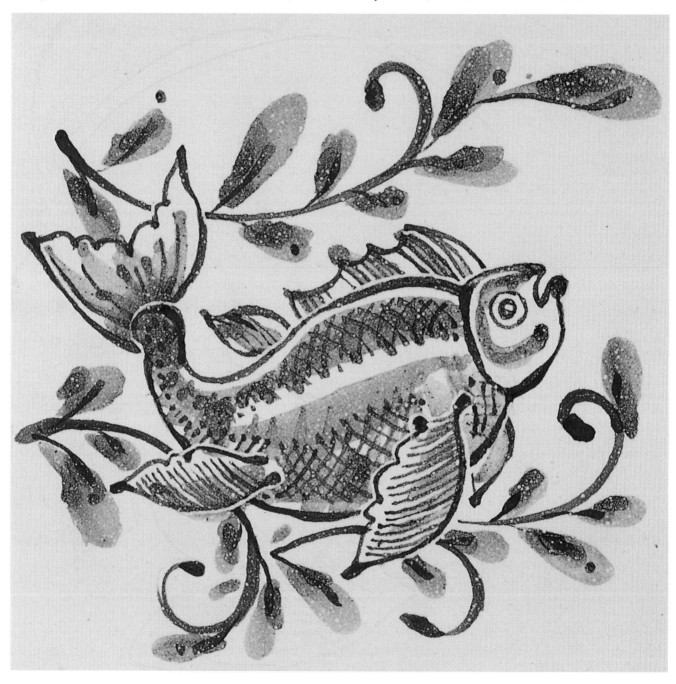

BLUE AND WHITE BRUSH SHAPE AND CONTOUR

Here varying intensities of cobalt carbonate and water are applied with soft-tipped calligraphy brushes to create outline and brush shapes. The glaze has been toned down to a softer cream colour by the addition of one per cent of rutile to the recipe.

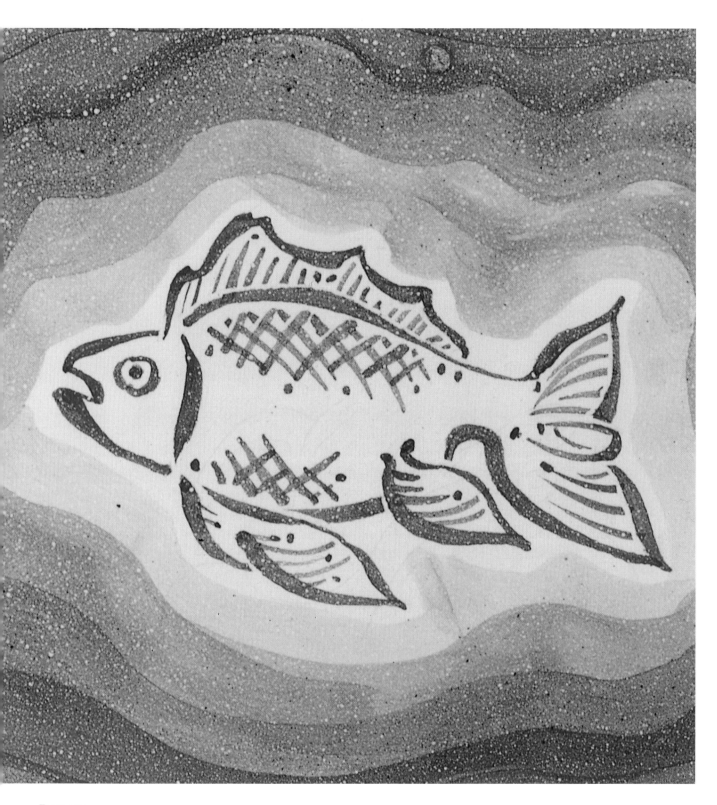

BLUE AND WHITE OUTLINE AND BACKGROUND WASH

The image has been painted with a controlled fluctuating outline and details. Graded cobalt wash strokes from light to darker towards the outside are applied with a square-tipped soft brush. The body of the fish itself is left white by omission.

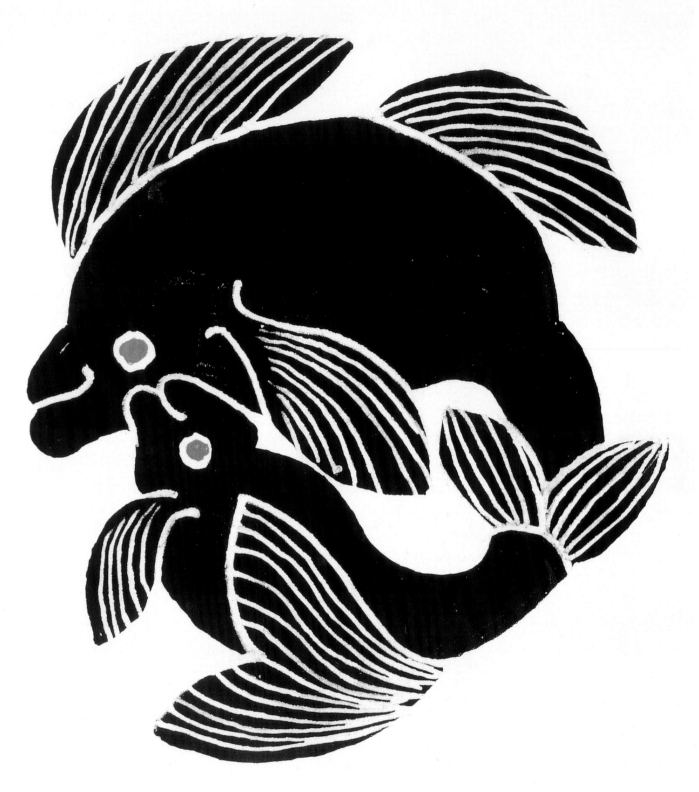

Two colours

In this image, strong graphic visual impact is created through the use of solidly applied black stain on white, with fine *sgraffito* detail. Added punch occurs through the use of a very small quantity of bright red.

68

4. Using wet-brush techniques

Some of my favourite techniques fall into this category. Here is where I feel that maiolica as a paining medium is both distinctive and unique, for its possibilities of complex colour blending and visual richness.

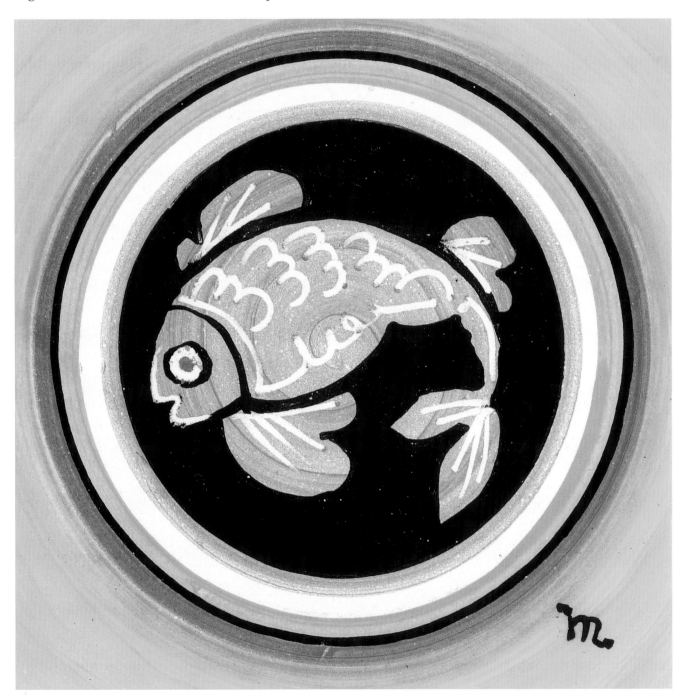

UNBLENDED SUPERIMPOSED COLOUR

Four colours and black have been used in this image that is contained in a circle with all brushwork done on a rotating banding wheel. The inner turquoise circle has a black inner frame and outline drawing superimposed, with the black background then filled in over the turquoise. *Sgraffito* details are added.

UNBLENDED JUXTAPOSED COLOUR

The various fishes here have been painted with a small round-tipped brush loaded
with a colour-stain mix of six pure colours and black. *Sgraffito* details have been lightly
added with a fine bamboo tool.

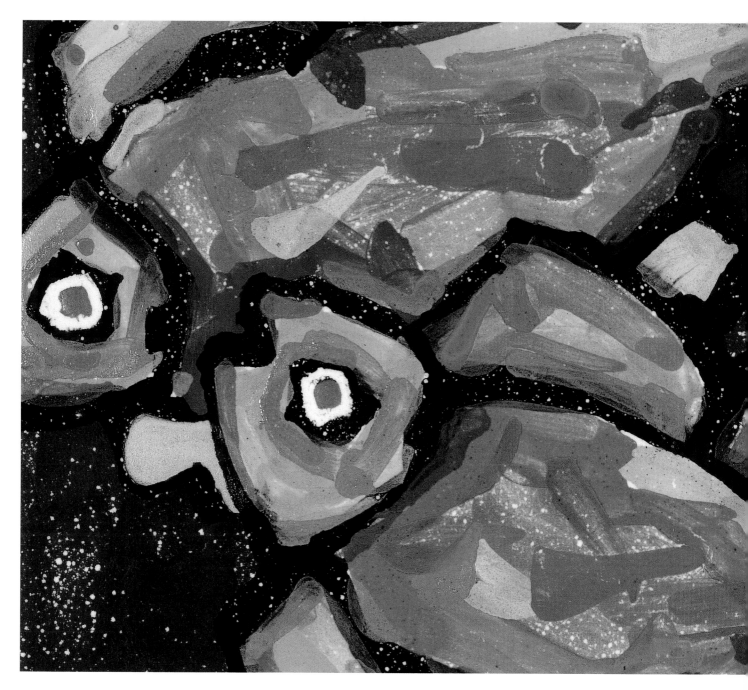

UNBLENDED LAYERED COLOUR

Using soft round brushes, image and background colours are juxtaposed
and overlapped in a controlled pattern with no surface blending, and
minimal *sgraffito* detail. Colour mixtures are kept to a medium-thick consistency
for more intense colour.

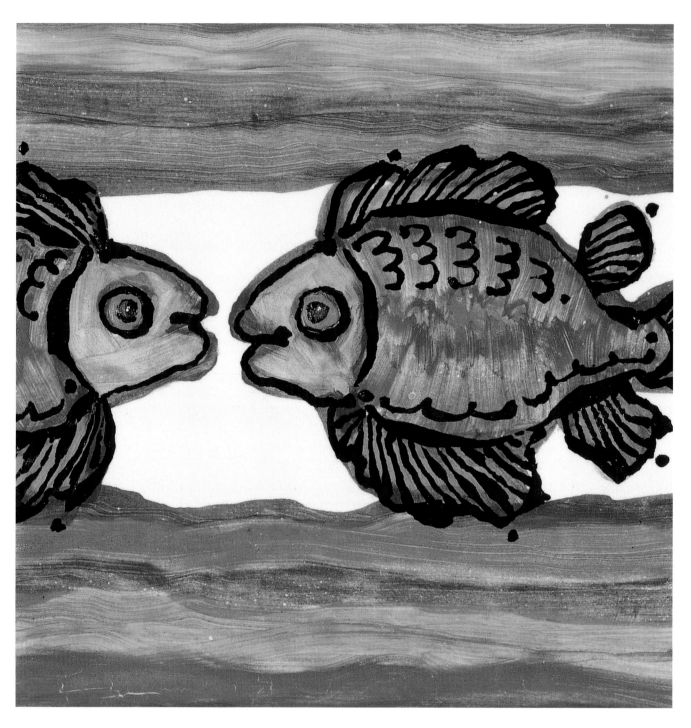

BLENDED COLOUR WITH BLACK LINE

Colours are laid down in their respective areas with a soft full brush, then blended
on surface with a stiff, not-too-wet, round-tipped brush. A fine black line contour
drawing is superimposed with a fine calligraphy brush.

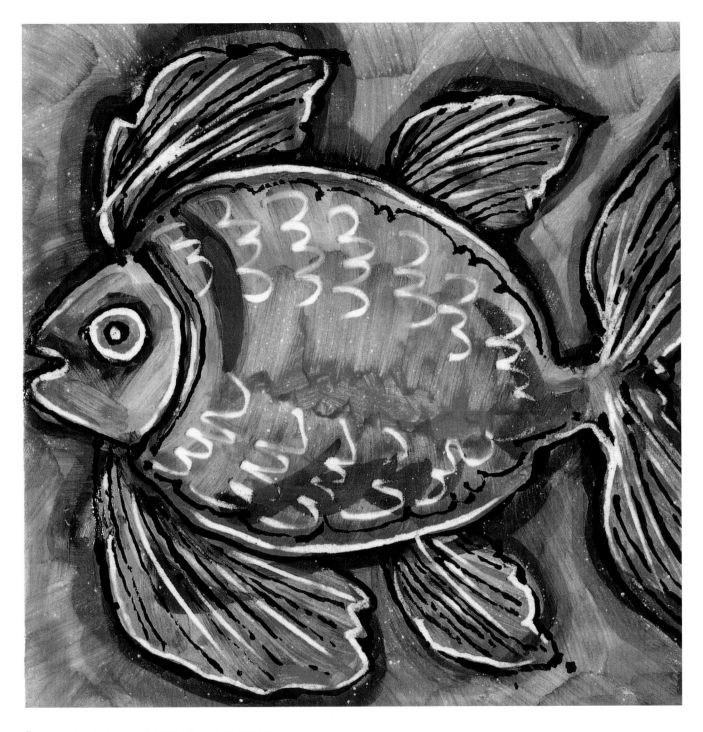

BLENDED COLOUR WITH BLACK LINE AND *SGRAFFITO*

The image has been outlined in a thick dark stroke using a soft-tipped full brush. If the
image is unfamiliar I might lightly sketch the pattern first on-glaze with a soft lead pencil.
This sketch can be rubbed away for corrections, and will not remain visible after firing. All colours
are applied loosely to image and background with a soft, well-loaded brush,then blended
on-surface with a stiff blunt brush, using deliberate directional strokes to create surface
movement. The texture of each brush stroke will show in minute detail. For larger areas, a larger
brush is used. A fine black outline is superimposed onto the image with a fine-pointed calligraphy
brush, followed by a quick, light accenting in white *sgraffito* line through the colour.

5. Using sgraffito

Sgraffito (or *sgraffiato*) – from the Italian for 'scratched' refers to the technique of scratching through one layer to another of contrasting colour below. Being a sketch artist, I tend to use this technique a lot to create white line drawing or to accent details on fields of solid colour. When drawing through the colours to the glaze surface below, the touch must be light to avoid scratching through to the clay body, which might cause the glaze to crawl. It is also best done when the surface has been dried for a few minutes, to avoid damp line edges from curling off. I remove the powdery residue with a vacuum cleaner, otherwise it remains as dark, rough sprinklings along the *sgraffito* line.

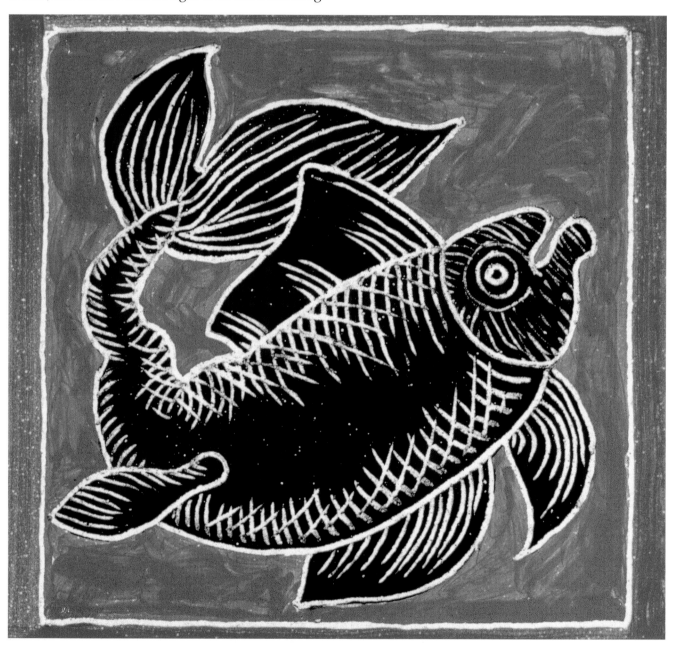

FINE LINE AND CONTOUR

Using a sharpened, flat, pointed bamboo tool, I create a fine line drawing with contour details
in a minimal three-colour palette. The effect is very much like that of a simple woodcut or engraving.

74

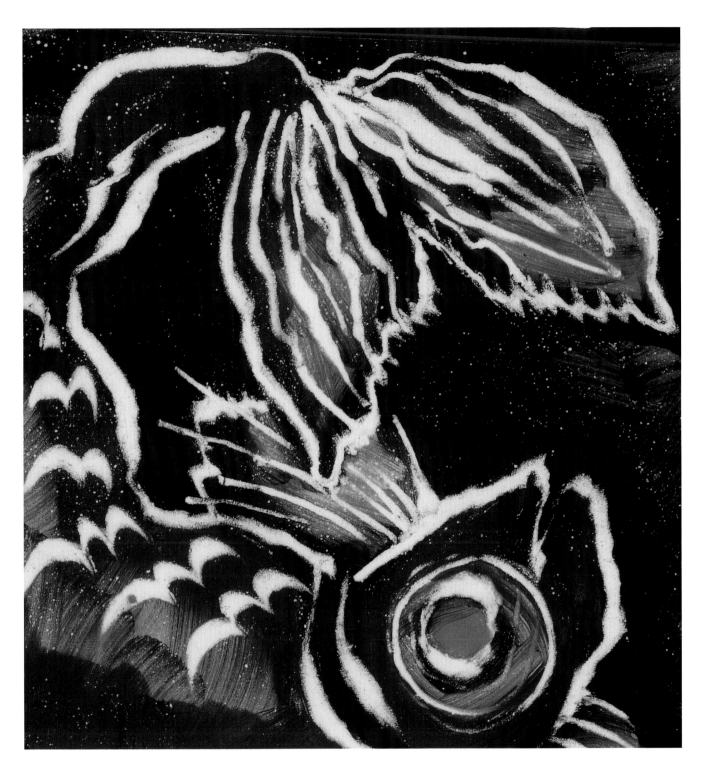

FLUCTUATING LINE

After the colour areas have been loosely applied and wet-blended, the image itself
is defined using an outline of controlled shape. For this I use the tip of a small,
pointed plastic spoon, which responds to light pressure to create a line of fluctuating
width. As an image expands in size so must the relative proportion of line thickness,
and the appropriate tool. For fine detail I will use the bamboo tool, or a sharp-pointed
flat metal tool, made from a hacksaw blade.

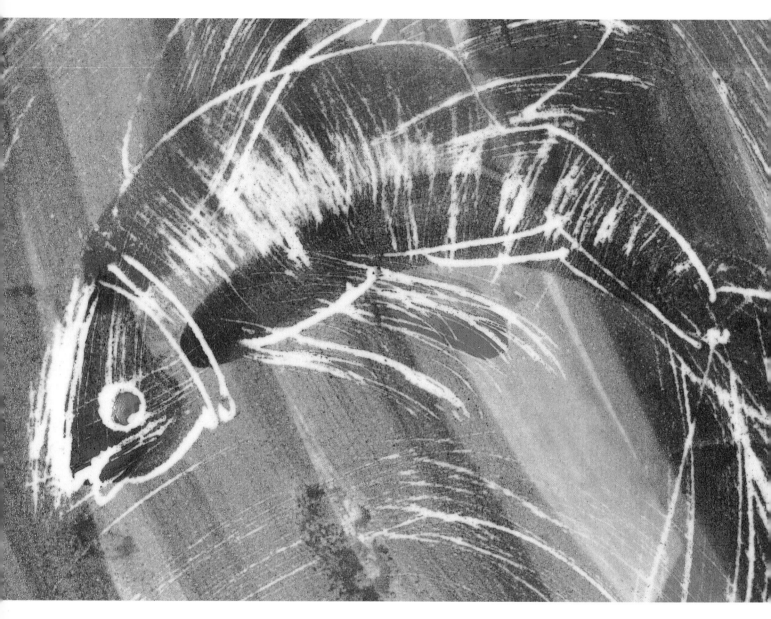

BRUSH *SGRAFFITO*

Here a broad-stroked cobalt wash is painted on a matt glaze surface, with small
additions of green and bright red stain, to form the background for a very loose
sgraffito outline sketch. Details and movement in the form of parallel lines are created
using a small stiff-bristled scrub brush.

6. Using dry-blending techniques

The charm and advantage of these techniques are the soft, pastel-like effects created, as well as the fact that there can be a little relaxation of the usual meticulousness of brushwork. The finger, here, is a more important tool than the brush.

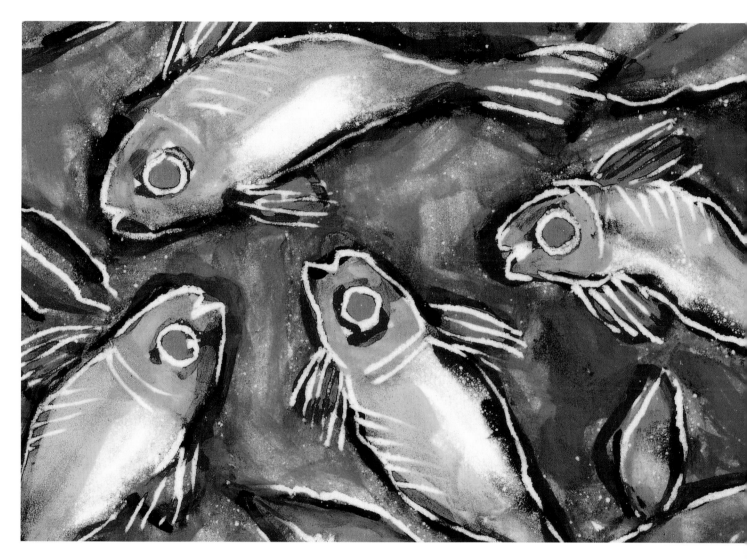

ON-SURFACE SMUDGING

Colours are loosely and fairly thickly applied with a soft brush in the same way as in wet-blending. White areas can be left for highlights. A dark outline around any shapes will help to delineate foreground and background. Instead of wet-blending, the colours are smudged on-surface using the finger, with visible directional strokes. A light *sgraffito* drawing redefines the softly blurred image. The absence of gum or binders in the colour mixture promotes easy blending. Once blended, however, the surface becomes too rough for additional wet brushwork. If upon completion a piece is fully covered in colour and needs to be handled, it can be sprayed two or three times with a standard charcoal/pencil fixative. This hardens the surface entirely and makes for easy handling.

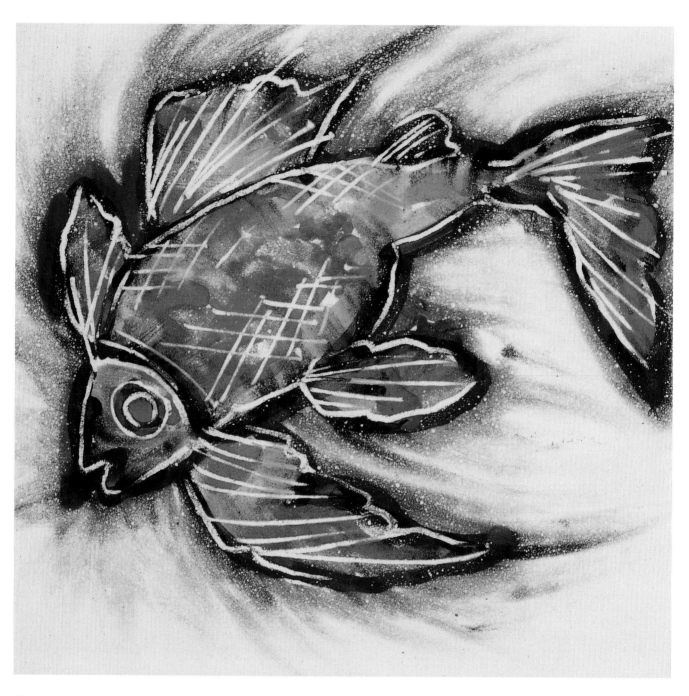

SMUDGING FOR MOVEMENT

After colours have been applied within the image outline, they are smudged on-surface. Outward smudge lines from the dark contour onto the white glaze create a very soft-edged sense of movement.

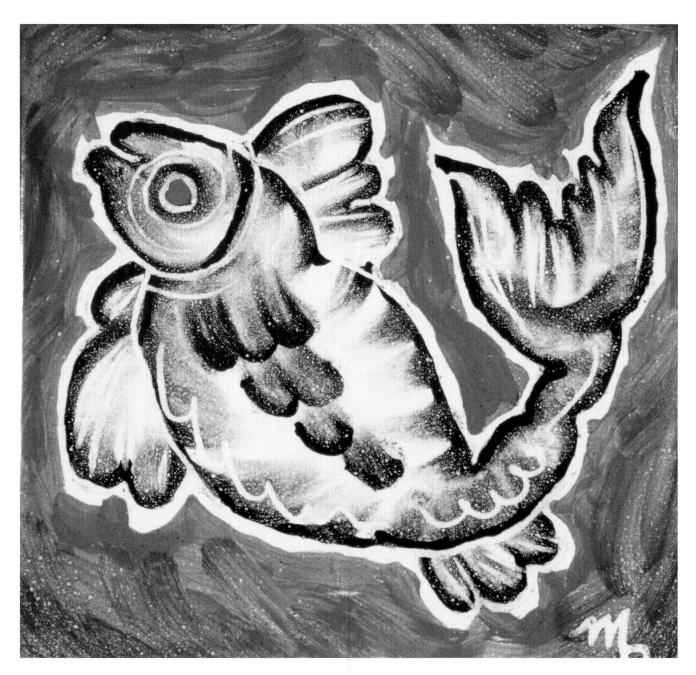

SMUDGING FOR CONTOUR

Using only a black stain outline drawing surrounded by a wet blended two-tone
blue field, an effect of volume and contour is created by repeated curved
smudge strokes, from the edge to the inside of the image. Details are picked
out in *sgraffito*.

7. *Using glaze as texture*

Some of these techniques might be more suited to non-functional pieces, in a sculptural or mural context. The emphasis here is on surface texture as well as colour.

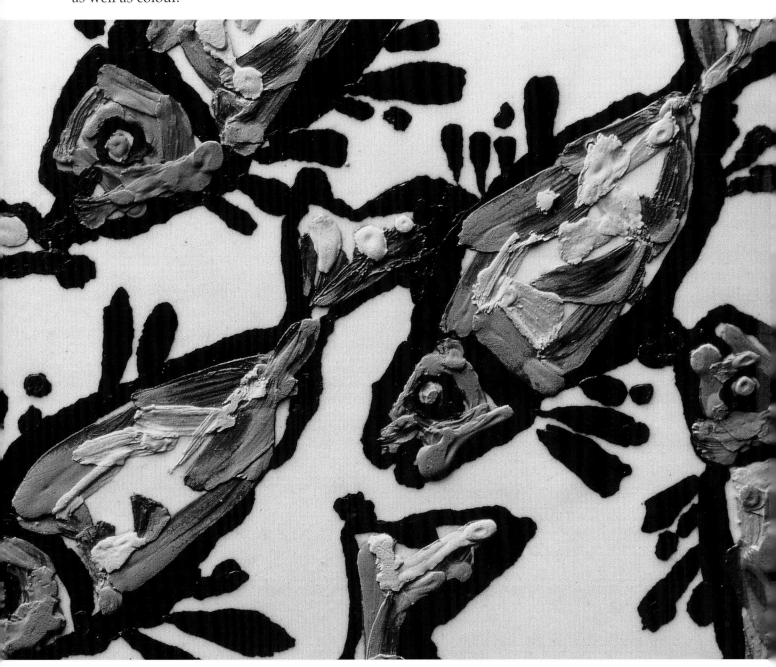

FRITLESS STAINS

In this image, the fish motifs have been painted with a soft brush and a colour mix made up of thick, entirely-fritless stains on a matt maiolica surface. Normally, fritted stains take on the surface characteristics of the glaze below; they appear glossy on a glossy surface, matt on a matt surface. In this example, the lack of frit allied to a full-matt surface creates a very dry, textural effect.

80

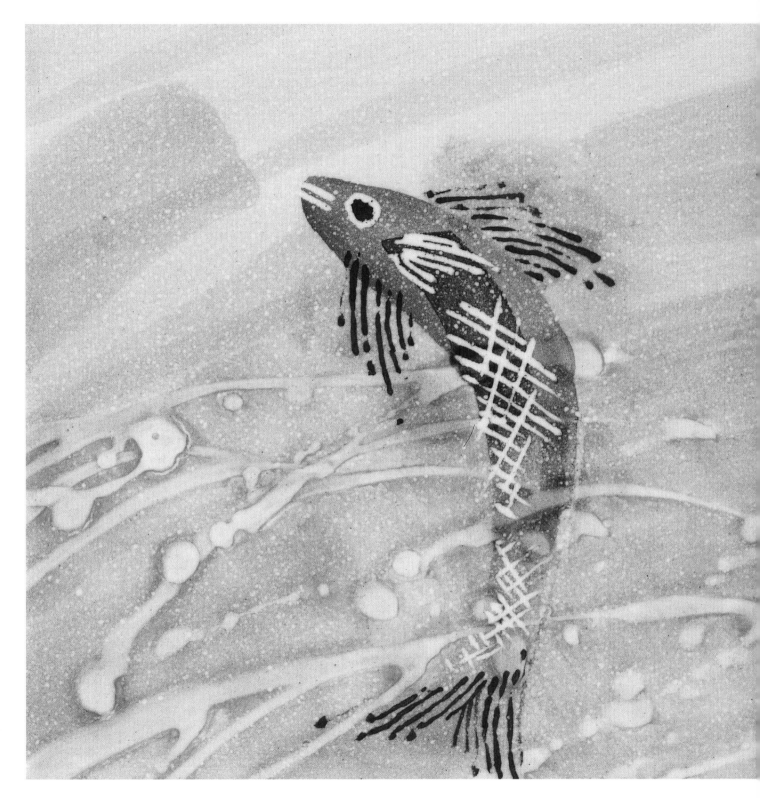

POURED MATT GLAZE

Matt maiolica glaze has been trailed in loose, splashy curves over my regular glaze, using a rubber squeeze bulb trailer (available from any pharmacy). A very diluted cobalt wash was brushed over, and colour pooled around the edges of the raised trailed areas. A mauve brush shape, cobalt line, and *sgraffito* highlights create the image of a fish leaping from the waves.

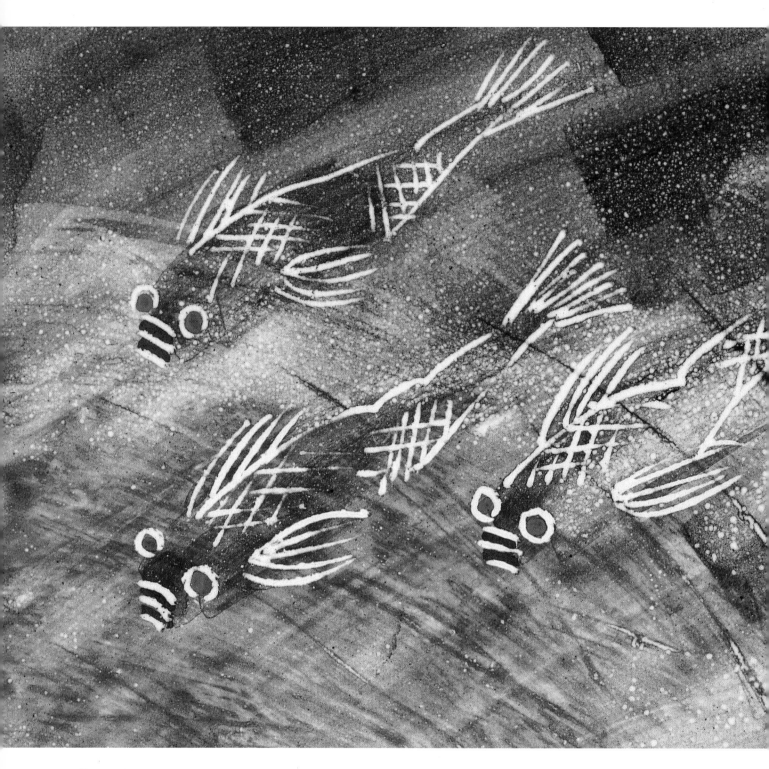

GLAZE *STUCCO*

This makes use of the fact that colour on-surface will respond in terms of intensity to any pooling over textures (voluntary or accidental) on the glaze surface below. To encourage this, I sometimes take a coarse house-painter's brush, and *stucco* over the smooth, raw-glazed surface in controlled directional strokes with additional glaze before doing any colour work. In this image, cobalt wash brushed against the *stucco* strokes creates colour gradations where the mixture has responded to the rough surface. Mauve, green and minimal bright red with *sgraffito* complete the image.

82

8. Using poured stains

Interesting abstract effects can be created here, making use of the fact that overlapping stains will create some transparency effects and intermediary colours.

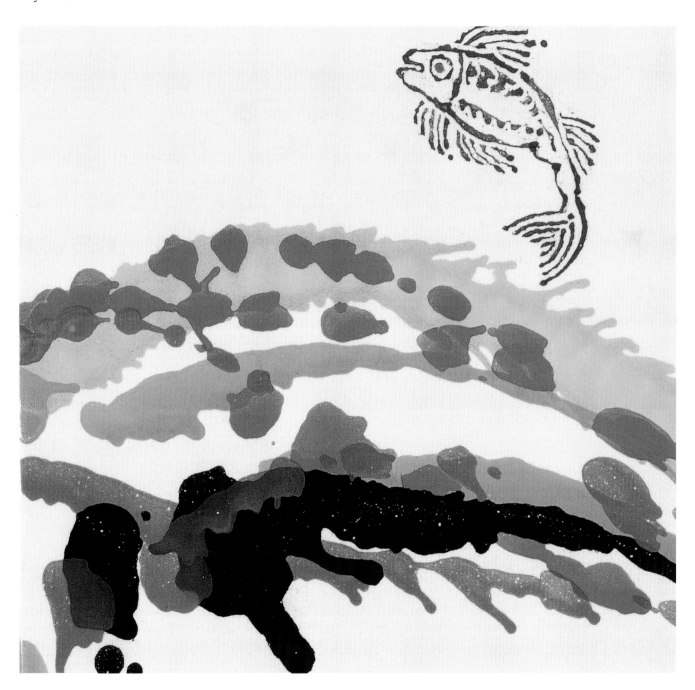

POURED STAINS ON WHITE

Using the bulb trailer, several well-stirred colour-stain-and-frit mixtures have been poured and splashed across the white-glazed surface in controlled overlapping curves.
The small cobalt line drawing of the fish was added subsequently.

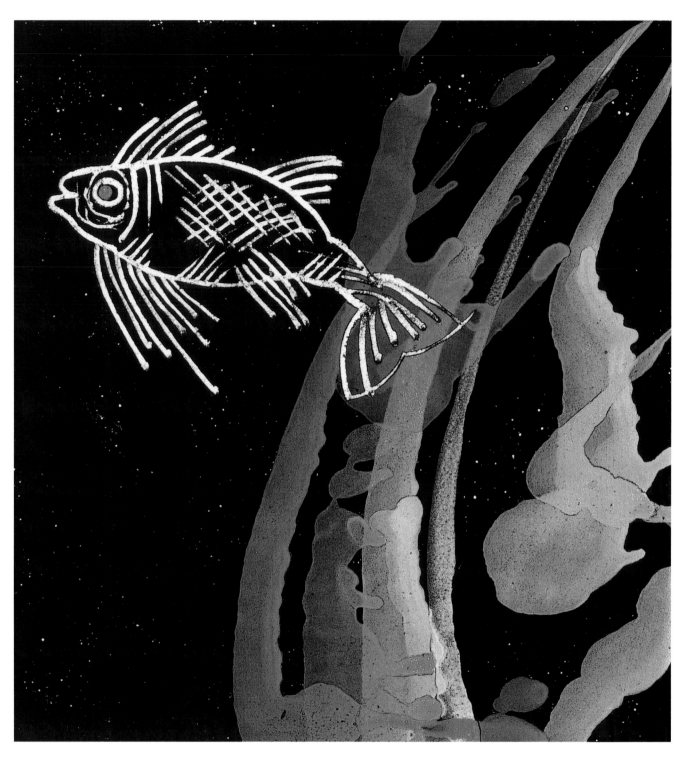

POURED STAINS ON BLACK

The entire glazed surface has been treated with a solid wash of black stain, before
the pouring of the coloured stains, as above. The fine-line *sgraffito* drawing of the
fish cuts through all the colours below.

9. Using coloured glazes

The use of colour-trailing as a technique is one most often associated with slips under a transparent glaze. With tin glaze, rich opaque colour effects can be achieved by the addition of coloured stains to the base glaze itself. I usually do this in very small quantities (six parts of wet glaze to one part dry colour mix, without extra frit). Since it would be prohibitively expensive to saturate a large quantity of glaze with colour in the above proportions, the answer might be to spray or air-brush large glazed surfaces to be covered with coloured stain mixtures. A small quantity of colour-saturated glaze can then be used for limited area details or accents.

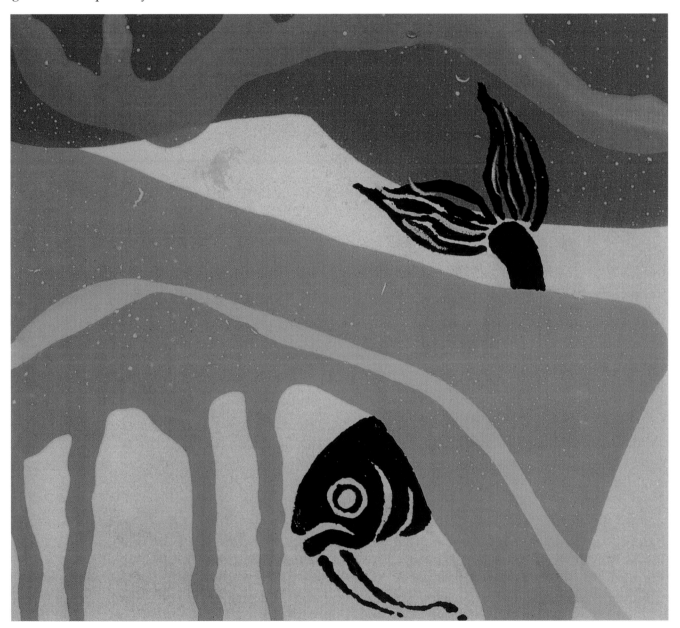

POURED AND TRAILED COLOURED GLAZES

Using a small spouted cup for the wide poured patterns, and the small rubber bulb for narrow lines, coloured glazes have been systematically poured and trailed over a saturated yellow maiolica glaze. Black fishes were carefully painted in around the trail lines, and accented with *sgraffito*. Where colours overlap, the *sgraffito* line can reach more than one colour.

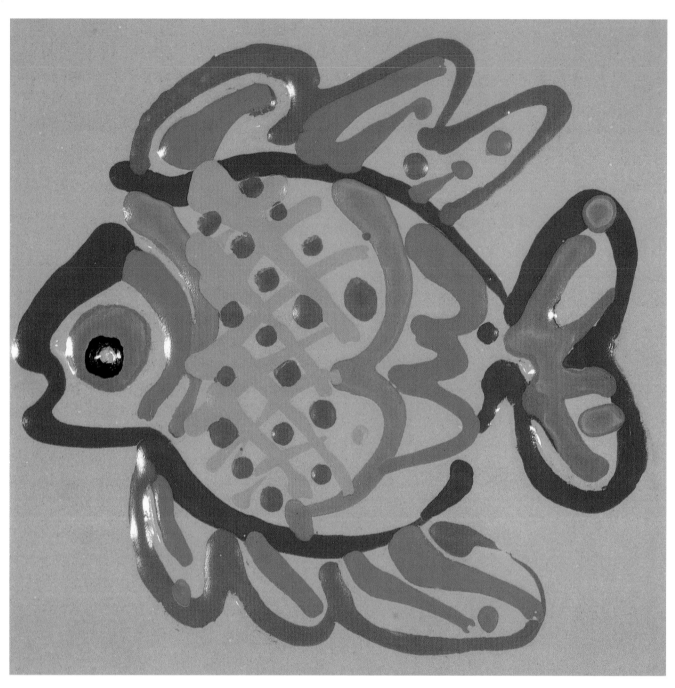

GLAZE TRAILING

This technique, using the bulb trailer and saturated coloured glazes, promotes a soft, rounded and rather simple line drawing. The glaze might need to be slightly thinned, if the line is blocked and too short. If, on the other hand, it is too splashy and uncontrolled, the mixture is too thin. This technique requires a very sure and quick hand, and a feel for when the bulb will empty, and stop your line.

10.   Using stencils

Stencils are an easy and practical way of creating a repeated image. I use cartridge paper, which can stand up to repeated wetting and use. The fish in this case has been cut from a piece of paper, giving me two stencils: the inner shape being that of the fish shape itself, and the outer, the background shape around the fish.

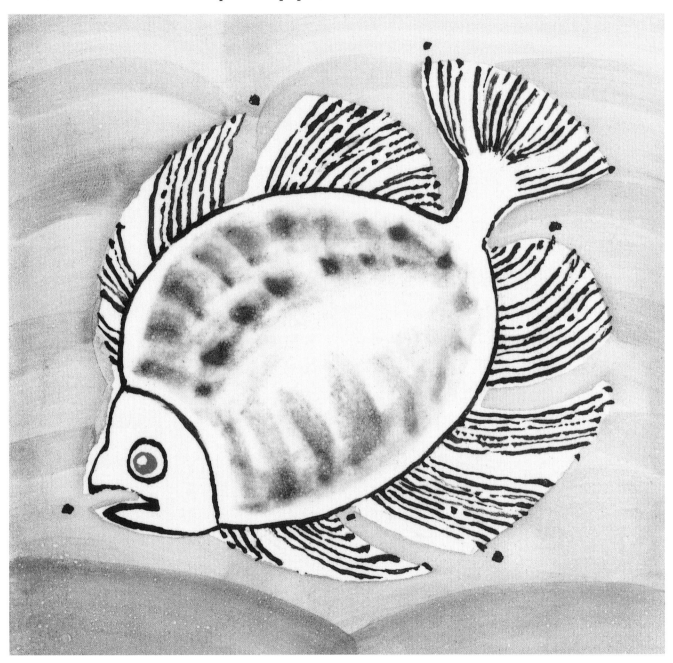

SHAPE STENCIL

The inner fish stencil is dampened lightly and laid onto the glazed surface.
A light turquoise wash is laid over the entire surface, including the stencil,
with a soft, wide brush. When the stencil is removed, this leaves the white
fish shape. Cobalt outline, stippled copper brushwork, and a red eye complete
the image. Note the soft-edged effect of the copper.

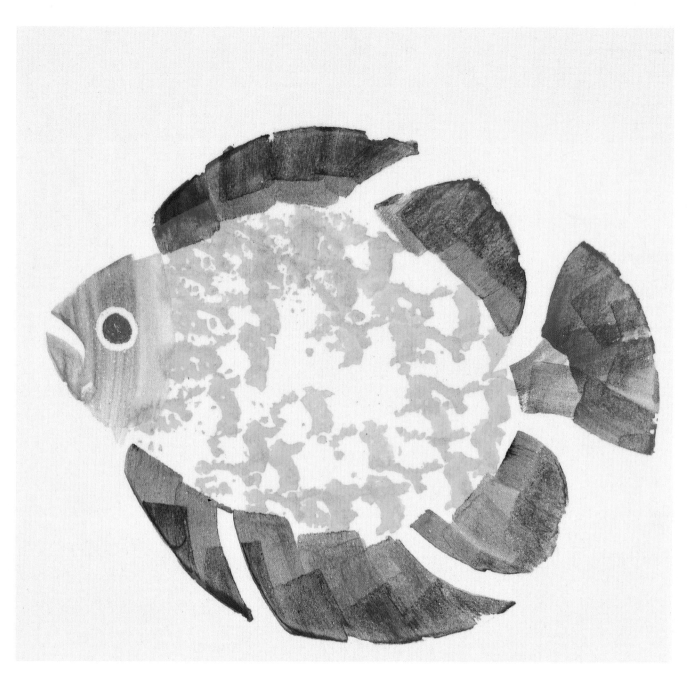

BACKGROUND STENCIL

This time the outer stencil has been used to block off the white surround area.
Head, fins and tail of the fish have been painted with a square-tipped brush
in an outward stroke over the stencil edge, creating a defined fish shape.
The yellow body has been applied with a sponge.

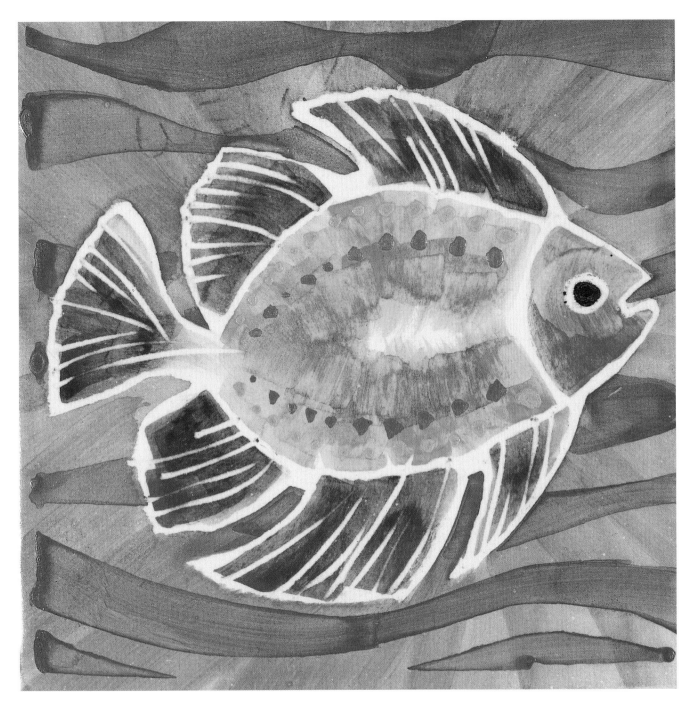

DOUBLE STENCIL

In making this image, three stencils have been used: an inner fish-shape, the outer background-shape, and a third wave-pattern stencil. The inner fish-shape stencil is first laid down to resist a light green surround wash, and then removed, leaving a white fish shape. The outer fish-shape stencil is carefully laid down to cover the green wash and the body of the fish is painted in. The outer fish-shape stencil is then removed and the inner fish-shape stencil laid down again to cover the now-coloured fish body. The third wave-pattern stencil is laid over this, and a blue wash applied over the cut-out gaps of the wave-pattern stencil, from left to right. The two stencils are removed, and *sgraffito* details are added.

11.   *Using resists: latex and wax*

Both water-based latex and wax emulsion have the advantage of being fairly easy to use and clean up. The best kinds of brushes to be used here are good sable or fine synthetic, since Chinese calligraphy brushes tend to lose their shape. I keep separate wax and latex brushes; both need to be cleaned immediately after use with soap and warm water.

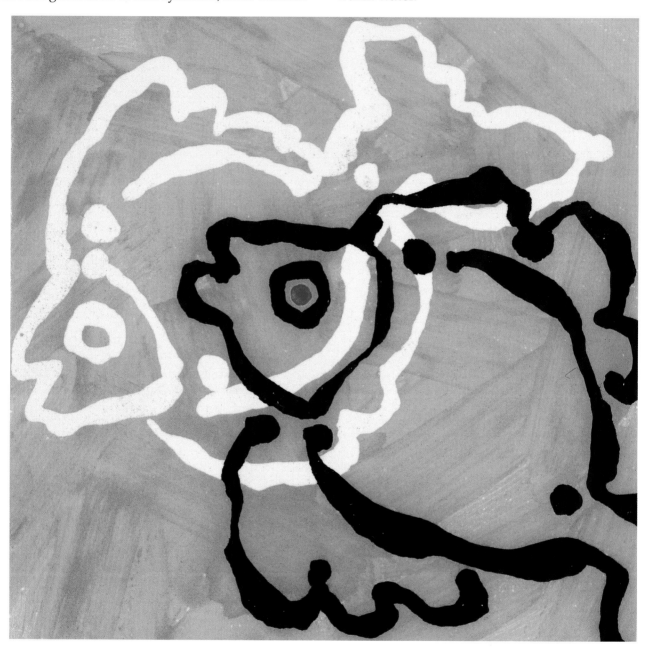

LATEX LINE

The advantage of latex over wax is that masked areas can be worked over later. Using a flexible point-tipped synthetic brush, the white outline of the fish is laid down. The surface must be smooth if the glaze surface is at all powdery or smudged, it can be dabbed smooth with a well squeezed out sponge – otherwise the latex may not adhere cleanly. A few minutes later yellow wash is laid down in a rotating motion. With a sharp blade, an edge of the latex is carefully lifted, and the remaining latex pulled away. The black fish-outline is then painted in over the wash and resisted areas using a fluctuating brush stroke.

90

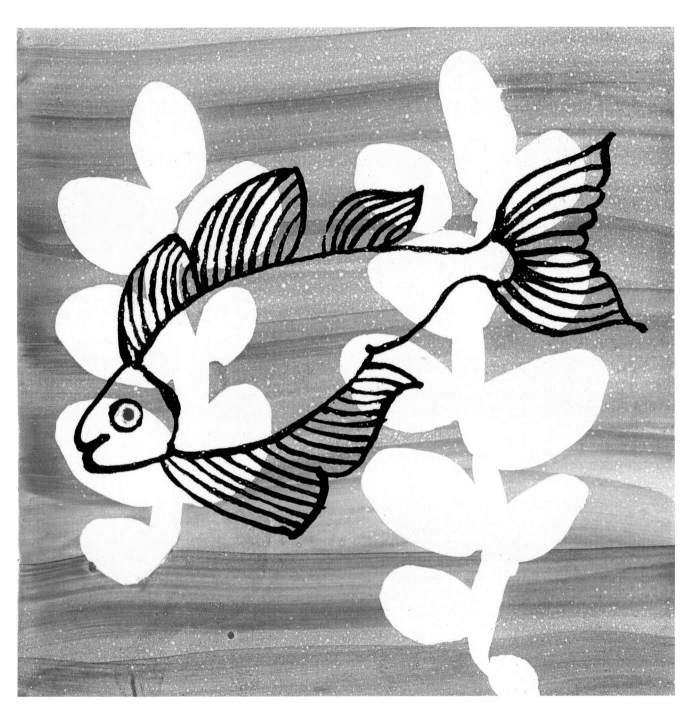

LATEX SHAPE

Using a wide, rounded brush, latex shapes are laid down in a plant pattern,
and washed over with graded green and turquoise stains. The latex is
again carefully peeled away, and a fine black-line fish drawing superimposed.

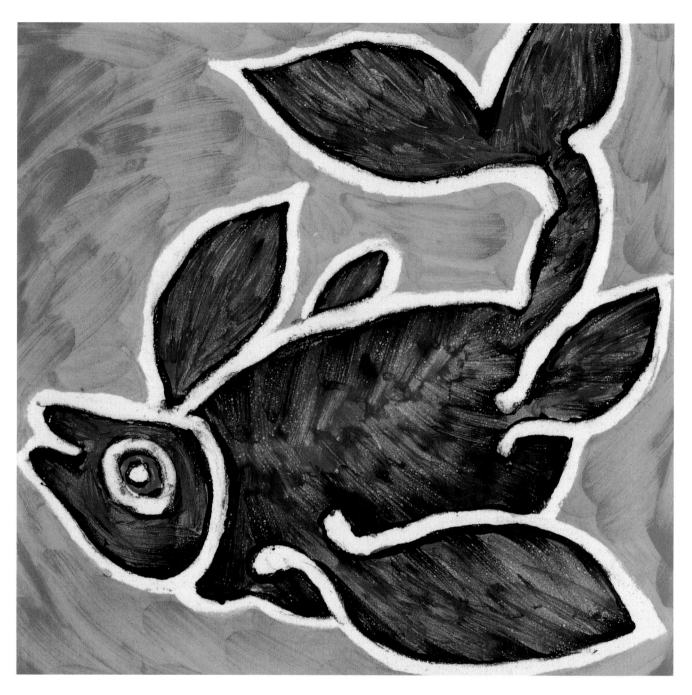

WAX LINE

I prefer cold-water-based wax to hot wax, because it is easier to handle and clean,
and has less burn-off smell. The fish image has been outlined in wax with a flexible,
point-tipped brush. Good quality sable brushes are preferable, because they best keep
their shape. Once the wax has dried, outside yellow and green stains are loosely brushed
on and wet-blended. The wax resists the colour and leaves a white line. The inner part
of the fish is also blended, with a black edge blending in, giving more contrast to the
white line. Beads of colour on the wax can be dabbed off with a not-too-damp sponge.
If the wax is too thick, it will curl off, and needs dilution with water. If it is too thin, the
colour will adhere to it and not sponge off easily. This may also occur if the wax has not
been allowed to dry on the glaze for at least an hour, and/or if the glaze coating is too thin.
For the wax mixture, I tend to favour a consistency just a little thicker than milk.

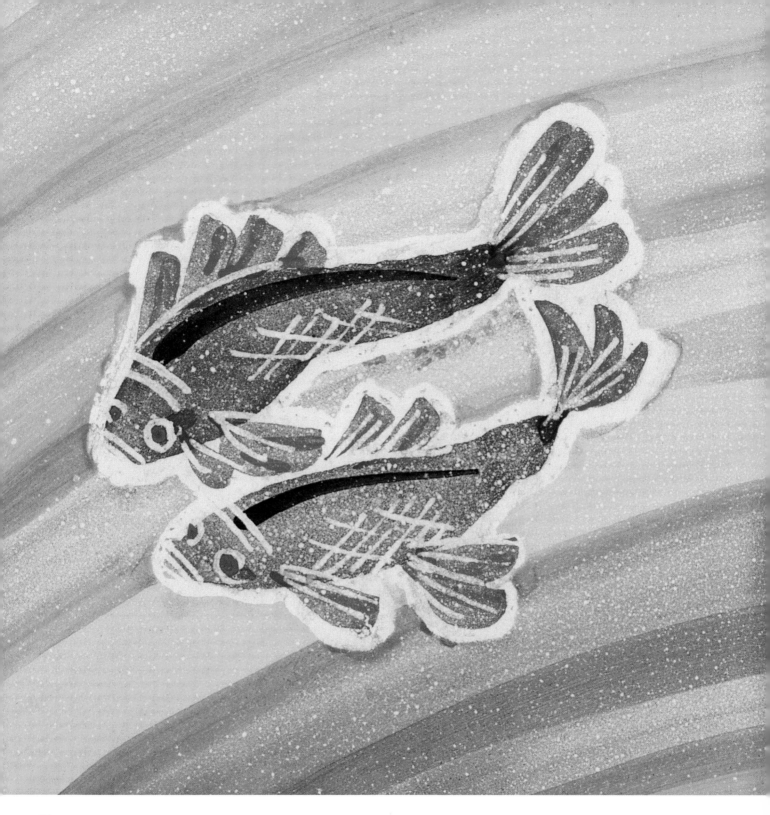

WAX SHAPE

In this image, the two fish have been painted using various brush shapes, with brush line and *sgraffito* detail. A layer of wax is carefully dabbed over the fish, taking care not to smudge or move the colour below. Once the wax has dried well, a coloured wash is applied over the entire surface in a diagonal stroke, using a wide, soft, square-tipped brush.

12. Third firing: copper and stains

Although any third firing process is an added procedure, the inherent advantage is the very fluid quality of brushwork possible on an already fired surface, not to mention the possibility of simply wiping down an error and starting again. Most raw-glaze painting cannot be corrected in this way.

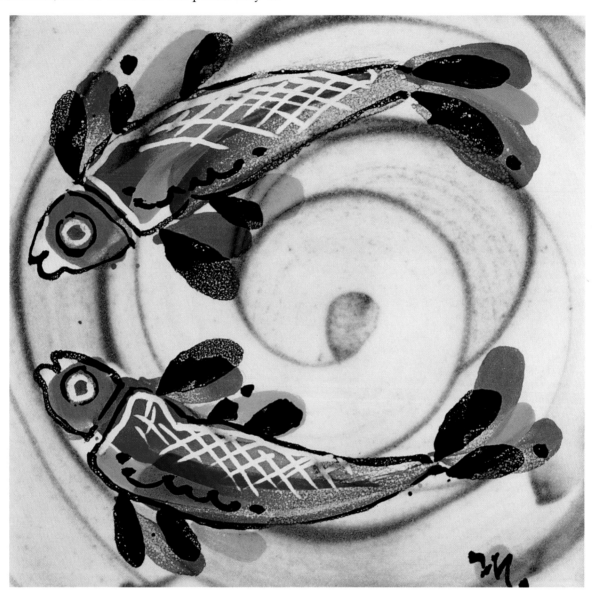

COPPER WASH

A copper-carbonate-and-water mixture is especially attractive for its smoky, watery quality, and for the visible gradations of transparency occurring in a single brush stroke. The fishes were initially painted in-glaze with coloured stains, using brush shape, line and *sgraffito*, and then fired. Using a slightly thick, almost grainy copper mixture, the entire surface was loosely brushed. The gesture and brush shape define the pattern. (In this instance, a medium-stiff, square-tipped brush was used.) Underlying colour, or white, can be highlighted again simply by carefully wiping away the copper from those areas. The piece is then refired at the normal glaze temperature, or just a touch cooler.

94

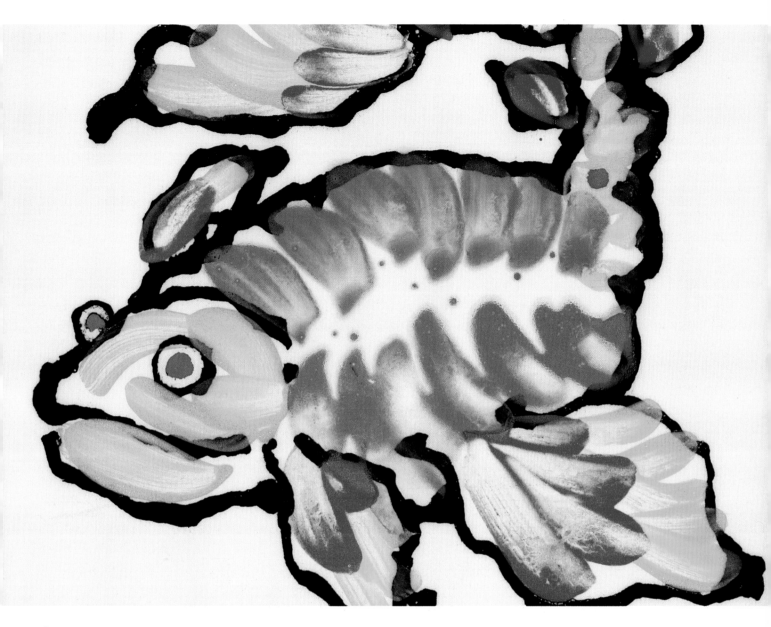

STAINS AS ENAMELS

This is a technique I use when I wish to repair or enhance an area of weakness,
or when I am looking for the effect of colours shimmering through each other, rather
than being blended together. The stain and frit mixture is mixed up with very little
water almost to paste thickness, and applied over existing fired colours, or white.
In this instance, the fish outline was painted in black and fired. The bright colours
were applied in paste form, using a soft, round-tipped brush, and then refired again
(best done in the kiln's cooler area). For some sculptural pieces I may want an intense,
layered, even a textured look, and will apply the colour mixtures almost like thick
oil paints. Matt and dry surfaces are created by the controlled omission of frits in these
mixtures for varied surfaces.

13. Third firing: lustres

Maiolica has been associated with the use of lustres almost since its very inception, from the early Hispano-Moresque wares (see picture on p. 12), to the most contemporary work. For some of the reduction lustres, the technical challenges of achieving good lustre are considerable, but the gradations and subtlety of colour change achievable make this well worth the effort. (See picture on p. 42) Oxidised metallic lustres tend to be more flat and uniform, and the challenge here for me is finding the appropriate balance of lustre to glaze colour on a given surface. I find at times that too much blank gold – on a ceramic surface, for example – can give an effect of tawdriness (which might be fun) but with the kind of wall-to-wall surface painting I tend to favour, there is not much room for a flat metallic lustre complement. I think that in all cases, lustre needs careful planning, so that it becomes an important and necessary adjunct to the image, rather than an afterthought detail. This initial planning has to occur right from the beginning, since two decorating processes and two glaze firings are involved, and need to be coordinated.

There are many kinds of lustres and ways of using them. Some of these include bronze, copper, silver, platinum, and burnished gold, as well as coloured transparent and mother-of-pearl lustres. They can be used with lustre pens, overglaze resists, marbleisers and other techniques for varying effects. I have concentrated on simple brush effects using gold lustre. What is basically required here is a variety of suitable sable brushes for line or filling-in, the lustre itself, lustre thinner, and lustre brush-cleaner. It is best to keep separate brushes for each colour of lustre. The fired glaze surface to be decorated is cleaned with acetone or denatured alcohol (*not* rubbing alcohol). Hands should also be clean, since any grease on-surface will inhibit lustre adherence. Lustre is applied in a thin, even coat, using a straight stroke, in a medium application. If the lustre is too thick it can be thinned, but very minimally with the lustre thinner. If the application is too thick, the colour disappears after firing, leaving a powder residue. If it is too thin, the colours are not vivid, or the golds tend to a transparent blotchy purple tone. Uneven edges can be cleaned up with a razor. Lustre is best left to dry overnight before firing. If the tin glaze itself is normally fired below 1040-1060°C, small hairline cracks might appear. This is the soft glaze moving under the lustre in the third firing. It would be better to raise the glaze-firing temperature to at least 1046°C (Orton large cone 05) or more. The third lustre firing itself occurs in a very well-ventilated kiln to about 717°C (Orton large cone 018). If the finish is dull or powdery after the lustre firing, or even burnt off, the firing may have been too hot, the lustre too thickly applied, the heat in the kiln poorly circulated, or there may have been inadequate ventilation. Having survived all of the above pitfalls, some of the effects of lustre are well worth pursuing for the added spice and richness they can provide.

The following three images are of simple gold lustre fired in oxidation at 717°C (Orton large cone 018).

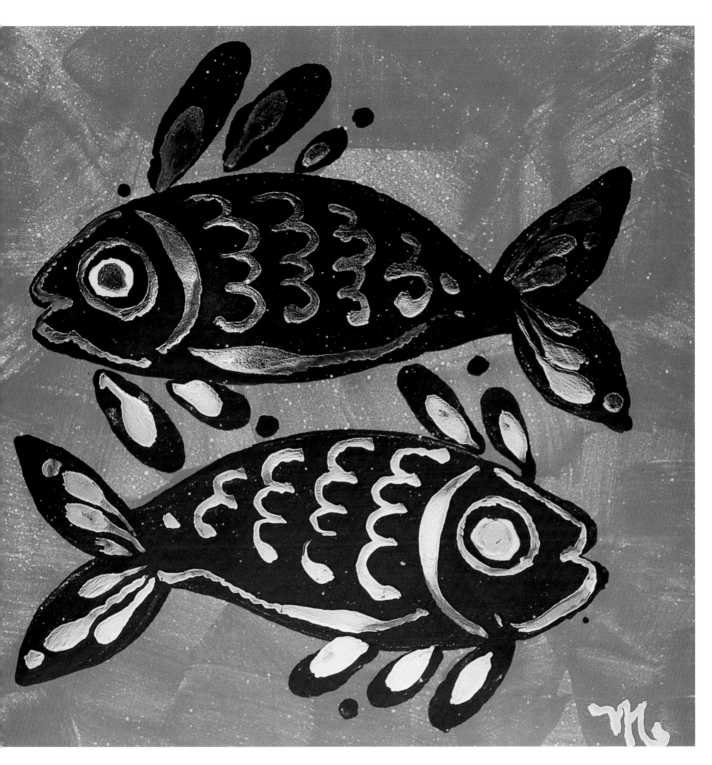

LUSTRE DETAIL

In this image the gold lustre has been applied to the black fish with a fine-tipped, flexible, medium sable brush. The planning element to include the lustre as a design component is very evident here, since the black fish-silhouettes on their own would be too incomplete to support the image.

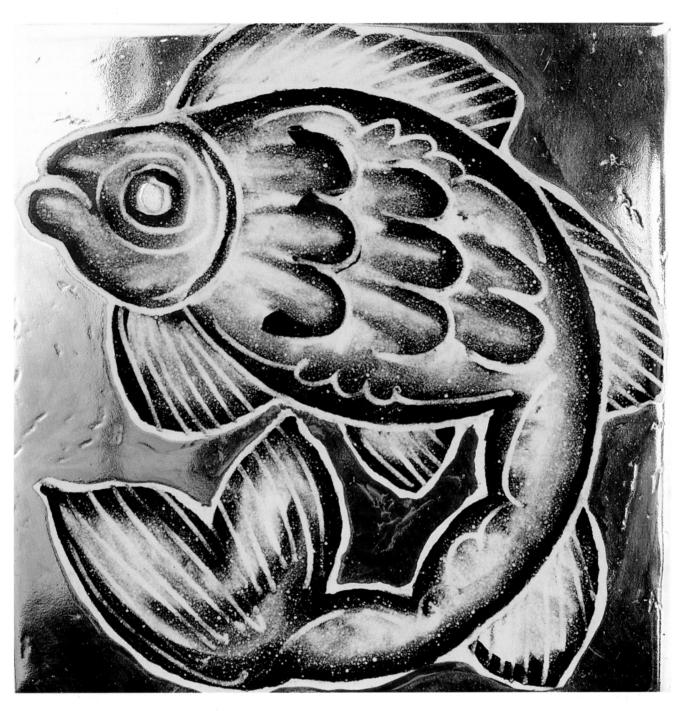

LUSTRE BACKGROUND

I have always been fascinated by old Russian and Greek Orthodox icons, with their simple figurative painting and flat gold backgrounds. In this image the colour palette and graphics have been kept to simple black and white, with brush outline and contour smudging. The massive even gold background pushes the image forward for strong dramatic contrast.

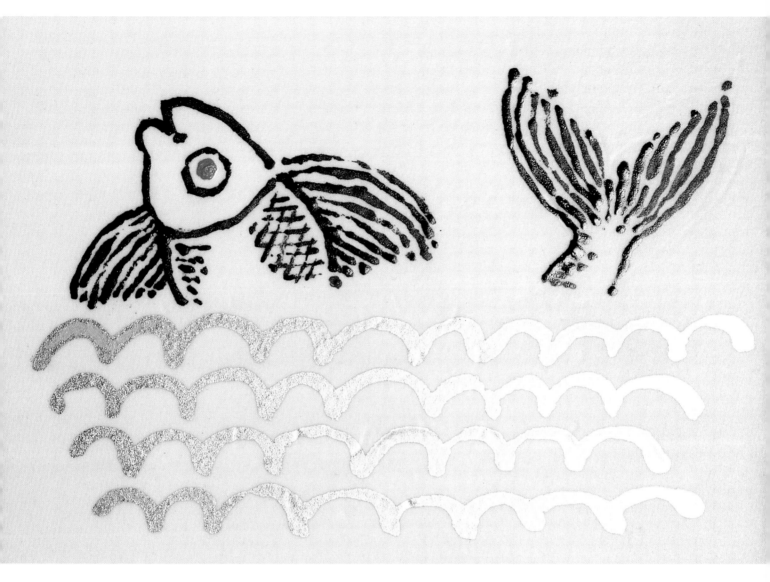

MATT LUSTRE

Lustre will assume the surface (gloss or matt) of the glaze to which it is applied. The black stain drawing of the fish in this case also tends towards a matt finish, complemented by a fine-line matt gold lustre wave pattern. If I wish for a matt lustre effect on a shiny glaze surface, I will simply rub down the shiny lustre with very fine steel wool. Matt gold leaf carefully applied to the glaze surface is another option.

The following two images show pieces that were reduction-fired in Alan Caiger-Smith's wood-firing kiln. The red-gold lustre pigments are mixed with ochre clay and gum arabic on a glazed tile surface for a controlled and easy flow. Once applied to the piece, they are fired in a pre-warmed kiln over an eight- to nine-hour period up to 650°C with a number of small reductions toward the end of the firing cycle, and with clear burning periods between reductions. As the pieces emerge from the kiln they are dusty and dingy, and need to be rubbed down — then the true lustre colours and gradations emerge. (For further information about lustre-firing techniques see Alan Caiger-Smith's book, *Lustre Pottery*.)

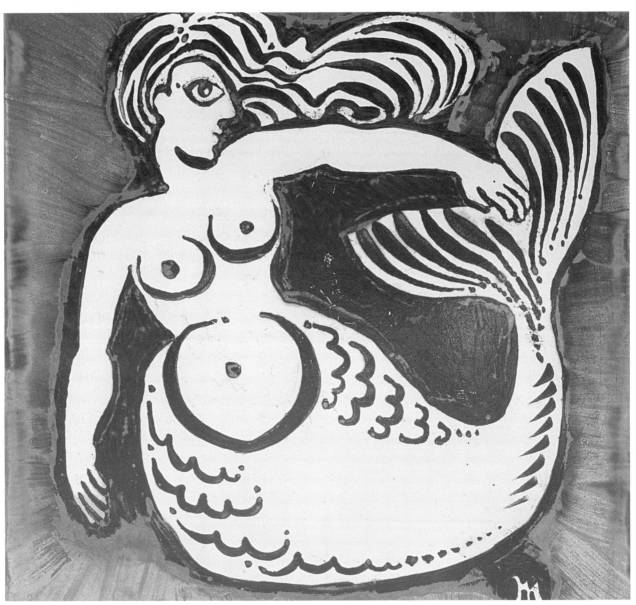

LUSTRE PAINTING: 'MERMAID'

In this image the mermaid has been painted on the fired white tin glaze using
a pointed sable brush and even, fluctuating strokes, to create controlled line
and brush shapes. The background has been painted in with a wider wash brush
using a thinner lustre mixture. In reduction, where the lustre is thinner, the colour tends
to gold. Where thick, it is a deep metallic red.

100

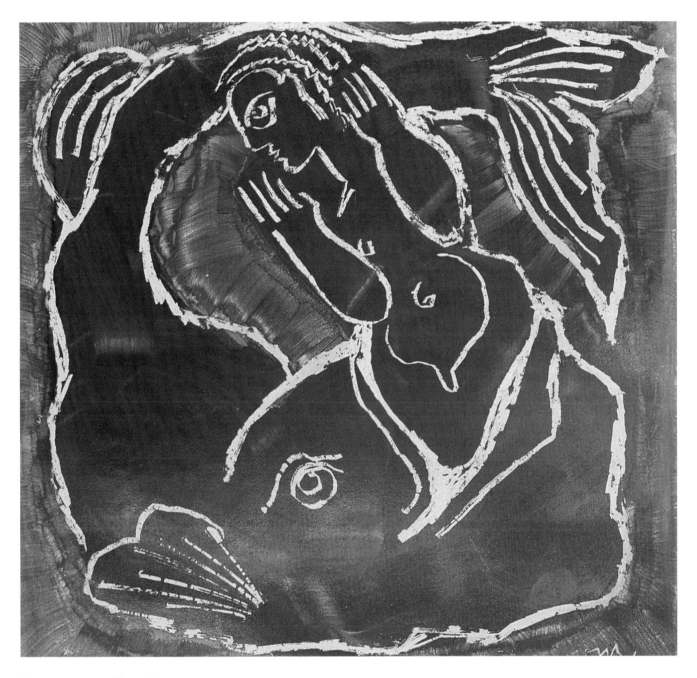

Lustre *sgraffito*: 'Jonah'

Here the image has been painted with red-gold lustre, with dense application to the figure area, and a lighter application for the background. The outlines have been scratched through the dried lustre to the white fired glaze below using a razor.

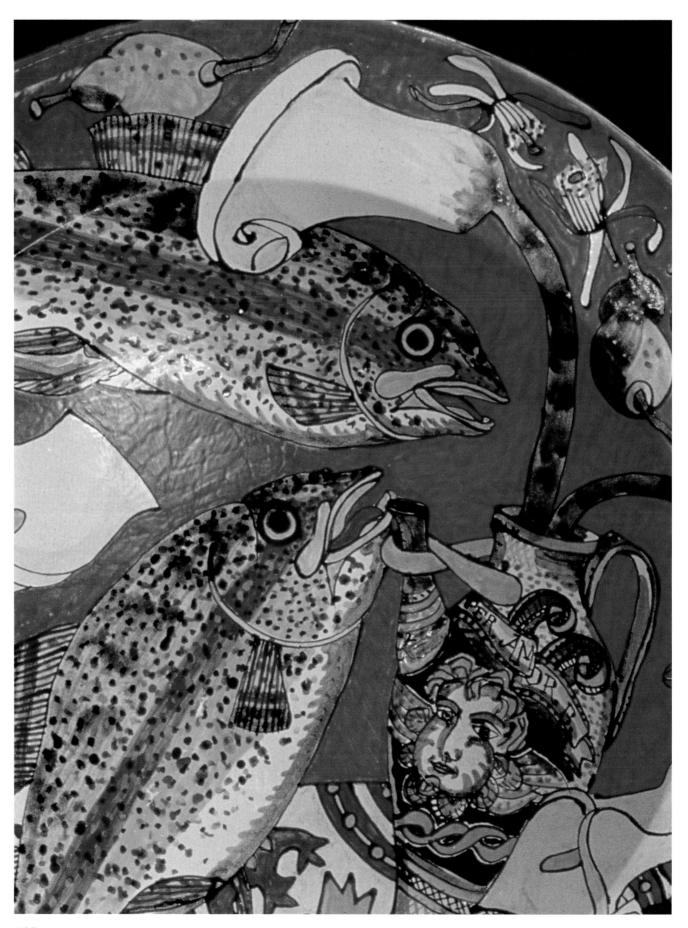

Contemporary Expressions

'The modern artist has set out to conquer eternity, and the designer to conquer the future; the craftsman allows himself to be conquered by time. Traditional yet not historical, intimately linked to the past but not precisely datable, the handcrafted object refutes the mirages of history and the illusions of the future. The craftsman does not seek to win a victory over time, but to become one with its flow. By way of repetitions in the form of variations at once imperceptible and genuine, his works become part of an enduring tradition.'

OCTAVIO PAZ

Artists are obliged to work within the physical constraints of space, scale and the nature of materials. These constraints have to be accepted, worked around and used to advantage. The physical framework within which the ceramic artist works comprises clay, glaze and firing, and all the related technical considerations. Artists also work within an external cultural framework. Although we are motivated by inner compulsions to create and communicate, and by the urge to develop an individual form of expression, we do not work in a vacuum. What ceramic artists produce, for instance, can be constrained by the contexts of past ceramic culture and present-day arts and applied arts in which their work is perceived. We are influenced, as well, by material and economic considerations, and by a highly specialised marketplace with very defined show and sales venues. Cultural frameworks, and their effects, change. Consider, for example, the 1950s and 1960s in the UK, when early tin-glaze practi-

tioners such as William Newland and Alan Caiger-Smith encountered great difficulties in having their work accepted. The mainstream ceramic culture of the day was that of high-fired stoneware and porcelain, with an associated

OPPOSITE: ALEXANDRA COPELAND (AUSTRALIA)

RAINBOW TROUT PLATTER (DETAIL), d. 65 cm, 1996.
This piece was conceived as a presentation piece for a passionate trout fisherman. For uniformity of surface to accommodate complex painting, this large shallow platter was made using a jolley-mould system. Dense colour pigments are continually ground in small quantities throughout a slow application process. All drawing is freehand, and the complete image can take more than a full day to complete. The matt red ground is designed to contrast with the shiny fish, and to resemble Chinese cinnabar red lacquer.

Photograph: Leigh Copeland

'I am a compulsive artist. I have always drawn and painted. The strange shapes and colour combinations of plants and insects in my garden are recorded; patterns are invented; humorous schemes sketched and coloured. I grew up in a community of painters and potters whose art books broadened my horizons.

I rarely make preparatory sketches. I love the way the hand can run the brush over a curve. The eye adjusts the line and the hand obeys the eye, if not, the eye can improvise as it goes.

With enormous help from Leigh Copeland, I have spent years experimenting – always with a mental picture of the hoped-for result. Colour recipes accumulated slowly. A personal palette was achieved. I feel I am almost where I want to be with maiolica.'

Alexandra Copeland

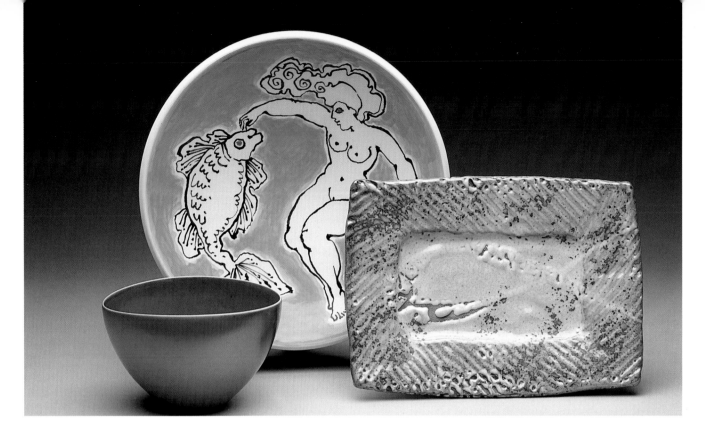

THREE CONTEMPORARY EXPRESSIONS

These three pieces, although greatly different, express distinct and valid characters.

Left: Gwyn Hanssen-Pigott (Australia)
Bowl, d. 65 cm, 1997. Wood-fired porcelain, wheel-thrown and altered.
Character: Contained, linear, cerebral, serene, delicate, contemplative.

Rear: Matthias Ostermann (Canada) in collaboration with Peter Collis (New Zealand)
Plate, d. 27 cm, 1995. Slip-painted earthenware with oxidised, transparent glaze.
Character: Colourful, whimsical, lively, warm, narrative, evocative.

Right: Eric Wong (Canada)
Plate, d. 25 cm, 1996. Press-moulded, rope-patterned stoneware, with slip and shino glaze; gas-fired reduction.
Character: Abstract, visceral, relaxed, earthy, vigorous, spontaneous, solid.

Photograph: Jan Thijs

Anglo-oriental aesthetic valuing purity and integration of form, function, materials and process. The language of maiolica, in contrast, expresses ideas through exuberance of surface treatment and imagery. Both these ceramic forms speak out distinctly, and have long-standing traditions supporting their aesthetic validity in any debate. Yet for the longest time, the high-fire aesthetic was dominant, at least in English-speaking countries.

In recent years, we have seen great expansion of eclecticism within the ceramic spectrum. All forms of expression – from functional to funky, from austere monochrome to wildly coloured, from pure vessel to sculptural – now jostle comfortably alongside one another. Each has its own message and following, each contributes in its own way.

Another illustration of the play of changing culture and tradition can be seen in the contemporary ceramics of Italy and Spain. Here, in the birthplace of maiolica, I could find no examples of contemporary tin glaze for this book. Studio ceramists in these countries prefer media such as stoneware and raku. Perhaps this is a simple reaction against the factory-made, tradition-inspired maiolica ware that seems to fill every shop window in these countries (see picture on p. 105).

Similarly, the effect of material and economic factors can be seen in the wealth and variety of earthenware from the former Eastern-European countries. This is an expression of a ceramic tradition formerly constrained, in some places, by the unavailability of abundant electricity, and the consequent need to keep to low temperatures.

Finally, it is important to keep in mind the context in which work will be seen and sold. The boundaries between fine art and applied art and crafts have become less rigid. The eclecticism of current ceramic expression has opened the way

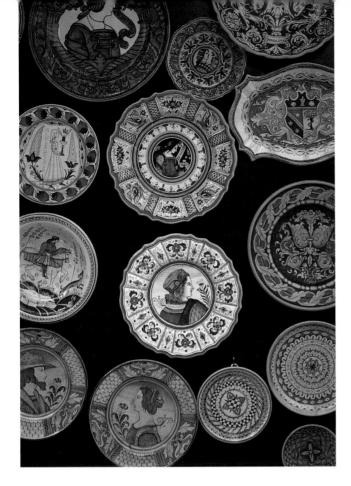

CERAMICS IN SHOP WINDOW, DERUTA, ITALY

Photograph: Matthias Ostermann

for different kinds of venues. Since access to these venues plays a significant role in the appreciation and sale of work, makers have to include consideration of them in their production strategy. That is, makers have to answer such questions as: Will this piece be a functional pot, to be sold among many in the lower-price range, or is it a one-off conceptual piece to be shown in a more highly-priced gallery setting? Or can it be both?

Ceramics have always been one of the most versatile and expressive of the arts. Contemporary maiolica, in particular, is exceptionally rich in this regard. As a medium with its stable white ground clearly holding line and colour, it is especially attractive to those preoccupied with narrative and surface decoration. The whole history of maiolica – and particularly the Italian *istoriato* wares of the *cinquecento* – provide evidence of the attraction of tin glaze for artists.

The images collected in this chapter reflect the vision and enormous diversity of work of contemporary ceramists from around the world. Some of them (such as Arbuckle, Caiger-Smith, Carnegy, Fine, Hilpert-Artes and Neave) are full-time tin-glaze practitioners. Others (such as Cochrane, Derval, Dipeta and Pereira) have made a brief foray into maiolica from other ceramic backgrounds. Then there are those artists who normally work in a non-ceramic medium but who, like Picasso and Chagall, have been seduced by the mystery and challenge of clay and glaze – in this instance, of tin-glaze maiolica. What has struck me as remarkable in looking over the work of so many different people is their great inventiveness, and the variety of both their technique and expression.

For the sake of simplicity and visual variety, I have organised the imagery by context rather than artist's nationality. This sampling is incomplete. There are probably many ceramists whose work should surely be included, but whom I did not know about, or who were unable to participate. Artists from some countries, notably the USA, may seem to dominate this collection, but that is due to the size of the USA, its proximity to and close ties with Canada, where I work, and to the open-minded nature of the North American ceramic milieu, which leads to great diversity of work. Most of the work in this section is electric-fired in oxidation at standard low-fire glaze temperatures of between 950 °C and 1100 °C. Any special firing conditions or specialised techniques are noted in the captions. Each artist has described their work and made personal statements giving insight into the abstract concepts that precede and accompany the making of any work – statements on their motivations, inspirations, obsessions, and points of view.

From the traditional

In some parts of Europe, maiolica or *faïence* work is still being produced in much the same way as it was centuries ago. Computers may be storing glaze recipes now, but all the hand-forming and decorating techniques, and above all, the image inspiration remain very much rooted in tradition. Entire volumes could be devoted to this kind of work, but I have chosen the following two. One is a traditional factory concern in the Netherlands, the other a traditional operating studio in the old Provençal town of Moustiers-Sainte-Marie in France.

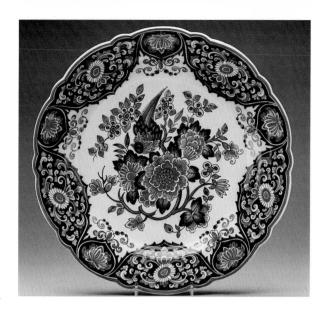

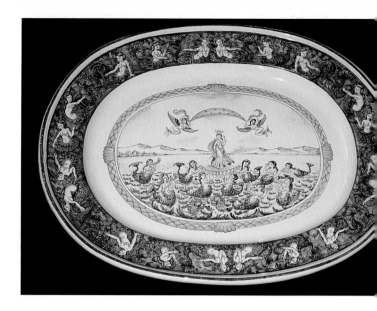

KONINKLIJKE TICHELAAR MAKKUM (THE NETHERLANDS)

PLATE, d. 32 cm, 1996.

This earthenware was made from Frisian sea clay mixed with marl (a crumbly earthy material with a good deal of calcium carbonate). Once purified the clay was shaped by hand-moulding (slabs were wet-thrown over moulds attached to the wheelhead), and by semi-automatic turning, or by casting. After a slow bisque firing to 1040°C, the yellow bisqueware was dip-coated in white tin glaze (from a centuries-old recipe). Decoration was applied by ornament-artists having received at least a five-year training in the factory. Patterns were outlined using the traditional pouncing method, in which charcoal powder is dusted through pin-pricked paper stencils, and in-glaze painting was meticulously done using fine cow hair reservoir brushes and metal oxide mixtures, including cobalt and copper. Wares are placed in saggars and carefully fired to 1000°C.

Photograph: courtesy of Koninklijke Tichelaar Makkum

The Royal Makkum pottery and tile factory is very old. It is not known when it was created, but a record exists of a sale made in 1594. The Tichelaar family has been connected with the pottery for more than 300 years. A farmer's son called Freerk Jans came to Makkum and bought the existing pottery. He worked as a maker of tiles or bricks, a *tichelaar* in Old Dutch, so he used Tichelaar as his surname. Since Freerk Jans the pottery has been handed down directly from father to son; the current owner, Pieter Jan Tichelaar, is the ninth generation of his family to run the enterprise.

The most important products in the past were household utensils such as dishes and plates, as well as both plain and decorated tiles. The factory now makes a large range of ornamental earthenware – plates, dishes, pots, vases, bowls, figurines, tiles, some 900 items in all – and all are shaped and painted by hand.

MORÉE ET MÉRÈT (FRANCE)

PLATTER, d. 46 cm, 1997.

This platter was made in much the same way that such pieces have been continually made in Moustiers-Sainte-Marie, Provence, since the 17th century. The piece is drape-moulded over plaster, fettled and sponged, then bisque-fired to 1020°C. After dipping in a tin-opacified glaze, it was painted in-glaze with metallic oxides, and glaze-fired to 980°C. The theme is an invented one, playing with a mythological fantasy, in the style of old French *faïence*.

Photograph: Pierre Mérèt

'The production of our studio consists for the most part of reproductions taken from old photos or old documents, and for these there is a great demand. Beyond this we produce our own creations, but still technically and visually with a traditional *faïence* framework. There is always gratification in dealing successfully with this most temperamental medium, as well as having personal contact with our clients and the public right here in the place where we live, and where the work is made.'

Pierre Mérèt

Early practitioners

The following five artists are notable for being ground-breakers at a time when maiolica was not so much in vogue. In the UK William Newland and Alan Caiger-Smith diverged from the Anglo-Japanese high-fire aesthetic, and in the south of France, Gilbert Portanier, Jean Derval and Jean-Paul van Lith were among the first to revive the use of tin glaze in a very contemporary context. An interesting development here by Derval and van Lith was the use of low-fire reduced copper reds.

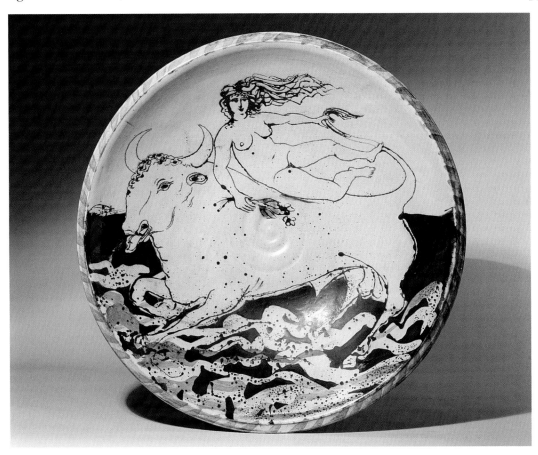

WILLIAM NEWLAND (UK)

LARGE BOWL: 'EUROPA AND THE BULL', d. 61 cm, 1965.
This large, rare bowl is an example of the early revival of tin glaze in the UK after the 1950s. (For biographical information on Newland, see Daphne Carnegy's book.) This wheel-thrown bowl was decorated with Newland's special technique of etched wax and wax resist. The leatherhard piece was coated with wax and the design etched through into the clay. A black glaze/clay/manganese mixture (suitable for raw firing) was applied to the etched areas. After bisquing, wax and surplus glaze were burned off, leaving a fine-line pattern in black. The piece was then covered in tin glaze, and further wax resist and in-glaze pigments were applied. After firing (to approximately 1100°C) the initial black glaze had burned up into the tin glaze for a soft, dark, textural effect.

Photograph: courtesy of Christie's Images

' "Style is the person – himself, herself" said Oscar Wilde in *De Profundis*. "To discover the self and develop it to its full realization that is our duty." Each potter or painter or barrister – each "self" is like a big mixing bowl: it's what you put in that counts. The bowl is open, receptive, from the early years of life.

Reflecting back on the early 1950s and the then-influential Bernard Leach ... we didn't want to sit in the heart of London, poised with a Chinese brush in hand painting bamboo. At the time our mixing bowl was full of Picasso, Miro, Matisse, Artigas, Le Corbusier, and Gropius; painters Klee and Kandinsky, poets WH Auden and Louis MacNeice...'

William Newland

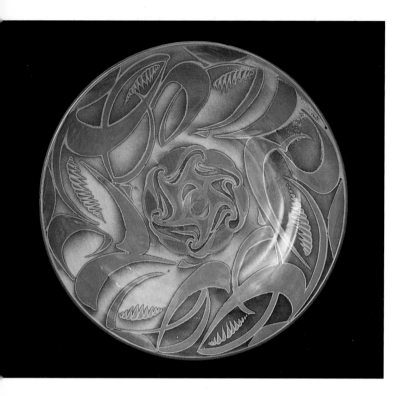

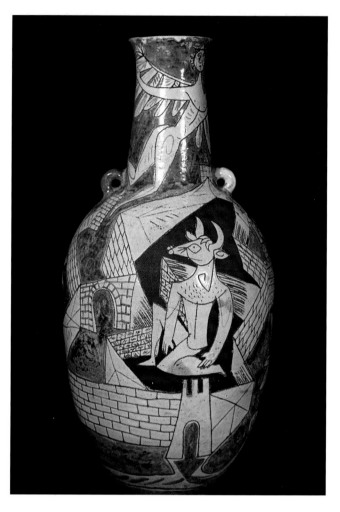

ALAN CAIGER-SMITH (UK)

LARGE DISH, 41 cm x 7 cm, 1997.
This wheel-thrown dish is made of a light red clay, tin-glazed with wood-fired reduction lustre pigments of vapoured silver and copper red. The lustre is fired in a pre-warmed kiln over an eight- to nine-hour period at up to 650°C, with clear burning periods between a number of small reductions toward the end of the firing cycle.

Photograph: Ken Dickinson

'I am working from a vague dream-ideal. It's an asymmetrical dance, a sequence of chasing rhythms moving inwards, outwards, and around in relation to an undefined centre. Something like it occurs when leaves are whirled by the wind. The movement is always unpredictable, always coherent, though there is no logical structure. I think this idea recalls the very beginning, when the form was soft clay, rising and spreading on the wheel. Thus the shape-making (the first process) and the decoration (the last) come together through their connection with the invisible centre. I decorate in many different ways, but I keep coming back to this dream. It's as old as the hills, perhaps even older, but it continually renews itself.'

Alan Caiger-Smith

JEAN DERVAL (FRANCE)

VASE: 'MINOTAUR', d. 78 cm, 1954.
This vase was wheel-thrown from finely grogged Vallauris clay, washed with an iron/manganese slip, and fired to 980°C. A subsequent coating of tin glaze was scratched away in part to reveal the dark slip base. Other areas were covered with copper oxide in a diluted lead base and, finally, black fine-line and cobalt details were added. This vase was wood-fired in reduction to 1120°C.

Photograph: Gaby Giordano

'During the last 50 years of working with clay, I have conceived many different kinds of work. I create not so much for myself; I see the artist/maker situated in the world of men, not the museum of personal experimentation. Art should be lived within a daily context. My favourite moments have been those related to the design and execution of architectural ceramics: the entire collaborative process including myself, the architect, the client, and the site, and all the tangible and exciting realities between conception and final installation.'

Jean Derval

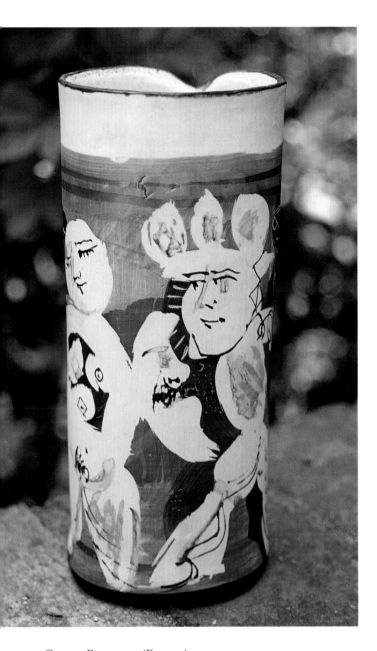

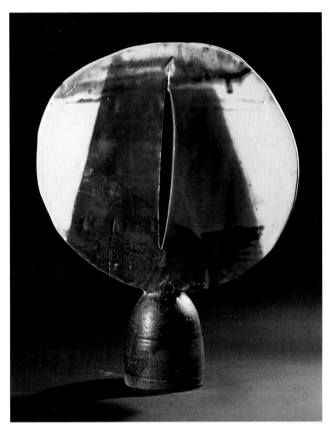

JEAN-PAUL VAN LITH (FRANCE)

SCULPTURE: 'ROUGE À FENTE', h. 53 cm, 1970.

This piece was constructed from a wheel-thrown base and joined, textured slabs. The central area was brushed with copper slip, and glazed with white tin glaze. Copper glaze was added to reinforce the red colour, which is the unusual result of low-fired copper in reduction. The work was pinewood fired to 1020°C. The piece was conceived as part of a group of slit and perforated objects, negating the idea of the ceramic container.

Photograph: van Lith ADAGP

GILBERT PORTANIER (FRANCE)

VASE, h. 28 cm, 1983.

This vase was slab-constructed of white earthenware, with both bisque and glaze firings to 1030°C. A thin coating of tin glaze covers areas of resisted iron-rich slip, and fine-line drawing is added in-glaze to the surface.

Photograph: Annette Chaillard

'Because it is asked of them, or because they feel they must, artists often have the tendency to play critic – that is, to analyze and explain their own work. I prefer not to provide the sources to my work, the keys to what lies behind it. Art is, above all a mirror in which the viewers are reflected. To them I leave all final conclusions.'

Gilbert Portanier

'I never said to myself: "I want to be a potter." I was attracted to ceramics by smells of gold wafting out of the staircase of the small building adjacent to the town school in Argenteuil, where an old couple decorated trophies and vases in their apartment. I have never forgotten those smells, and they are the same as the ones in my workshop today.

The main thing for me is to keep having fun. I have always found the way to do so. Ceramics is also a way of life, an art of living.

And I have learned the lesson of the masters. I believe only in passion, patience, and strenuous work ... and to top it all you need phenomenal luck.'

Jean-Paul van Lith

Functional

Most people becoming involved in ceramics have usually begun as potters. Some have branched out to other three-dimensional expressions, others have specialised in pot-making only, and yet others (myself included) have a foot in several camps. There is a great satisfaction in producing a vessel for use, regardless of any metaphoric role it may play.

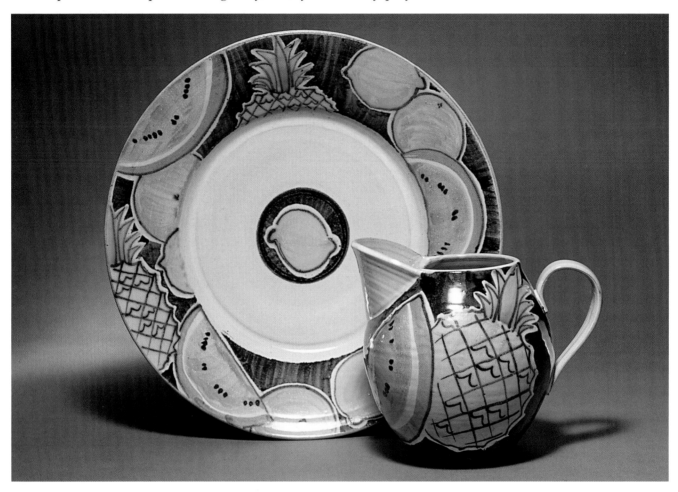

DAPHNE CARNEGY (UK)

DOMESTIC GROUPING, PLATE: d. 33 cm, JUG: h. 17 cm, 1992. These pieces were wheel-thrown using a red earthenware body bisqued to 970°C and glaze-fired fairly high to 1145°C. After glazing, the designs were lightly marked out in soft pencils, then areas of solid colour were filled in (using oxides and/or commercial stains), the palest colours first, with darker colours overblended for subtle gradations. Wax was used to outline the shapes, clearly separating motifs and fine outlines from the darker background.

Photograph: Stephen Brayne

'Ever since my workshop training in France I always knew that I wanted to make thrown domestic ware. My choice of tin-glazed earthenware as a medium was based on several factors.

- It offered infinite colour possibilities – the luminosity, depth, and texturing of the pigments in fusion with the glaze being peculiar to this medium.
- It represented a challenge to create my own personal language of painted decoration.
- I had for a long time admired the strength of early tin glaze, notably Islamic and Hispano-Moresque, designs.
- The European peasant pottery tradition presented me with a pedigree of the integration of surface and form in a utilitarian object, an integration to which I aspired.'

Daphne Carnegy

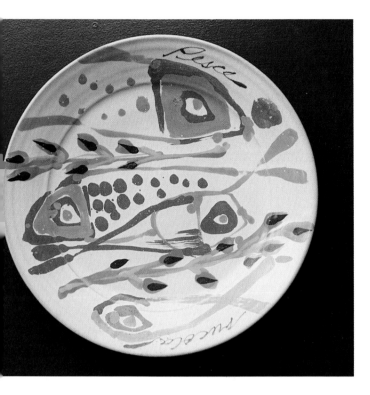

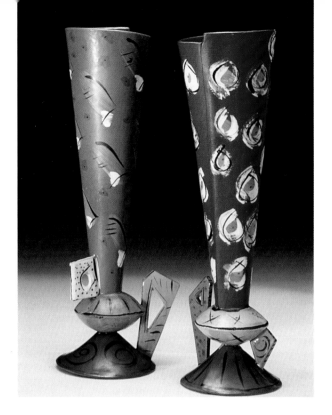

ANNE AND JOHN CRAWFORD (NEW ZEALAND)

FISH PLATE, d. 42 cm, 1997.

This plate of thrown red earthenware, one of a series of wares for domestic use, was glaze-fired to 1110°C. The loosely painted colour mixture (painted in-glaze) contains not only frit but also some of the base glaze. Brushwork was quick and gestural and food themes recur both in images as well as words.

Photograph: John Crawford

'As a child I was always being told that my colouring books were a disgrace ... all those colours going all over the lines. I decided early on that I liked them that way – they seemed more real. Never have I had a desire to replicate an image. What I want to, always, is, to "remove" an image from reality; only in this way, only by taking them over into my own reality, could I make things live. So it is with my work today.

I work directly, using memory and impulse. Themes for my work are drawn from my sense of place. In this fish plate, the theme is the catching of fish from our ever-present ocean.'

John Crawford

STEVE HOWELL (USA)

FLOWER VASES, h. 46 cm, 1996.

These pots are hand-built, assembled from slabs of clay which have been wrapped around styrofoam shapes and to which press-moulded sections have been added. They are glazed with stiff, opaque stain and oxide-saturated glazes (four to seven per cent colour to the base) which fire to 1060°C. The colour patterns are applied, glaze on glaze, using brushes or a glaze trailer. The opacity of the glaze allows clear superimposition of one colour on top of another.

Photograph: Randall Smith

'I have always thought of myself as a painter who makes pots. My primary sources of inspiration have been painters from the 1860s to the present. What really makes my heart soar are the colours of Monet's haystacks, the wonderful compositions of Matisse's cutouts, and the sombre intensity of Rothko's painting in the chapel in Houston. One of the prime reasons I find such joy in painting is that the artist is responsible for every mark on the canvas. The process will not make the image better. If the artist doesn't do it, then nothing will be there. Much of ceramics depends on process and faith to produce the image ... but not maiolica. With maiolica, the potter is responsible for the image, just as with painting. I appreciate that responsibility very much, as well as the truly unlimited colour possibilities (also as in painting), and the notion that the colour I put on the pot is what I will get back. Maiolica really allows me to paint my pots, just as I would a canvas.'

Steve Howell

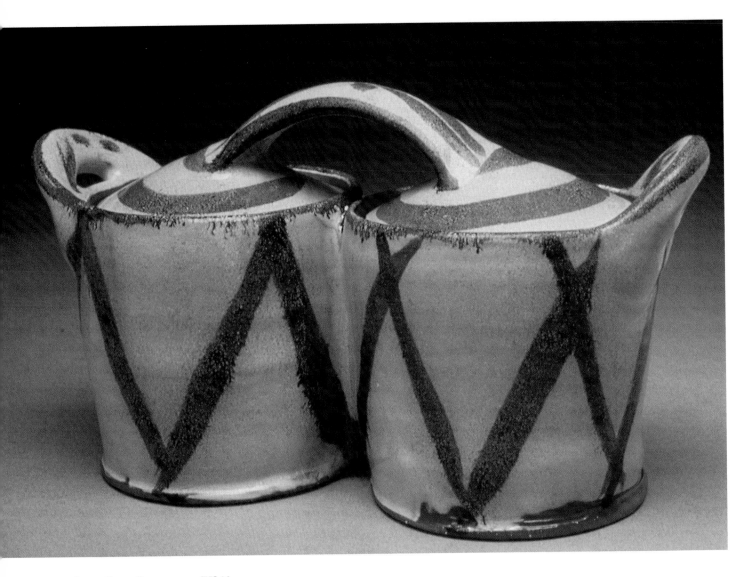

STEVE DAVIS-ROSENBAUM (USA)

DOUBLE JAR SET, d. 28 cm, 1996.

These pots are wheel-thrown red earthenware, altered and assembled off the wheel. The maiolica glaze is then painted with coloured stains mixed with varying fluxes that are designed to react with one another in the kiln and cause flashing. If the base stain is tin/vanadium it will turn pink/orange-red when mixed with gerstley borate, or deep yellow when mixed with ferro frit 3124. If colourants contain chrome, the resulting chrome/tin flashing adds variation to the surface of the pot. These pots were glaze-fired to 1060°C.

Photograph: Geoffrey Carr

'Much of my pottery originates in the basic human joys of eating and cooking with all their overtones: fireside, nourishment, caring and celebration. I make my pottery based on my personal domestic needs and life-style choices; and the focus of my production is everyday dishes for use in cooking, dining, and home decoration.

During the past ten years I was involved in making salt-glaze fired stoneware pottery rooted in the Leach tradition. About three years ago I made a "life change" and switched my production to maiolica. I approached making maiolica through the East, by looking at T'zu chou pottery. The forms and bold lines used in the decoration on the pottery gave me a direction. My later investigations in Islamic and early Italian maiolica pottery gave me a deeper appreciation of the relationship between form and decoration; challenging my ideas on how to interpret this process in my pottery.'

Steve Davis-Rosenbaum

112

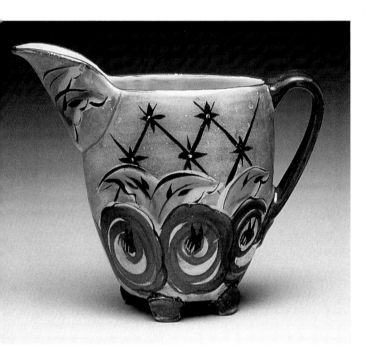

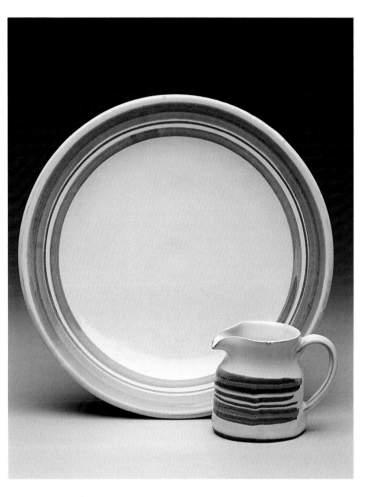

POSEY BACOPOULOS (USA)

BEAKED PITCHER, h. 19 cm, 1996.
This pot is a combination of thrown, altered, and hand-built slab components, made separately, then assembled. The piece was fully dipped in maiolica glaze, and painted with both oxides and commercial stains, fluxed with equal parts of ferro frit 3124 and gerstley borate. The foreground was painted first, then waxed so that the next layer of decoration could be added. This layer was then waxed, another layer added, and so on. Background, border and grid pattern were painted last. The yellow background was given an added coat of sprayed oxide for further colour depth.

Photograph: D. James Dee

'I try to create pots that enter people's everyday lives in a direct and intimate way. My goal is to integrate form, function and surface so as to bring balance and excitement to my work. The decoration of my pots is a direct response to the textures and forms that surround me. I strive for lively expression of line, pattern and colour. My hope is that my pots invite use, and that my pleasure in making them is shared by those who use them.'

Posey Bacopoulos

ELIZABETH NEAVE (IRELAND)

DOMESTIC GROUPING, JUG: h. 9 cm, PLATE: d. 23 cm, 1995.
The pots were wheel-thrown from local Irish earthenware and covered with a zircon-opacified glaze fired to 1060°C. The glaze was brought into a slightly warmer, cream colour range by adding a small amount of rutile to the base recipe. The banded borders were painted in-glaze with cobalt and copper carbonate, and with iron chromate.

Photograph: Jan Thijs

'The first 25 years of my working life were spent as a teacher of young children in Sydney, Australia, and later in London. I came to pottery rather late in life, and for the next 25 years worked with Philip Pearce in his Shanagarry Pottery, in Ireland. I now have a simple workshop at home where I make modest pots for functional use. My ambition was not to be greatly innovative, but rather, in a very healthy, traditional way, to produce tableware that is easy on the eye and comfortable in the hand. I prefer a simple banded pattern on a plate to overall decoration, so that the food itself becomes the important visual attraction.'

Elizabeth Neave

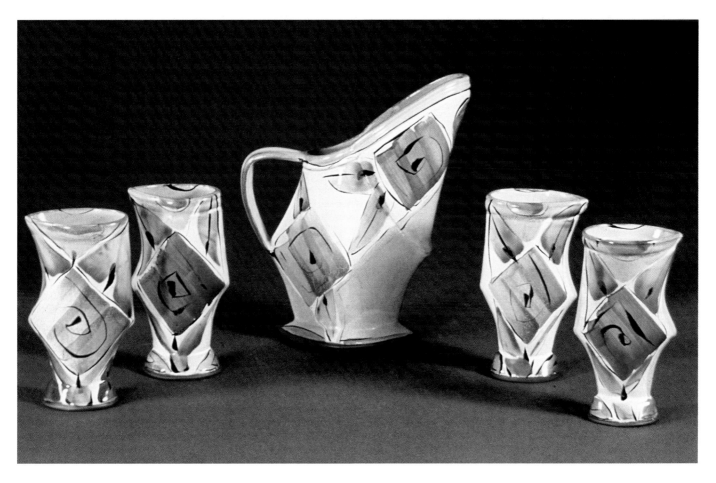

JANICE STRAWDER (USA)

PITCHER AND TUMBLERS, h. 32 cm, 1992

This pitcher and tumbler set was constructed using slab-built earthenware, with bottoms coated with terra sigillata. Bisque-firing was high (to 1040°C) and slow, to avoid the ever-lurking white-spot problem. The maiolica glaze has been painted with various stains combined with gerstley borate and cobalt carbonate, using bamboo, *hake* and water-colour brushes. Glaze firing was to 1060°C, with a 20-minute soak at the end.

Photograph: Janice Strawder

'Clay is a material which can directly and intimately transmit my touch to others. Therefore it is important that the user be a participant and as such complete the piece through use. For this reason I choose to make functional pottery.

I have always held great faith in things that grow and change. Much of my inspiration comes from nature, particularly floral and vegetative. In my work I strive to interpret the logic I observe in nature; to express rhythms and patterns through surface decorations as well as form, and to include those surprises nature provides for those who look closely.'

Janice Strawder

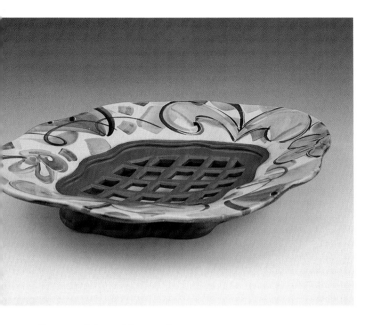

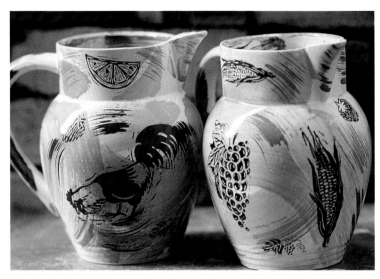

RICHARD MUND (CANADA)

FRUIT PLATTER, 36 cm x 46 cm, 1997.

This drape-moulded platter with wheel-thrown foot had its perforations cut while still on the mould to alleviate stress. Once dry, the bottom and inside were brushed with several coats of terra sigillata. After bisquing at 1015°C, exposed clay areas were brushed with wax-resist before a double-dip glaze decoration was done (with a variety of brushes), and *sgraffito* detail added. Glycerine added to the colour/frit stain mix promoted flowing brush strokes. Glaze firing was to 1168°C, with a gradual rise in temperature and a slow soak toward the end.

Photograph: Jeff Chown

'My initial inspiration to make decorated maiolica came from a Stanley Mace Andersen cup and saucer. Instantly captivated by the fluidity and freshness of colourful brush strokes, it wasn't long before I became dedicated to this technique.

The fruit, flower and leaf images in my work are used for their colours and shapes; they are vehicles which enable me to create playfully active patterns.

When decorating I try to respond directly to the form, giving equal consideration to the whole surface., by using a harmonious palette of complementary colours. I strive to develop work that is confident, energizing and lively.'

Richard Mund

LISA KATZENSTEIN (UK)

TWO JUGS, h. 23 cm, 1993.

These two pieces were slip-cast and then bisqued and glazed at the same temperature (1060°C). The glaze was leadless and zircon-opacified. Background pastel-toned colours were loosely applied with coarse, wide brushes, then fired in-glaze. Original on-glaze motifs in the form of linocut-type decals or transfers, were then applied and third-fired at 800°C with a 20-minute soak.

Photograph: Lisa Katzenstein

'In this work from the early 1990s I wanted to develop a line of functional tableware which used all the colour and softness of maiolica but did not necessarily relate to its long and venerable history in Western ceramics. My inspiration came from abstract painting and from printed ephemera such as fruit boxes. This was especially important since in Britain maiolica pottery tends to be associated with the tacky souvenir pieces people buy when on summer holidays in Italy or Spain. I did not want to be associated with that kind of pottery. I've since turned my attention to making one-off, hand-built pieces which aspire to be three-dimensional abstract paintings.'

Lisa Katzenstein

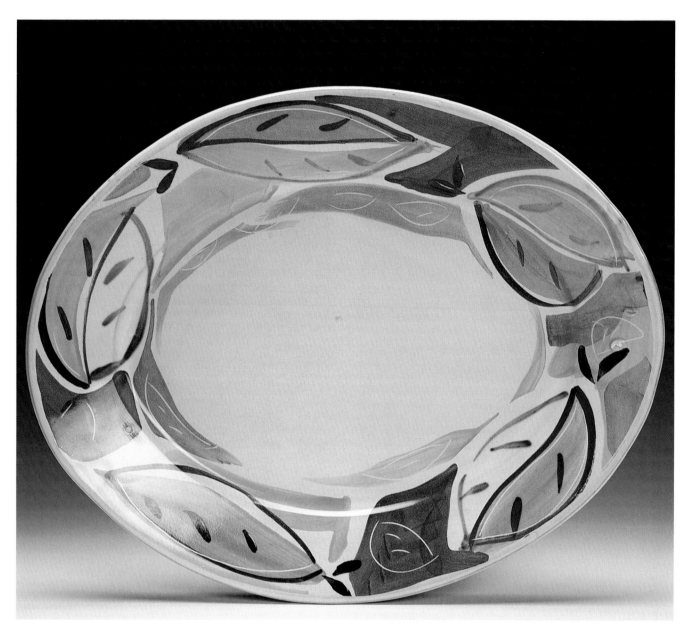

MEGAN PATEY (AUSTRALIA)

OVAL PLATTER, d. 42 cm, 1997.

This shape was drape-moulded, and painted in-glaze using quick, broad strokes to block in the main design with wide, flat brushes. Latex was used to block out some white areas. The placement of the initial brushstrokes is crucial to the vitality of this work, and the whiteness of the glaze always remains an integral part of the design. Contrasting thinner descriptive lines pull the design together and define the motifs. Bisque firing was to 1060°C, and glaze firing was to 1115°C.

Photograph: John Lascelles

'The inspiration to make and decorate pottery comes, only in part, from my enjoyment of preparing and dis-playing food. There is another source: a vague idea, lurking in the back of my mind, of "grasped spontaneity". I see this spontaneity in other pots or paintings – in, for example the work of French potter Catherine Vanier, paintings by Matisse, decorations on Persian lustre ware.

I am more interested in the abstract use of imagery, colour and pattern combination in decoration rather than in the narrative approach. I love the way the maiolica glaze picks up subtleties of colour and delicacy of wash. I like working quickly and spontaneously, trying to express energy within brushstrokes. The maiolica technique suits my needs wonderfully.'

Megan Patey

116

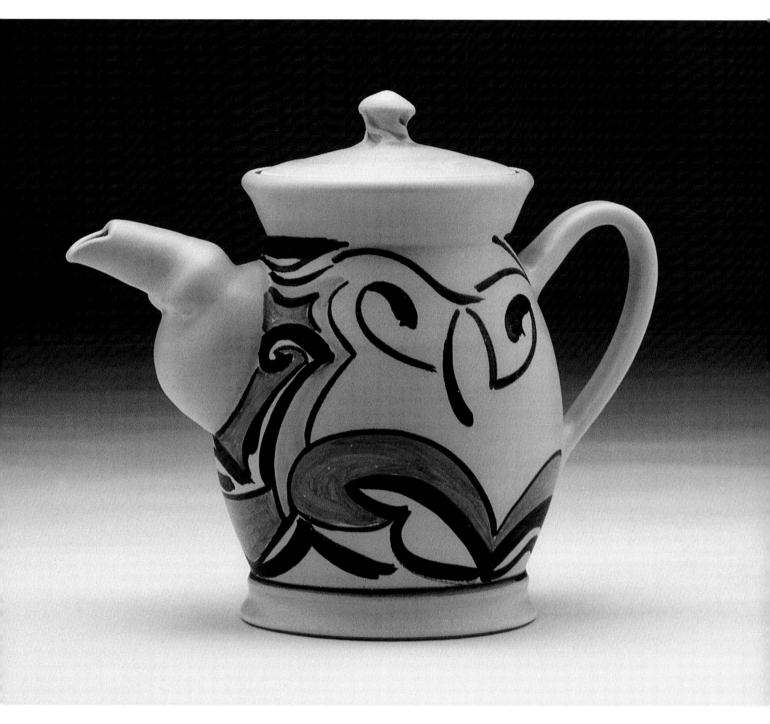

PAUL ROZMAN (CANADA)

TEA POT, h. 20 cm, 1996.
This wheel-thrown earthenware pot has a titanium matt glaze, fired to 1168°C. The abstractly conceived brushwork was freely applied, counterbalanced by large areas of white.
Photograph: Paul Rozman

'My aim is to make living a work of art by transforming the ordinary into the extraordinary. Pottery can provide meaningful aesthetic experiences because we interact with it daily, eating and drinking. Pots can delight us, humour us, exalt us, can express such qualities as romance, seduction, innocence, and flamboyance. When we experience these human qualities using pots we connect emotionally and become transformed by very ordinary actions. The mark of great art, after all, is its overwhelming capacity not to inform, but to transform.'
Paul Rozman

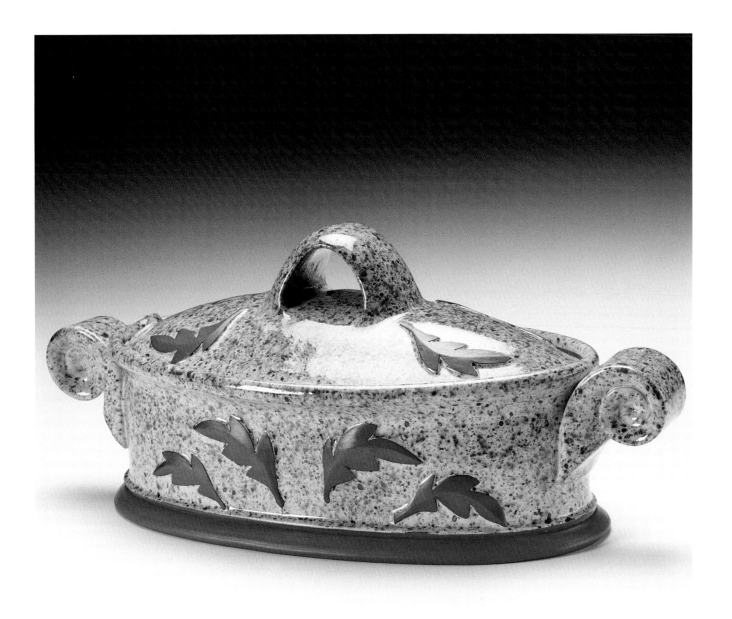

BRUCE COCHRANE (CANADA)

COVERED SERVING DISH, h. 10 cm; w. 10 cm; l. 24.5 cm, 1989.
This piece was thrown and altered, and the lid formed as an
inverted slab pressed into the oval flange of the pot itself.
Appliqué terracotta leaves were resisted with wax before
glazing, and the exposed foot treated with terra sigillata.
Copper and cobalt oxide were 'spattered' over the maiolica
glaze. The piece was fired to 1040°C.

Photograph: Peter Hogan

'How can I make a teapot, butter dish or salad bowl that
continues to engage its owner, to intrigue and satisfy,
with repeated use, and that provides a sense of the
process and connection to the maker? Balancing of
artistic expression and sensitivity to functional design
continue to provide the challenge, motivation and passion for making pottery.

Selection of materials (porcelain, earthenware or
stoneware) is made to accommodate ideas about form,
and where and how it functions. The thrown earthenware
forms are manipulated off-wheel to express the gesture of
containment and serving. Exaggeration is often used to
overstate the function.

Maiolica overglaze decoration is minimal in favour of
a rich contrast between the revealing terra sigillata and
the fat coating of opaque glaze. This combination main-
tains a sense of volume and flow in the fired form.'

Bruce Cochrane

Sculptural

The following images achieve their validity more through their three-dimensional stance and conceptual role than through the kind of elaborate surface treatment and narrative more usually associated with tin glaze.

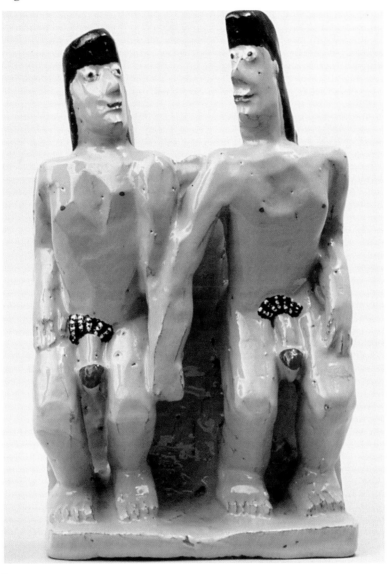

HYLTON NEL (SOUTH AFRICA)

SCULPTURE: 'BROTHERS', h. 28.5 cm, 1996.

Press-moulded and carved red earthenware, covered in a semi-opacified pea-green tin glaze, with black and red overglaze enamel details.

Photograph: David Barrymore,
Courtesy of The Fine Arts Society, London

'About work, what can I say? I am surrounded by examples of old ceramics from all traditions, not all tin glaze by any means. All things picked up here and there. I also have English things, Chinese pots, bowls from Afghanistan.

These are my inspiration. I look at the colours, the shapes, the brush marks, and then do what I can. My inspiration also comes from the fact that I must earn my living, that I like ceramics very much and feel that since such things always break, they must be constantly replenished. For a guiding principle, I try to make things such that were they to appear in a junk shop with no one to speak for them, they would nevertheless be a bit interesting and maybe make someone want to own them.'

Hylton Nel

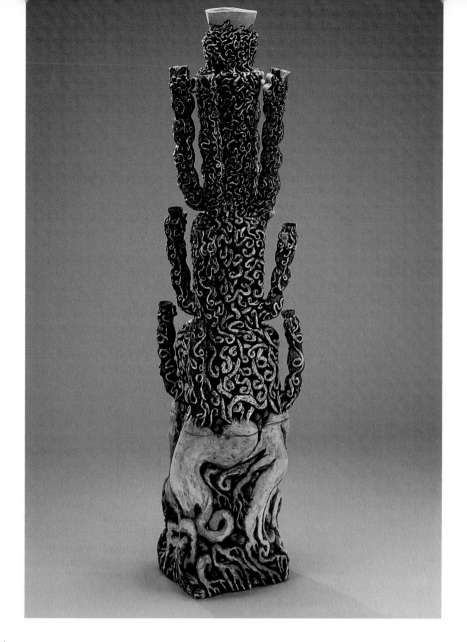

DEIRDRE DAW (USA)

TULIP VASE, h. 160 cm, 1995.

This monumental piece was built up into a double-walled structure using the coil method and a specially conceived semi-vitreous terracotta clay body. Additional carving and shaping was done as soon as the clay was leatherhard. After a low bisque, the maiolica glazes were painted on thickly in some areas, using a liberal amount of GMC gum mixture (100 g to 4 *l* hot water, shaken, and left overnight). A variety of watercolour and *sumi* brushes were used to paint on a 40:60 mixture of frit and stain, and other glazes and terra sigillata combined with the maiolica to create varied surface textures. The glaze firing was to 1060°C, with slow preheating to ensure stability of so large a structure.

Photograph: Koichro Hayashi, SF

'I've been fortunate enough to visit the Victoria and Albert Museum in London, the entire fourth floor of which is devoted to ceramics. The exciting ceramics I have seen there are still fuelling my work. Particularly interesting is the tin-glazed Hispano-Moresque work of eleventh and twelfth-century Spain, which blends the differing aesthetics and values of its Islamic, Christian and Jewish makers. This work encourages me in my belief that it is possible for all kinds of people to coexist fruitfully in this world. Aesthetically, combining two, three or more unlike ideas can be a rich method of developing challenging work.

The seventeenth-century Dutch tulip vases, some over four feet in height, have inspired me to try to combine the monumental tulip vase with the double-walled and pierced forms of Persian ware. I have made a roomful of these double-walled tulip vases over the past three years, and feel I still have not exhausted the possibilities of this format.'

Deirdre Daw

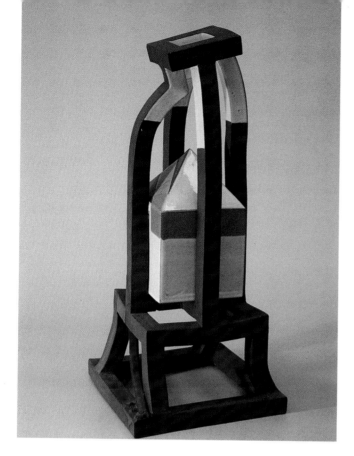

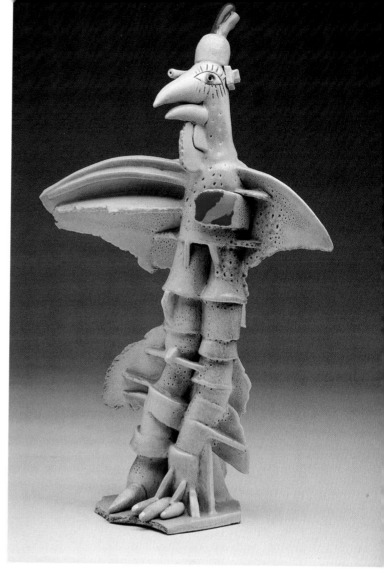

LUDMILA KOVÁŘÍKOVÁ (CZECH REPUBLIC)

SCULPTURE: 'THE CAGE', 51 cm x 24 cm x 24 cm, 1995.
This complex sculpture was made in two distinct phases.
The central 'caged' object was first assembled from joined
slabs, bisqued to 900°C, glazed with white tin glaze and fired
to 1000°C. Blue transfers were then applied, but not fired.
The pedestal form and clay structure were made from hol-
low, square, extruded tubes. Once the pedestal shape was
assembled, the initial fired slab shape was put in place and
enclosed by the cage structure, which was then joined to the
pedestal. Once dry, the entire structure was bisque-fired to
900°C, more glaze was applied with brush and spray gun,
and the structure was given a final firing at 1100°C, fusing
both transfers and 'cage' glazes.

Photograph: Ludmila Kováříková

'I am fascinated by architecture, its geometry and strict
functional discipline. The architecture of past cultures,
such as the Mayans, Aztecs and ancient Egyptians, and
also Czech functionalism before the Second World War –
all these have served as an inspiration. Some other particular touchstones are the traditional buildings in southern Moravia, where I live, the sculpture of Henry Moore,
and the purposeful objects created by various ethnic cultures. I work with such themes as gates, cubes in motion,
hearts, cages, cats, angels, boars, fortresses, riders and
most recently, thrones.'

Ludmila Kováříková

VLADIMÍR GROS (CZECH REPUBLIC)

SCULPTURE: 'IKAROS' (ICARUS), h. 38 cm, 1995.
The components of this sculpture were wheel-thrown,
assembled and altered, with additions of cut and torn clay
slabs, for irregular jagged edges. Tin glaze is thickly applied,
in some areas over a pre-applied brown glaze. Where the
underlying glaze is thick, it breaks through in darker, textural blotches. The piece is sprayed with pink stain, dusted dry,
and then saturated selenium red and a yellow glaze are
brushed on for added detail. Glaze firing is to 980°C.

Photograph: František Chrástek

'Most of my creations are humorous, hopefully with a
flavour of playfulness and wit. I usually work on a series
of pieces that are thematically connected, with, if possible, an underlying current of satire. One such series in
progress is called "Great Moravia", and will consist of
representations of famous local ancestors portrayed in a
humorous and exaggerated way. I enjoy provoking and
watching a reaction.'

Vladimír Gros

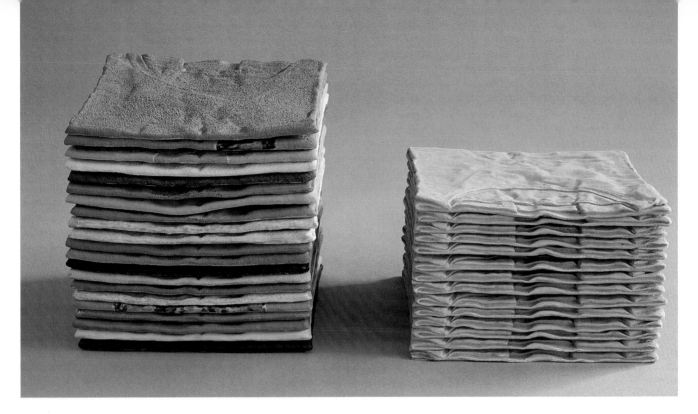

ABOVE: ANNETTE MEYER (GERMANY)

SCULPTURE: 'T-SHIRT STAPEL' (PILED T-SHIRTS),
h. (left) 35 cm, (right) 22 cm, 1996
This sculpture consists of two stacks of slip-cast clay folded T-shirts. The left pile consists of 21 separate pieces, each glazed with a different coloured tin glaze. The 14 pieces in the right pile were bisqued only. The work was fired to 1040°C.

Photograph: Matthias Hempe

'One thing that influenced this work is the idea of paper cut-out dolls with their various little clip-on costumes. The squareness and flatness of a folded T-shirt – flat, like paper, yet three-dimensional; a folded-over shape – becomes symbolic of duplication, of returning. Like clothing on the body, glaze becomes a metaphor for covering. The banality of the T-shirt itself is transformed by its sudden appearance in permanent fired clay, to reveal an article of clothing, or the personality of its wearer. Colours are similar, but not the same. Each fired T-shirt can reside on its own, or as a part of the larger entity, the pile.'

Annette Meyer

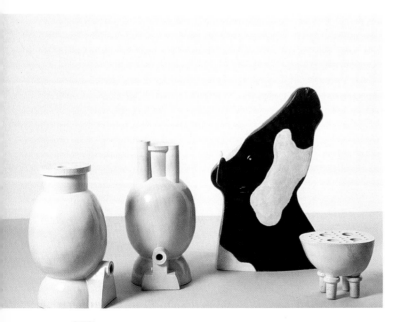

LEFT: FRITZ VEHRING (GERMANY)

SCULPTURE: 'KREATUR UND APPARAT' (CREATURE AND APPARATUS), 83 cm x 120 cm x 250 cm, 1996.
The individual components of this grouping were constructed of thrown and slabbed elements of grogged stoneware clay. White tin glaze, allowing a faint blush of terracotta colour to appear, as well as black in-glaze colour, comprise the glaze surface. The work was fired at 1040°C.

Photograph: Mark von Rahden

'Fritz Vehring's precisely contoured sculpture associates and relates the generic functions of both cow and machine. The necessary elements that comprise both creature and apparatus become a related entity, by nature of their actual similar construction and organic appearance.'

Bettina Zöller-Stock

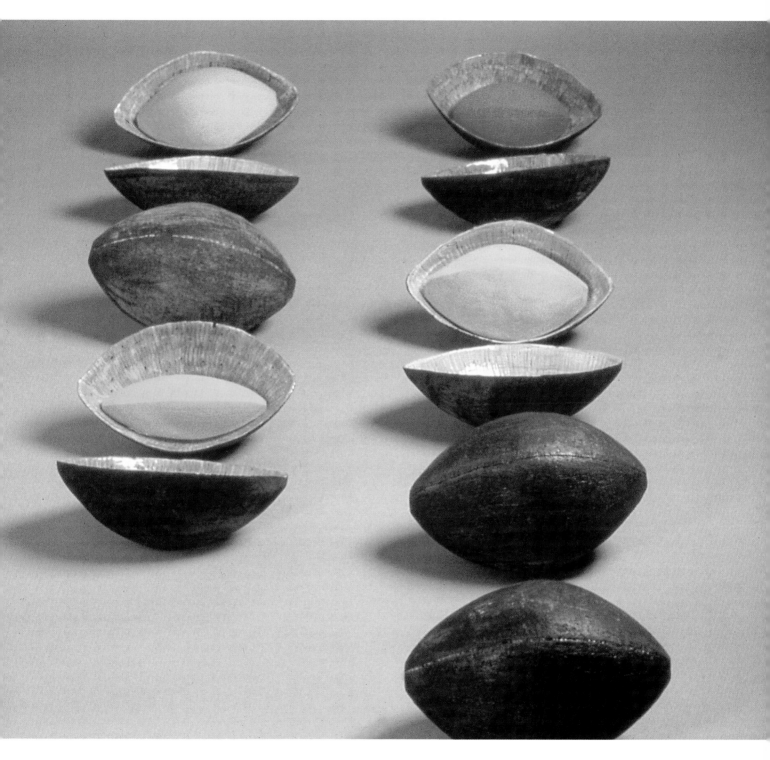

ULRIKE MÖHLE (GERMANY)

INSTALLATION: 'FRÜCHTE' (FRUIT), Each: 25 cm x 15 cm, 1996.
Each of these pieces has been slip-cast and the interiors
glazed with saturated coloured maiolica glazes. Exterior surfaces have been covered with black porcelain slip, for a dry-
surface contrast. Work was fired to 1040°C.

Photograph: Mark von Rahden,
courtesy of Fritz Vehring

'In this work the maiolica technique allows me to use
strong, vibrant colours that create the necessary tension
between a rough, unprepossessing exterior, and an exotic
interior, as is often found in the case of tropical fruit.
Painting and colour work here have to more do with
colour layering and depth and plasticity, than with the
painted image.

Ulrike Möhle

Object and image

This necessarily is a large section because for so many ceramists the prime attraction of maiolica is the melding of surface painting with ceramic object forming. Although most of the pieces shown here could be said to be vessels, some even functional, I perceive them primarily as images in themselves, or as vehicles for displaying images.

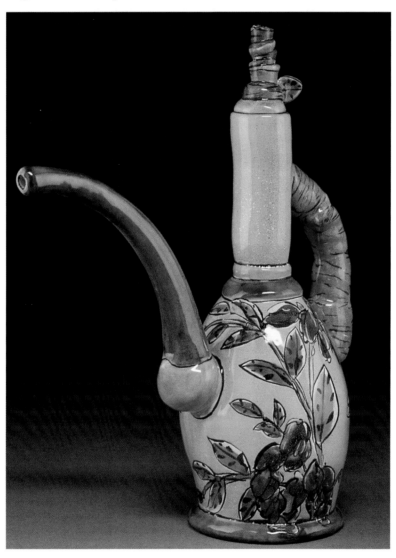

LINDA ARBUCKLE (USA)

TEA POT: 'SPRING IN MARDI-GRAS COLOURS', h. 35 cm, 1995.
This work is composed of thrown, altered and hand-built sections, and was glaze-fired to cone 03 (1101°C). To enable a broad sweep of background colour to be applied, images in the foreground were protected with wax resist. The bottom surface has been sealed with terra sigillata to reduce porosity and give a finished, terracotta look.

Photograph: Offices of Instructional Resources,
University of Florida

'My interest is functional pottery, and I enjoy appealing first through the senses in a domestic setting. I've always loved the personal experience of indulgence in function, like a hand-made postcard sent to a friend. Tableware, by nature, tends to be positive in attitude. I want the work to have strong forms and cheerful, spontaneous surfaces: properties that are direct, but that engage the viewer over repeated readings. Maiolica is a challenging vehicle that allows an extended choice of palette and active brushwork to investigate surface on form.'

Linda Arbuckle

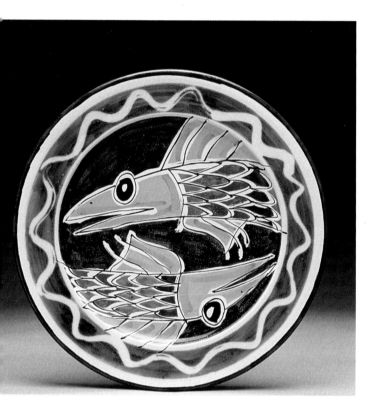

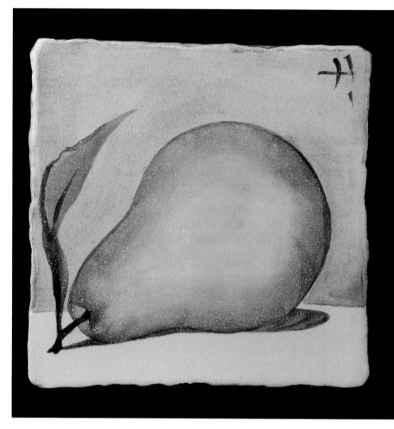

JENNIFER DAWSON AND IAN MACRAE (AUSTRALIA)

PLATE, d. 27 cm, 1995.

This collaborative piece, thrown by Ian Macrae and decorated by Jennifer Dawson, was bisqued at a high temperature of 1100°C. White outlines and patterns were freely brushed on the glaze with rubber latex, and coloured stains were liberally applied within the white borders. Once the latex was removed, fine black-line details were added over the previously latexed area with a traditional Italian maiolica decoration brush of very fine long hairs emerging from a thicker brush reservoir. The final glaze temperature was 1060°C, lower than that of the bisque.

Photograph: Victor France

'My love of vibrant colour and the inspiring drawings of artists such as Picasso, Egon Schiele and Brett Whitely have led me on a convoluted journey to the technique of maiolica. Both my desire to express myself in energetic drawing and my love of loose line work and bright colour are accommodated beautifully in this wonderful medium.

Most of my work takes the form of functional vessels. In contrast to traditionally understated tableware, however, my exploration of surface patterns, use of personal icons, and love of ceramic technology result in colourful, highly patterned pieces.'

Jennifer Dawson

XENIA TALER (CANADA)

TILE, 10 cm x 10 cm, 1997.

This white earthenware tile, after glazing, had its pear image pounced onto the surface with graphite through a cartoon, in the traditional manner. A fine liner brush created the outline, and underglaze colours were delicately added and blended on-surface. The tile was fired to 1040°C.

Photograph: Amir Gavriely

'Painting, and the mastery of its technique, always drew me but, sadly, I began to suspect that with the confusion of contemporary painting, only in ceramics was one still capable of making something truly beautiful.

My inspiration comes from great painting through the ages, but I'm especially interested in Chinese brush painting for its economy of gesture and for its treatment of space. Design and perfect arrangement are very important, as I want each tile to stand alone. Maiolica is a demanding but addictive technique. The challenges it presents – the necessity for sensitivity, speed and decision – are a constant source of pleasure and excitement.'

Xenia Taler

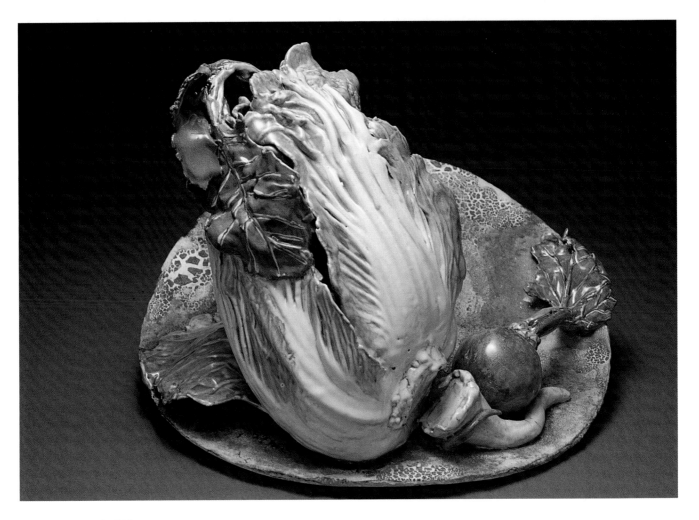

PHYLLIS KLODA (USA)

SERVING DISH: 'OOOH LA! VEGETABLE HOT DISH',
26.5 cm x 35.5 cm x 33 cm, 1996.

This multiple-fired, complex piece was hand-built from press-moulded sections, and a repertoire of slip-cast shapes created from plaster moulds of vegetables and found objects. These various pieces were assembled for the desired shape. Red and white earthenware slips were used for casting and in the hand-building process. Fragile parts were coated with paraffin in the leatherhard stage to prevent breakage during handling in the dry stage. The work was low-bisqued to 950°C. An air-brushed thin coating of maiolica glaze was fired to 710°C to provide a hard surface for colour application. A second glaze firing occurred at 1115°C. Then another coat of glaze was added, and the piece fired yet again to 1015°C. Overglaze enamels (China paints) were then applied, and fired one or more times for additional layers of colour depth and surface detail.

Photograph: Phyllis Kloda

'I consider myself a curator or orchestrator of objects depicting humour, fun and sensuality. These qualities are portrayed through the use of moulded vegetables and implements in tandem with muted colours. The vegetables represent social values, human relations and emotions. By taking objects such as a beet and a carrot and entwining them, these objects appear in an unfamiliar context. We consume such foods daily, but rarely stop to see their beauty, colour and sensuality.

Vegetable folklore, I find, is rich with numerous metaphors. Vegetables are colourful, with a variety of protective outer surfaces, yet internally yielding; much like people, they have their soft, vulnerable sides. They also have physical characteristics similar to those of males or females. The beet, a very intense vegetable, symbolises female genitalia, passion, immediacy and other feminine characteristics. The carrot, on the other hand, symbolises male genitalia, and promised or illusory rewards. Awareness of the clichés, the pretenses, allows me to manipulate my vessels and fully understand the forces behind them.'

Phyllis Kloda

126

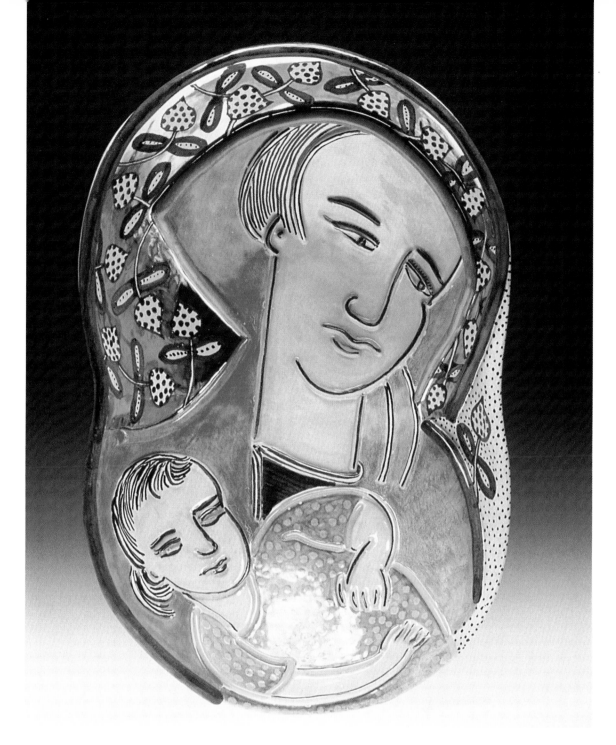

ANDREA GILL (USA)

BOWL: 'ROUMANIAN ICON', 45.5 cm x 30.5 cm x 12.5 cm, 1997. This bowl was made from press-moulded terracotta clay (slabs made on a slab roller) with coil decoration applied to the moulded form. The bisque was sprayed with a maiolica glaze, with laundry starch used as a hardener in the glaze. Colour stains, mixed with water, lead frit, and some glycerine and laundry starch were painted onto the unfired surface, and fired to 1040°C. Commercial gold lustre was then applied fired to 720°C. The reference in this image is to Roumanian reverse-glass paintings.

Photograph: Brian Ogelsbee

'Pottery form has long been used as a site for the painted image. My work continues this tradition, using pattern, layering and linear motifs to activate the surface. The maiolica tradition is one of the most painterly of all decorative techniques. My approach has never depended on the movement of the brush, but on a more geometric division of colour. The images and patterns are often borrowed from historical references, with changes in scale and colour. My visual language is influenced by Matisse: his flat shapes of colour, his simplified figurative forms, and his use of pattern floating over pattern.'

Andrea Gill

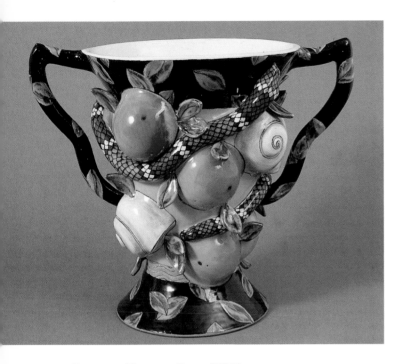

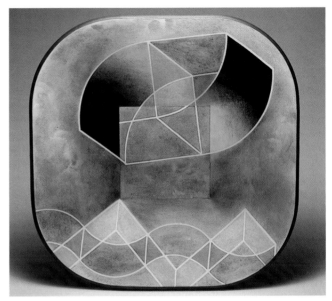

ANGELO DI PETTA (CANADA)

Plate, d. 30 cm x 30 cm, 1987.

This plate of slip-cast earthenware with a titanium-rich glaze was fired to 1015°C. The glaze's rich, matt-vellum surface has a softening effect on colours. Once applied, it was sealed with a charcoal spray fixative, which gives a stable surface for drawing. With each layer of stain, whether wet or dry, more fixative was added, giving free play to underglaze and copper pencils, copper foil tape and coloured glaze. The design was outlined in thin strips of masking tape, then filled in.

Photograph: Angelo di Petta

'In 1973 I was awarded a scholarship to study ceramic design at the Istituto Statale d'Arte per la Ceramica in Faenza, Italy. It was at this historical centre for painted ceramics that I was introduced to maiolica. Although indifferent to the historical imagery, I was attracted to the forms, colours and smoothness of the surfaces.

Imageless, reduced, high-fire stoneware had been my only experience in ceramics, but on my return from Italy I began working with earthenware. I didn't envision any imagery for it, although I was interested in maiolica. Then, after revisiting Italy in the early 1980s, my interest was rekindled and with excitement I began my first experiments with this technique. I used a titanium-based glaze with promising results, and began to design a series of square-shaped plates with imagery evolving from the formal geometry of their shapes.

Design has played an important role in my development as a ceramist. It seemed appropriate to me that the form and the applied imagery should be in harmony, so that one would be meaningless without the other.'

Angelo di Petta

FARRADAY NEWSOME SREDL (USA)

VASE: 'VASE WITH SNAKE, ORANGES AND MOON SNAILS', 38 cm x 43 cm x 30.5 cm, 1995.

This vase was hand-built using a combination of wheel-thrown and coiled elements. Handles were generally extruded, then shaped by being laid on templates that had been sketched on paper and cut out. Relief elements were press-moulded in simple, hand-made plaster moulds, or freely formed. Bisquing occurred at the high temperature of 1145°C for a mature, dense body. For full, fat and fluid results, colour was applied on the white maiolica undercoat in the form of full-bodied coloured glazes rather than the usual oxide or stain washes. The final glaze firing was to 1040°C.

Photograph: Farraday Newsome Sredl

'I am a potter living in the Sonoran desert of Arizona, and my studio is my home. Maiolica allows me a bright and painterly use of glazes on a red-clay body. I like the lively richness of red terracotta clay, and I find that putting on an initial ground of white glaze is analogous to gessoing canvas in preparation for painting.

I use layered glazes rather than the more traditional washes and lustres. This enables me to build up a fatter, more complex glaze surface. The resultant translucency allows for visual mixing of the layers, and a depth and fluidity of colour.

My pottery tends to be generously sized and robustly built, qualities which I feel are in the spirit of the glazing. I aim to express optimism and sensuality, and to affirm the beauty of life and the natural world.'

Farraday Newsome Sredl

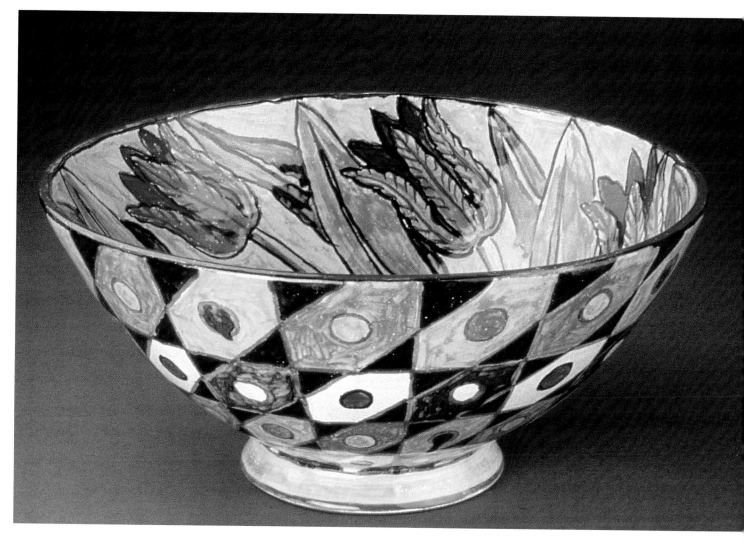

TERRY SIEBERT (USA)

BOWL: 'PERSIAN HARLEQUIN TULIP BOWL', 30.5 cm x 15 cm, 1989.
This thrown and trimmed bowl was carefully dipped in
maiolica glaze, with attention paid to assure a clean bisque
and a very even glaze coating. Decorating stains and oxides
were mixed with frit, water, and a spoonful of starch or glycerine (which helps colours to flow well and prevents smudging). Bright, opaque colours were applied thickly for maximum density and effect, with special attention paid to visible brush strokes. Both glaze and bisque firing were to
1060°C, for optimal clay clearance and glaze fit.

Photograph: Roger Schreiber

'Growing up in an historic New England town, in a house
full of books, history has always been important to me.
Many of the forms and patterns I use in my pottery have
their roots in ancient Persian, Spanish and Italian ceramics and decorative arts traditions. My pottery forms echo
the strong, simple shapes of European folk-pottery. I like
full-bodied forms with prominent bases, rims and spouts,
and thick, gestural handles. In other words, I value forms
that are functional as well as beautiful. I strive for decoration that interacts with the pottery form, enlivens its
surface and creates the illusion of depth. This I accom-
plish by the layering of pattern upon pattern and by playing colours off one another.

Many of my designs are inspired by my love of gardens and the intricacies of nature. My harlequin and
checkerboard patterns provide a counterpoint for the floral and plant motifs. They refer to the architectural elements of a garden (tilework, pavement, trellises, etc.).
Thus I combine the intricate with the simple.

The whole process is one of forming connections
between my self, my life, the natural world, other cultures, the artists who came before me and those who now
find meaning in my art.'

Terry Siebert

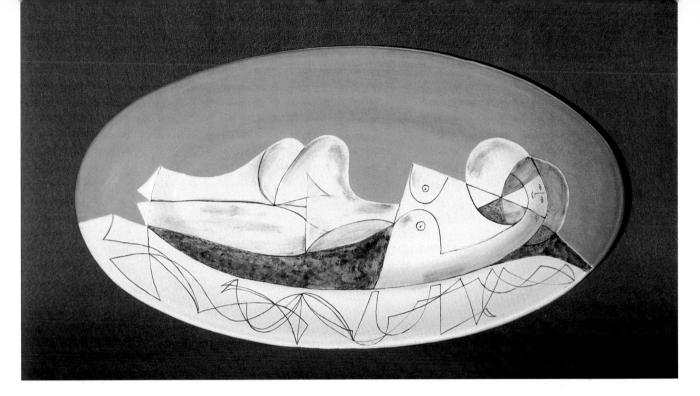

ABOVE: GEORGINA FINE (FRANCE)

PLATE: HOMMAGE À PICASSO, d. 60 cm, 1989.

This drape-moulded platter was bisque-fired to 1020°C and then glazed with a tin glaze, carefully scraped and wiped back to leave a visible red clay background. Fine-line drawing and details were painted in-glaze with metallic oxides, and fired to 960°C.

Photograph: Vania Fine, courtesy Atelier JMV Fine

'This work was created in the context of an exhibition of works on the theme 'Hommage à Picasso' at the Atelier JMV Fine in Moustiers-Sainte-Marie. The woman in the plate is comfortably reclining in its oval depression and the lines of her body are mirrored in the lower border.'

Georgina Fine

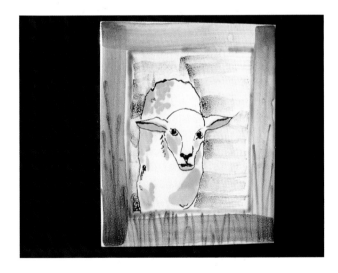

ABOVE: AGALIS MANESSI (UK)

TILE, 15 cm x 15 cm, 1995.

The tile used here is an industrially produced biscuit tile, covered with a commercial opaque, low-solubility glaze fired to between 1060°C and 1065°C, with a final half-hour soak. The image was sketched with a soft pencil, then standard oxides and stains, intermixed with diluted glaze, were applied in a broad wash, and fine-line drawing added. Vanadium pentoxide and potassium dichromate, two of the rarer oxides, were used for the way they interact with other colours and affect the glaze surface in subtle, lustrous ways.

Photograph: Bob Kessler

'A number of themes such as fruits, plants and flowers, still-lives, interiors, animals and people (figures and portraits) recur in the work. I paint and sketch these subjects in notebooks for future reference. My treatment is influenced by looking at a wide variety of painting and sculpture, from the classical to the contemporary. I try to capture the essence of my subjects as an illustrator would – accurately, but with a personal sense of expression and character. Through careful placement of the image within the form I try to achieve qualities of balance, harmony, and individuality in a quiet but, I hope, distinctive way.'

Agalis Manessi

130

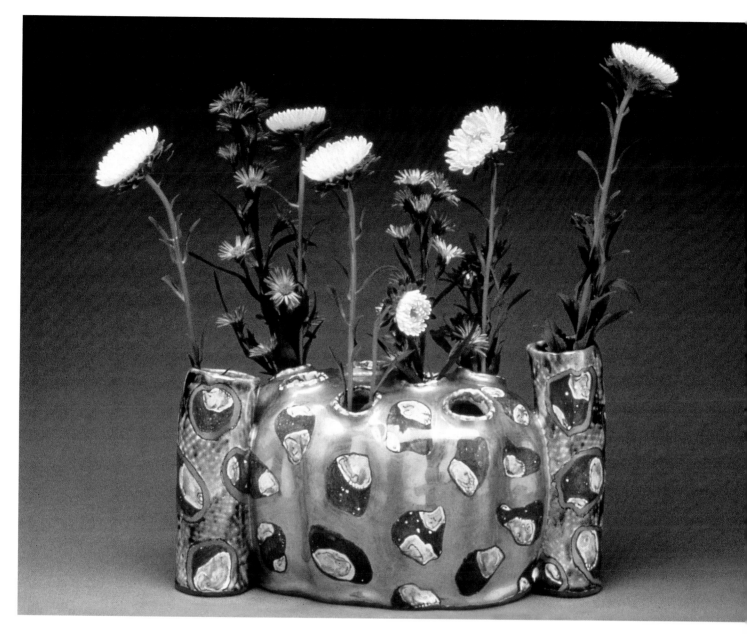

LIZ QUACKENBUSH (USA)

VASE: 'MOONVASE', w. 26.5 cm, 1995.

This piece was assembled from coiled and pinched forms of terracotta clay, bisqued to 1015°C and glaze-fired to 1115°C. Maiolica glaze was applied in three layers of hand-painting for a rich, fatty look complementing the loose irregularities of shape. A saturated colour effect was created by a thick application of cobalt and copper, with wax resisting some areas. Gold lustre highlights the main body of the piece.

Photograph: Liz Quackenbush

'These terracotta pieces are inspired by ceramics made during the thirteenth through the seventeenth centuries in France, Italy, Spain, Portugal and Iran. I call it a crazy quilt approach to ceramic history because I patch many different inspirations together. The clay surfaces are left irregular so that they look handled and handle-able. The bumpy surface underneath the gold lustre hearkens back to the hammered-metal dinnerware forms mimicked in earthenware in thirteenth-century Iran. My goal with this functional work is to bridge the gap between elegant china and down-to-earth pottery. I want to invite use, and at the same time, seek to subvert contemporary "run-of-the-mill" preconceptions of what functional pottery is or can be.'

Liz Quackenbush

131

Narrative

Again many pieces from other categories could be included in this one, but to me, the following works are specifically narrative: that is, the *raison d'être* for each piece is to tell a story.

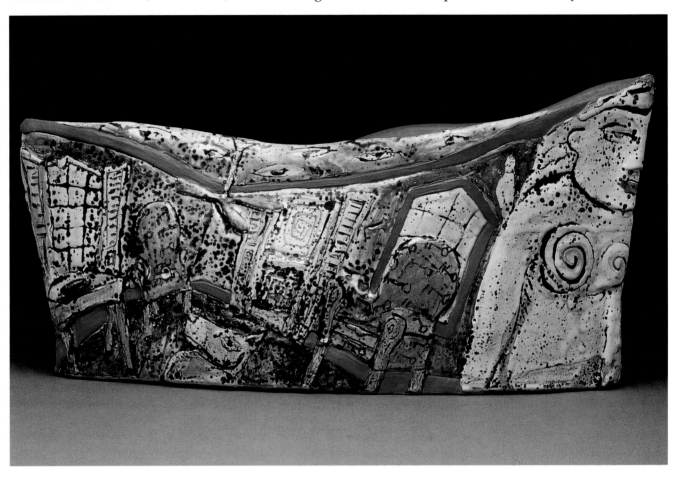

DEBORAH KATE GROOVER (USA)

VASE, 35.5 cm x 56 cm x 15 cm, 1993.

This open vase shape was constructed with thrown and stretched slabs, keeping the natural distorted profile of the slabs. Once assembled and joined, the image is loosely dictated by the shape, and emphasised through surface manipulation (i.e., bulging), and low-relief carving. Glazing is unorthodox; organic drips and spills are included and encouraged. A first dark glaze is applied, without opacifier, containing eight percent of black stain. Chosen dark areas are wax resisted, and the piece is dipped in white maiolica glaze. Fritted stains are then applied for details, and the piece is fired to 1060°C. The lower glaze is more fluid than the upper. This causes slight blurring of lines, and dark spots breaking through for a looser, more organic image.

Photograph: Walker Montgomery

'I was fortunate to have grown up in a region of the United States that has a long and rich heritage of story-telling. Legends of mythological proportion have been passed on through the generations by devoted family members seeking to preserve the past. I concluded long ago that knowing precisely where the reality ends and the myth begins is not necessarily the most important part of the story. (I have studied classical mythology, comparative religions, and southern literature.)

So that's how I approach my work. I tell stories. A little myth, a little reality, sometimes tragedy, sometimes joy. I make a visual record of my journeys using a personal iconography and classic archetypes.'

Deborah Kate Groover

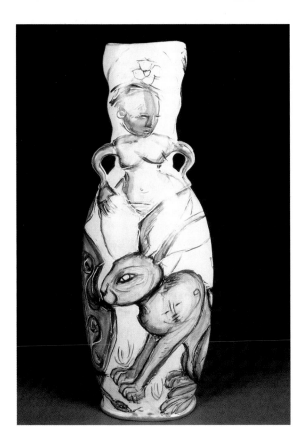

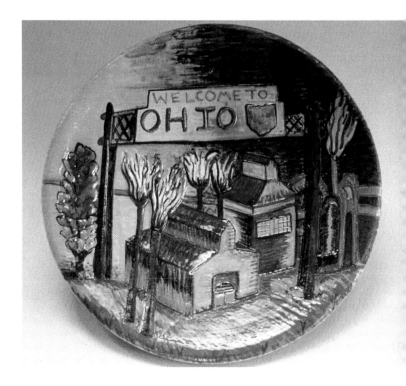

GINA BOBROWSKI AND TRIESCH VOELKER (USA)

VASE, h. 35.5 cm, 1996.

This work, from the physical building to the decoration, is entirely collaborative. The piece was thrown, altered and, as soon as the clay could be worked, assembled in sections. The surface painting is densely layered, visually obsessive, and intuitively derived, designed to restate the existing forms. Colours were painted in-glaze, using oxides and stain/frit mixtures, and the work fired to 1040°C.

Photograph: Triesch Voelker

'Collaboration, inviting the direct influence of another person, provides a way of stretching creatively. The focus of our endeavour is useful pots – pots that function both in daily use, and as individual objects. These works are imbued with fluidity of form, sense of touch, and a playful approach to volume, combined with strong, densely-drawn narratives that flow around the form.

The narrative is not an obvious one, but rather one that involves a liberal sense of play and association. The imagery is fuelled by our background in music and drawing; our lives as natives of semitropical New Orleans and Bunkie (in rural South Louisiana), where we lived; the high desert of New Mexico, where we now live; and our daily experiences of natural forces and mystical cultures. The spontaneous narrative quality of the imagery echoes that of the creative processes of children, visionaries, and self-taught artists.'

Gina Bobrowski and Triesch Voelker

MARY JO BOLE (USA)

'SOUVENIR PLATE', d. 20.5 cm, 1987.

This plate was drape-moulded over a carved bisque form to create the low-relief surface. After glazing, painted details were added using a combination of commercial stains and oxides, and the piece was finally raku-fired to give a smoky, mother-of-pearl finish to the glaze surface.

Photograph: Mary Jo Bole

'I grew up in Cleveland, Ohio. Its industrial landscape, considered forgettable by many, became for me a resource. I feel strongly about recording this left-over Victorian place and entwining these records through different materials. The souvenir enters my work in many ways; and I collect hand-painted souvenir plates. Maiolica adds the drawing medium to my work. It is an important ingredient in my layering of images and surfaces.'

Mary Jo Bole

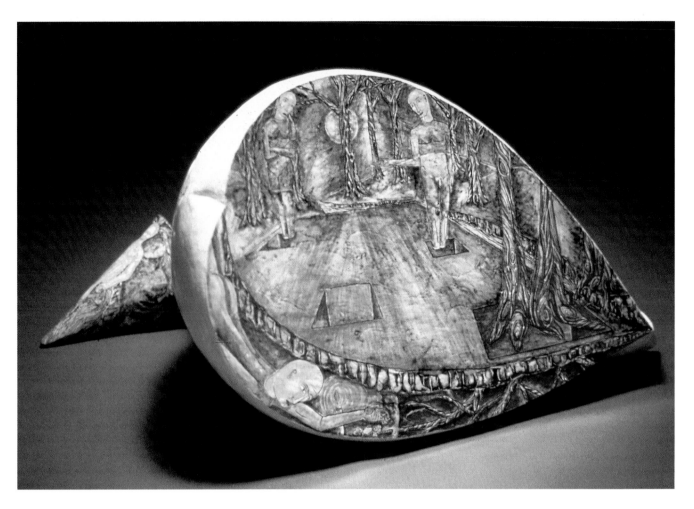

CHUCK AYDLETT (USA)

SCULPTURE: 'DECOY!', h. 56 cm, w. 71 cm, 1993.
This piece has been hand-built using slabs of clay, covered in part with terra sigillata (white area) and maiolica glaze. A combination of oxides and commercial stains were used to paint the detailed narrative. The work was glaze-fired to 1060°C.

Photograph: Chuck Aydlett

'A significant aspect of my maiolica painting and forms is the relationship between enhancing the form and camouflaging it in some manner. This push-pull effect will hopefully captivate the viewer and create more personal involvement.

My work deals primarily with human interaction. I strive to promote awareness of social issues and surreal situations. I work in a narrative style, engaging the viewer through pictorial imagery in painting and in figurative sculpture. Qualities of abstraction play a part in transforming these images into metaphors of our existence. How do images, symbols, and materials affect our senses? Where does curiosity take us? By questioning we can grow; curiosity opens many new doors.'

Chuck Aydlett

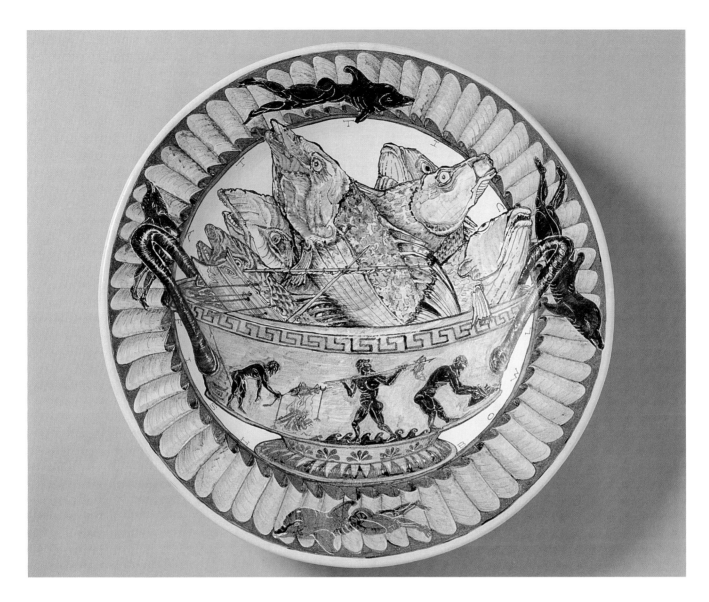

WILLIAM BROUILLARD (USA)

BOWL: 'ATTIC FISH BOWL', 66.5 cm x 66.5 cm x 12.5 cm, 1995.
This very large bowl is made from a heavily grogged red
clay, and has been thrown upside down over a convex-
curved bat to eliminate trimming, drying, and weight problems, and to allow immediate attachment of the foot ring.
After bisquing, maiolica glaze was applied and, after many
preliminary sketches, the pattern was sketched on-glaze in
great detail with a soft-lead pencil. Colours were applied
much like water colours on paper; glaze painting both sides
of the piece took from three to four days. The back was com-
pleted before the front. The piece was fired to 1060°C.

Photograph: Tony Grey

'With humour and whimsy as the backdrop, I have tried
to inject some familiar objects from both the natural
world and the man-made environment into the decora-
tive/commemorative object. Selection of the objects is
made with the overall objective of a contemporary por-
trayal using a historical format. The scale of the platters is
larger than would be appropriate for everyday use. This
gives them a slightly overblown sense of importance, and
makes them easy to see and understand at a distance.
They are meant for the wall and the table, with their large
size matching that of large gatherings or architectural
spaces.

I have tried to replace the historical patterns of the
maiolica style with patterns rendered from natural
objects or artifacts. Some of the objects are extensions of
my environment or reflections of personal interests.
Subject matter ranges from humorous depiction of everyday objects to gender stereotypes.'

William Brouillard

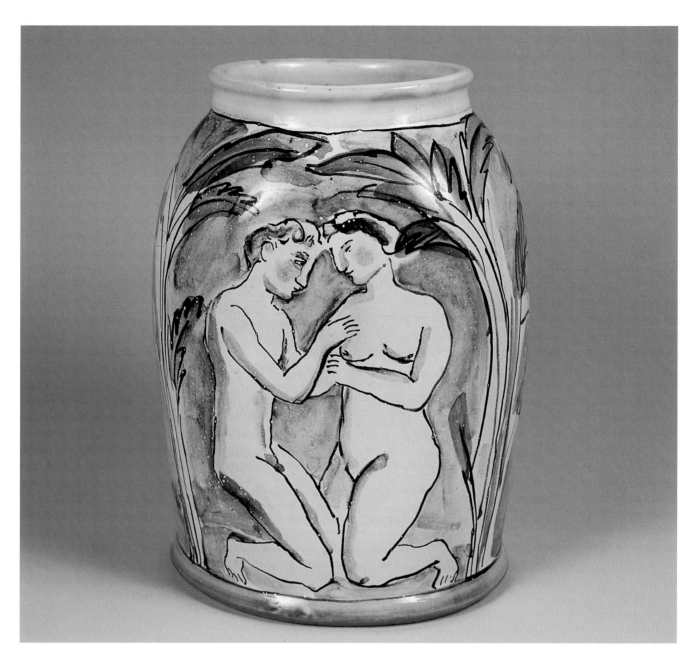

SIGRID HILPERT-ARTES (GERMANY)

VASE: 'FLASCHE MIT LIEBESPAAREN' (VASE WITH LOVERS),
h. 17 cm, 1997.

This vase is wheel-thrown and trimmed red earthenware, bisqued to 900°C. The tin-opacified glaze was dipped in the traditional way, and in-glaze painting was executed with fine-line and wash brushes, using a combination of oxides and commercial stains. Glaze firing was to 1080°C.

Photograph: Franz Zadnicek

'My mother was a painter, and I grew up in contact with many artists in the city of Dresden, in itself a beautiful place, full of great treasures. All of this encouraged me to be perpetually drawing and to choose a career in the visual arts. Painting seemed less practical than potting, so ceramic studies took precedence and maiolica happily combines the two. Some of the things that touch and inspire me are Arabian fairy tales – lively, erotic, and delicate; ethnic fabrics and carpets and woodcarving; stones, insects, butterflies, all kinds of plants; and the painters Matisse, Chagall, Picasso and Gauguin. All of these serve as food for inspiration. I have no desire to portray darker contemporary realities; rather, I try want to counterbalance them with optimistic and uplifting imagery.'

Sigrid Hilpert-Artes

Architectural

The works in this section were conceived as architectural installations, components of a larger-framework, such as a building or a public space. Their scale and complexity of construction sets them apart from pieces in other categories.

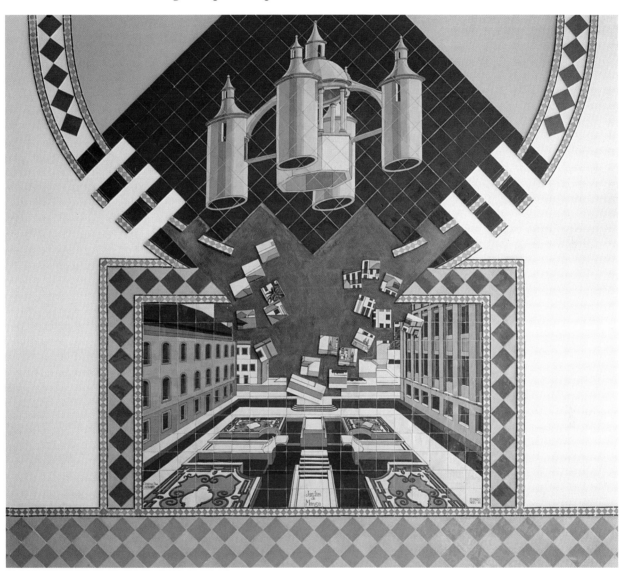

EDUARDO NERY (PORTUGAL)

TILE PANEL: 'JARDIM DE MANGA' (MANGA GARDEN), 4.7 m x 4.7 m, 1988. TILE LAYING BY AZULARTE, LDA, LISBON.

This large installation wall-panel, at the Centro de Emprego in Coimbra, Portugal, depicts a Renaissance fountain at the Manga Garden. The fountain seems to rise in space, simulating the explosion depicted on the panel centre. Tiles were hand-cut, glazed with a traditional maiolica glaze and decorated with oxides.

Photograph: Luis Filipe C. Oliveira

'There is a sense of ascension in the construction placed at the top of this panel, accentuated by diverse vectors of movement converging to a sky, which expands in a semi-circle. Nevertheless, the most dramatic effect derives from a sense of chaos expressed in the central part, where the impetus of the vertical trajectory of the construction seems to have destroyed the physical integrity of the panel itself, tearing off some tiles and spreading around all the rest.'

Eduardo Nery

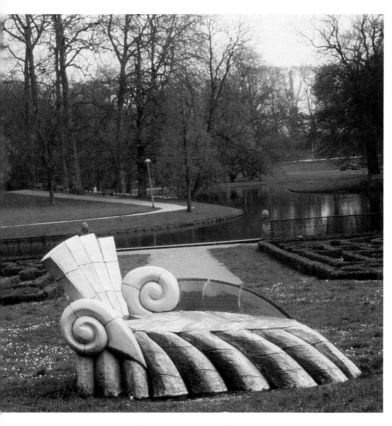

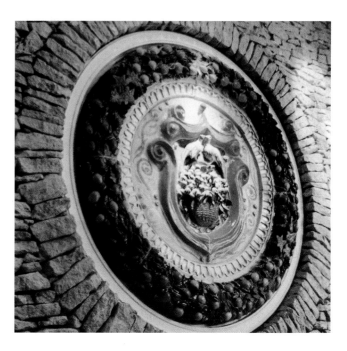

DORA DOLZ (THE NETHERLANDS)

SCULPTURE: 'CHAISE LOUNGE', l. 180 cm, h. 100 cm, 1988.
This outdoor sculpture, created in collaboration with the Structuur 68 Studio, was shaped out of wet earthenware clay in its entirety, and while still damp, cut into various sections, each of which was strategically hollowed to facilitate optimal (even) drying and firing. After bisquing, individual sections were glazed with tin glaze and painted with their respective colours. The bright red is added enamel in a third, lower-temperature firing. Once fired, all pieces were assembled and cemented to a central chassis.

Photograph: © Dora Dolz 1998 Vis*Art Copyright Inc.

'I was born and raised in Spain, and have always kept my strong affinity to bright Mediterranean light. There is a tenderness to maiolica colours that I find appealing, and thematically I lean towards depictions of landscape and still life. The scale is large because art is larger than life.'

Dora Dolz

JEREMY NEWLAND (UK)

PLAQUE, d. 1.8 m, 1992.
This plaque was commissioned for an Italian restaurant in Baker Street, London, and was inspired by the work of Della Robbia. The outer sections were press-moulded and worked over by hand, the inner section being entirely hand-modelled and sculpted. The green-leaf border was glazed in tin glaze over a copper wash, the fruit being glazed with underglaze colours under transparent glaze. The central fruit is tin-glazed with in-glaze colours added, and the basket and shield surround are white earthenware, with applied orange stain and transparent glaze. Bisque and glaze temperatures are both 1060°C.

Photograph: Jeremy Newland

'I owe almost everything I know to my father, William Newland, with whom I have often collaborated. I have specialised in large-scale architectural commissions (rather than domestic-scale work) perhaps because these were something William did so well, and because there is something attractive to me about the larger-than-life, overblown object. I am drawn to very simple, well-designed things: early Chinese pots, good Japanese design, the Zippo lighter, the Volkswagen Beetle...'

Jeremy Newland

Artists as ceramists

The artists in this section are in fact professionals in other fields who have used maiolica as another tool, one of many, to further their expression. Kunc is primarily known for his works on canvas, and the painters Nioré and Ceccarelli briefly worked in tin glaze in the context of a group exhibition organized by Atelier JMV Fine in France. Wernecke is a multimedia artist creating works on paper, raku-fired sculptural ceramics, and most recently, oversized wood sculptures for installation. Kruger is a notable jeweller, and has developed a range of porcelain and *faïence* works, in part through his association with the European Ceramics Work Centre in the Netherlands. Van Lith, with his background in metal and glass sculpture, could also be categorised as an artist/ceramist.

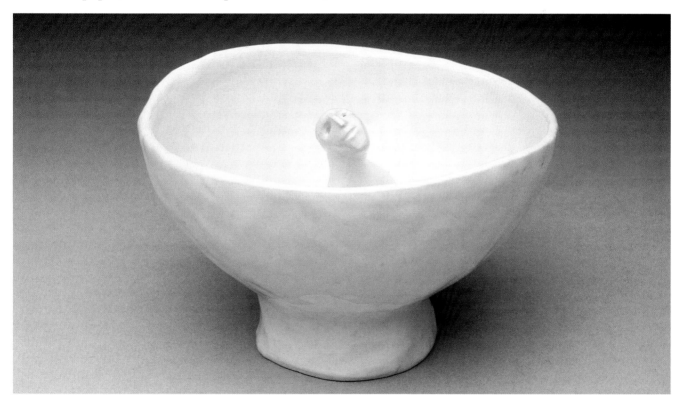

THOMAS WERNECKE (GERMANY)

BOWL, d. 15 cm, 1996.

This small bowl was pinched by hand, with the small head and foot-ring modelled and added. The white zircon-opacified glaze has been softened with the addition of a very small amount of rutile. A thin coating of glaze over the cream-coloured body emphasizes the modelled surface. The bowl was fired at 1040°C.

Photograph: Jan Thijs

'Drawing for me is working on paper. I draw people, landscapes, still lives. It is my personal entertainment while waiting at railway stations, etc. Everything I see becomes a source of inspiration and training for seeing form and proportion. Drawing is the basis for everything in art-making. 'Draw, Antonio, draw,' said Michelangelo to his student. Usually I ask the gods of fire to "paint" my ceramic figures; the little tableaux of figures and polished pots get their patina from the sawdust fire. Drawing on pots and plates is more difficult. The three-dimensional form must be combined with the drawn "illusion" of the third dimension. Once, when working with Matthias, he said "Watch out. With maiolica, every finger mark will show." So like a child I put my fingers in the colour pots, and paint cups with my fingertips.'

Thomas Wernecke

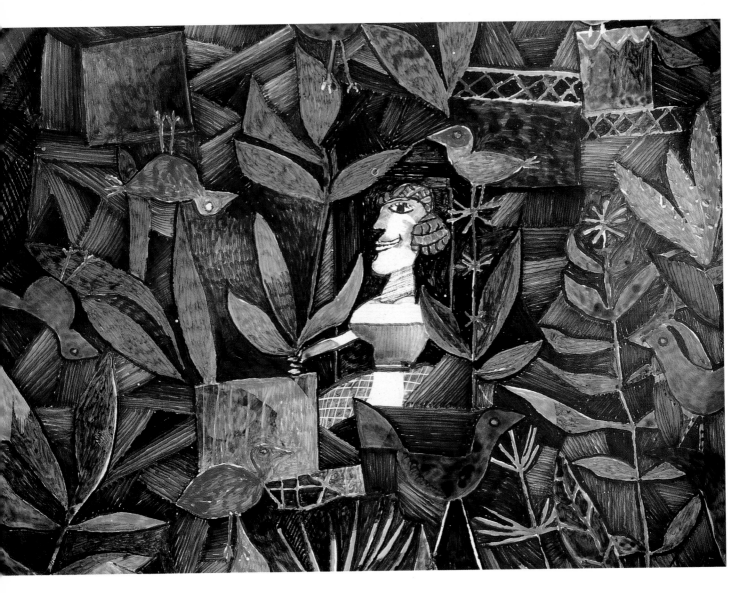

NIORÉ (FRANCE)

PLATE: 'LA SOUPE AUX HERBES SAUVAGES', d. 42 cm, 1997.
This plate was made at the Atelier JMV Fine. Throwing, trimming, and glazing were done by Johann and Vania Fine, the decoration by Nioré. Bisque temperature was 1020°C, and in-glaze painting with metallic oxides was fired to 960°C. Overglaze enamel details have been fired again to 780°C in a slow firing. In this instance, the theme was left entirely up to the artist.

Photograph: Vania Fine, courtesy Atelier JMV Fine

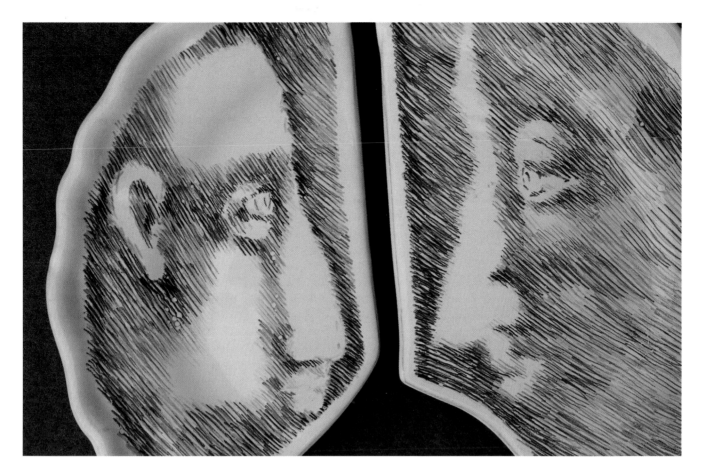

ABOVE: CECCARELLI (FRANCE)

PLATE FRAGMENTS, d. 24 cm, 1997.
Existing terracotta plate fragments were chosen, glazed, and decorated in-glaze using very fine line brushes and few colours, to create a very pencil-like drawing on-surface. The pieces were fired to 960°C.

Photograph: Vania Fine, courtesy Atelier JMV Fine

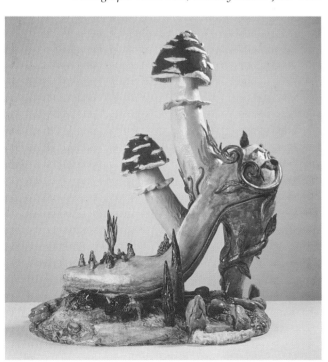

LEFT: MILAN KUNC (GERMANY)

SCULPTURE: 'WILD LIFE', 72 cm x 60 cm x 38 cm, 1995.
This sculpture is entirely hand-modelled, and assembled from red earthenware clay, hollowed out to facilitate drying and firing. Tin glaze is painted with commercial stains, fired to 1040°C, and bright red enamel details are fired to 780°C.

Photograph: Hans van den Bogaard

'I am more of a painter of images on canvas, but find ceramics the ideal medium for sculpture, for its immediate shaping possibilities, and the fact that glaze is the most durable of all colour surfaces. Maiolica in particular is like a watercolour medium, that three dimensionally and colourwise allows me to exercise my fantasy. My aim is to explore it fully as a very contemporary vehicle of expression. "Wild Life" is an icon of the American landscape, complete with high heels, Indians, and buffalo – a blend of myth and pop.'

Milan Kunc

141

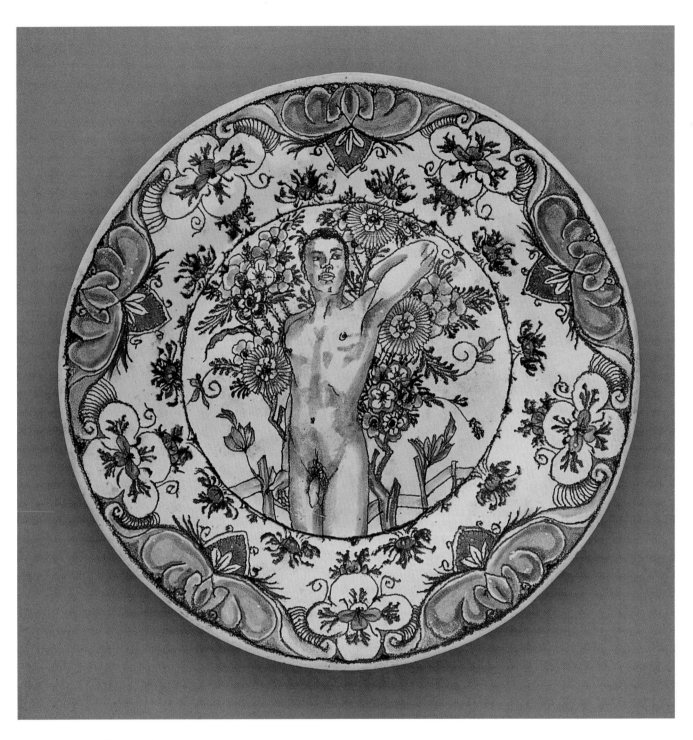

DANIEL KRUGER (GERMANY)

PLATE, d. 33 cm, 1992.

This plate has been drape-moulded and bisqued to 900°C. The tin-opacified glaze has been painted in-glaze with varying graded washes of cobalt carbonate, with added fine outlines. Glaze firing is to 1060°C.

Photograph: Wolfgang Pulfer

'This plate, in a self-consciously naïve way, is a derivation of Dutch delftware, which itself was intended to emulate Chinese porcelain. A familiar pattern serves as a background for a sensual male nude – an image not associated with this kind of decor. Yet seen in the broader context of my work, it is a continuation of the use of traditional forms and patterns. Like their predecessors, my images are poetic, amusing, titillating, or sentimental. They are intended to enrich and give pleasure.'

Daniel Kruger

Beyond maiolica

The works shown here by Kaagman, Parker and Schwarzbach are not, strictly speaking, maiolica. I have included them, however, because I feel their work is strongly related by tradition, technique or inspiration, to maiolica, and pushes its borders in interesting ways.

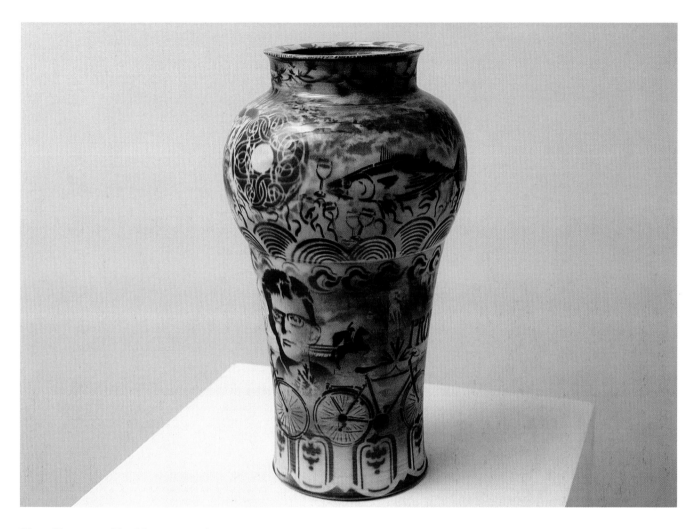

HUGO KAAGMAN (THE NETHERLANDS)

VASE: 'KAAGWARE VASE', h. 80 cm, 1997.

Created at the European Ceramics Work Centre in 's-Hertogenbosch, The Netherlands, this piece is by no means maiolica, but I have included it for its cheeky reinterpretation of Dutch delftware. It is, therefore, very much maiolica-inspired. The buff-coloured greenware was sprayed with a heavy zircon-whitened slip before bisquing to 1120°C. Hand-cut stencils (inspired by and cribbed from magazine illustrations) are used in conjunction with graded tones of cobalt sprayed through a Paasche airbrush onto the slipped bisque surface. The piece is then sprayed with transparent glaze and fired to 1200°C.

Photograph: Hugo Kaagman

'I was a graffiti artist in the 1970s, leaving images in public places and publishing a punk fanzine, using both the spray and stencil-and-collage method. I now do stencilling on canvas and ceramics, using pop images and clichés, blending game-playing and social commentary, piling pattern upon pattern. My pseudo-Delft ceramic work was originally intended as a parody of Dutch culture and all its corny landmarks, but gradually it turned into a romantic image of The Netherlands, with symbols and kitsch features as well. Tribal motifs from the land of the Nether are fixed into one big Dutch party; a pure pattern delight and the power of folklore reinstated into these post-modern times.'

Hugo Kaagman

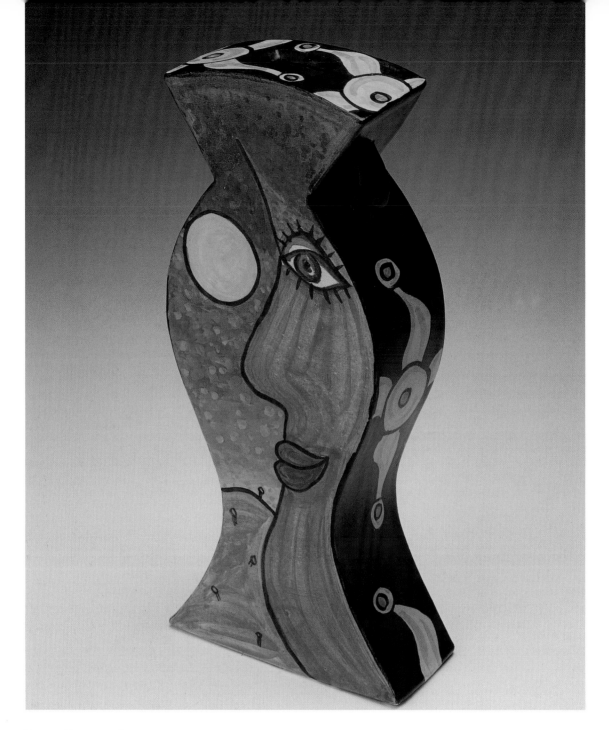

ANDREW PARKER (AUSTRALIA)

VASE FORM: 'SPIRIT OF THE SKY SERIES', h. 28 cm, 1997.

This ware is not true maiolica; it is actually low-fired stoneware, fired in gas oxidation to 1205°C. I have included it for its affinities with maiolica, which lie in the procedures by which it is made, and its colourful narrative. The piece was slab-constructed, glazed with a high-fire, semi-matte tin glaze, using zinc as its major flux. Colours were blended – some were mixed with equal parts frit, clay, and stain; others were mixed just with water – to create varying textures and intensities of colour. The colours were applied using a combination of blending and a Seurat-like, *pointillist* technique.

Photograph: Ian Hobbs

'The process of arriving at cone 6 (1222°C) was one of evolution. After having worked mainly in stoneware through my early potting years – the late 1970s and early 1980s – I dabbled in terracotta slipware, and gained a taste for colour and painting. Fitting slipware into my functional production proved difficult, so I introduced colour to my high-fire work, gradually reducing the temperature to facilitate a broad and bright palette. The imagery generally follows the ups and downs of life. It is personal, but broad and obscure enough as not to be too tacky. I see myself fitting into the long line of people who have told stories on pots.'

Andrew Parker

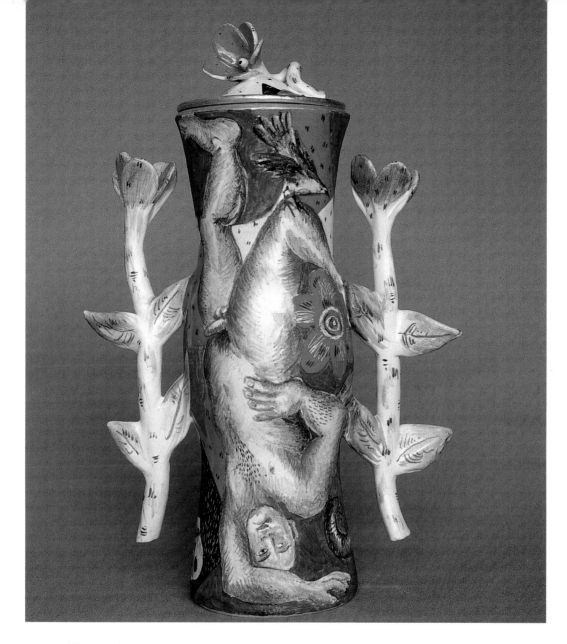

GEORG SCHWARZBACH (GERMANY)

JAR: 'BAROCK' (BAROQUE), h. 47 cm, 1996.

This piece was slab-constructed, with added modelled components, of a cream-coloured mid-range clay body. A silky-matt tin glaze was painted in-glaze using detailed fine-line-contour drawing and background colour fill-in. Black, grey, yellow, blue and brown stains were fired fairly high, to 1150°C. Overglaze enamels of yellow, selenium, red, turquoise and pink were fired to 850°C, and a final, third lustre firing was done at 750°C.

Photograph: Georg Schwarzbach

'Three sources of inspiration enticed me to pursue painted pottery. The first was an art teacher who unveiled the secrets of Delft tile painting to me. The second is one of the most beautiful kitchens in the world in a small castle in Munich whose walls are covered with colourful, baroque, ceramic paintings. The painters of the Blaue Reiter movement, who are very present in Munich with their vivid colour signals, are the third source of inspiration.

In the painting of my vessels I limit myself in my choice of themes to human beings, who expresses their wishes, fears, and yearnings on the vessel walls. The choice of such themes seems inescapable to me, given the close connection which has always existed between humankind and its vessels, both in their practical uses and in their transcendental meanings.

Formally, I see the contour of the vessel as a fundamental design factor. The edge of the vessel functions as a very expressive, clear line, which serves as a border between the object and its environment. I attach great importance to the spontaneity of this line within the painting.'

Georg Schwarzbach

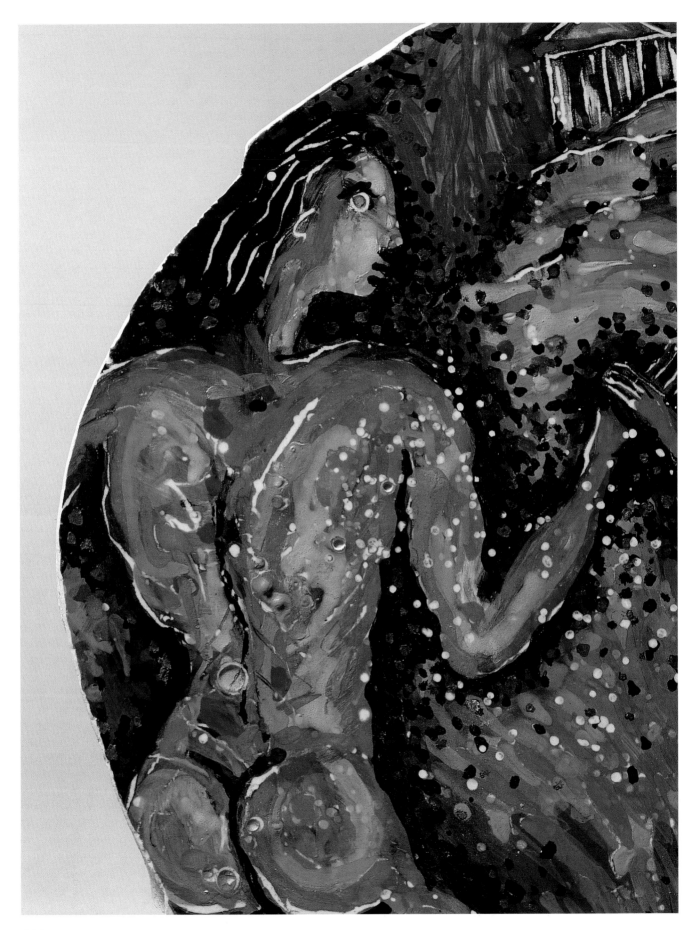

146

CHAPTER EIGHT

Troubleshooting

'The reward for being a good problem-solver is to be heaped with more and more difficult problems to be solved.'

R. BUCKMINSTER FULLER

'The most important thing to do in solving a problem is to begin.'

FRANK TYGER

I once heard someone describe the medium of tin glaze as the prima donna of all ceramics – high-pitched, difficult and exacting. I am inclined to agree. I come from a stoneware background, where crazing can be called *craclé* and throwing marks, varying glaze thickness, and glaze drips are the visible legacy of the making process, and hence attributes, not flaws. Not so with maiolica. For example, my first kiln-load of tin glaze came as a major revelation. My colours and brushwork, although faulty, were lively enough to excite me. However, the *dénouement*

LARGE PLATTER SHARD

This shard is a fortunate example of a piece exhibiting four major flaws, and an unfortunate one as regards possible sales. The left outer edge is a dunt line, where the rim of the platter cracked away because of poor construction. Large visible broken blisters indicate too-rapid cooling of the glaze, white spots indicate an insufficiently cleared bisque, and rough colour patches indicate too little frit in the colour mix. We live and learn.

came when I turned over the pieces and every drip, smudge and fingerprint was most painfully apparent, and certainly did not contribute positively to the work.

Since the field of ceramics is so diverse, and there are so many different aesthetic languages to be considered, I do not believe that there can be too much dogma about what is considered faulty in a work. Aesthetic judgments are very personal, and often cultural. Coming from a German background, I have in general shied away from tight, linear, controlled 'Bauhausian' forms in favour of looser, softer, oriental-type work. Asked once to judge a show of bowls for a local potters' group, I disappointed everyone enormously by picking out the most crooked and undulating pots. Obviously my standards were different from my hosts'.

Yet today, working in tin glaze, I am conscious of a need to create very controlled shapes to accommodate my painting. Where the visual language of wood fire speaks of visible making process and incorporating unforeseen fired effects, maiolica speaks a different language. It is about drawing and painting and controlled surface effects. Here throwing marks, or glaze irregularities, might well be considered undesirable.

Problems

I find that most problems that occur in the studio can be classified into two types: those that arise from actual incompatibility of materials and their misapplication, and those that result from simple

147

carelessness. Resulting flaws can be certainly seen as failings in technique, but their resolution sometimes can go well beyond rectification and lead to new technique. For example, I was once firing a load for a show deadline (at the last minute, of course). Going through a rather difficult emotional period at the time, I found myself in a state of some distraction. I arrive at the studio, find the kiln nicely warmed, turn it up to full power, and three hours later am wide awake to the fact that the kiln had not been pre-heating, but was in fact cooling from the last firing (which I had forgotten). It was now in the advanced process of a second glaze-firing, with all cones flat and out of sight. I sat beside the kiln for several hours with a bottle, trying to judge the colour of heat by eye (pretending to be a Japanese master potter), and finally when the tension became unbearable, shutting the kiln off and going to bed. For three days (*very* close to deadline) I waffled, and finally opened the kiln. It was one of the best ever, having refired to just below its normal temperature, and thickly applied stains had come up to an almost lustre-like surface. The show arrived in time and was a success. So, out of extreme carelessness and inattention, came a new firing technique.

Some problems can be the result of faulty materials, but this is fairly rare in my experience. Most problems can be resolved through analysis and re-testing, and a tightening up of habits and procedures. For the prima donna, this is especially true. *La Maiolica* demands great care in application and cleanliness in handling. When all care has been taken in the making, bisquing, glazing, painting, and glaze-firing, then the results are indeed worth it, but there are absolutely no short cuts. I have listed below my own repertoire of problems and their solutions, but it is to be remembered that all of these occur in the context of electric firing, and there are surely some that are outside my range of experience. For problems applying to reduction firing, or any other more specialised areas of technique, I highly recommend the book of Frank and Janet Hamer, as well as that of Harry Fraser.

1. Crazing

The most serious flaws in ceramics are those that have to do with clay-to-glaze fit; that is, with the ability of clay and glaze to contract more or less together when cooling after firing, and when heated and cooled in use. Craze lines throughout the glaze are the manifestation of a glaze too tight for the body, hence literally splitting, as would a too-tight garment. In some ceramic traditions, such as raku, crazing is in fact encouraged and enhanced as a special visual attribute. The problem of water seepage through a crazed glaze becomes irrelevant at high temperatures, since the body is fully vitrified in itself. However, at earthenware temperatures, especially for tableware, crazing might be considered a problem if too radical, since the body is rarely fully vitrified, and water seepage might occur. Most earthenware will craze in time, and I personally tend not to be too fussed by it. Sometimes concerns about hygiene are raised, but compared to breathing diesel fumes, handling money and door knobs, and using public toilet seats, eating or drinking from crazed pottery does not register highly on my worry index. However, for severe immediate crazing, indicating a fit problem, the answer might be to glaze a little more thinly, and/or to make an adjustment to the glaze recipe, slightly decreasing the relative amount of some of the higher-expansion materials such as frits and spars, and/or increasing the relative amount of some of the lower-expansion materials such as silica, whiting and clay. (Or, more precisely, decreasing the relative amounts of higher expansion oxides, such as potassium and sodium, and increasing the relative amounts of lower expansion oxides such as silica, boron and alumina.)

The more common crazing problem in tin glaze (and earthenware in general) is a long-term one, caused by moisture seeping into the exposed clay areas of a slightly porous body, causing it to expand and craze the glaze. One terracotta body I was using manifested this problem only during a hot, humid summer; suddenly my pots were an orchestra of pinging sounds – not my favourite music – for weeks on end. The answer here might be what commercial-industrial earthenware potteries do: fire the bisque to vitrification (i.e., over 1100°C), and then the glaze below that (say 1000°C and over). I am unwilling to accept some of the decorating technique strictures a higher-fired, non-porous bisque imposes (See Problem 7, 'Dull Surface colour'). Another solution might be to use a high-talc body, which will resist rehydration, although most such bodies tend to be more suitable for slip-casting than for other techniques.

I tend not to wax the bottoms of pots before glazing, but rather to scrape and sponge them afterwards, leaving a thin, glaze-water residue on the bottom which helps so seal the piece, but will not adhere to the kiln shelf. Some potters I know will use the ancient Greek *terra sigillata* technique (using a thin, deflocculated slip-mixture applied to leather-hard clay and highly polished before the bisque). This will sometimes help to seal exposed clay areas, and can make an interesting contrast to the tin glaze. Finally, some crazing in time can be avoided in an object being used by simply not subjecting it to repeated extreme thermal shock. Few pots will withstand the transition from freezer to hot oven.

2. *Peeling or shivering*
This, to me, is one of the nastier and least reconcilable of glaze problems. Again, it is a clay/glaze fit problem, basically the reverse of crazing. The glaze is under too much compression; that is to say the body contracts more during cooling than does the glaze. The glaze winds up 'bigger' than the body and will chip and peel off, or even crack the ware. This happens particularly along the rims and edges of a piece, where the glaze will lift off in slivers or leave a sharp, overlapping glaze crack line. There are a number of solutions to this problem. Wares could be glazed more thinly, with special attention paid to over-thick glazing on rims. Sometimes over-sponged rims on more sandy clay bodies can also prevent glaze adherence and cause peeling later. A slight lowering of the glaze temperature might help as well. Once, in order to solve a crazing problem, I gradually pushed up my temperature by three cones, only to find the rims of pieces starting to peel. I moved back down two cones, and both problems were solved – that was obviously my ideal temperature, where neither crazing nor shivering occurred. (You will be happy to know that the two are unlikely to occur on the same piece at the same time, God forbid.) Temperature change is not always an option, so it is still best to adjust the glaze for a better clay/glaze fit. By partially or fully replacing the existing frit with a similar, higher-expansion frit, and in general slightly

increasing the proportion of higher-expansion materials, the problem will generally be resolved (or, more precisely, by increasing the amount of higher expansion oxides such as potassium and sodium relative to the amount of lower expansion oxides such as silica, boron and alumina.) Design of a piece can also be a factor. I have rarely had large, round pieces peel, where the shape itself seems to evenly distribute any compression stress. Oval and rectangular pieces seem to be more prone, perhaps because of uneven lateral shrinkage.

3. *Dunting*
This is perhaps the most devastating problem. A dunted piece is pretty much irretrievable. Dunting is the actual cracking apart of a piece, body and glaze, due to extreme thermal shock. This usually occurs at the cooling stage in the kiln (where the piece can crack with a sound like a shot or, worse yet, on the shelf days later). It can also occur when the piece is subjected to thermal shock during use, such as being filled with boiling water. The causes of dunting are several. To begin with, small invisible cracks or flaws in the bisque will cause further cracking later on. The bisque should simply be examined or sounded for clarity of ring before glazing, and discarded if flawed. The main reasons for dunting are either (as for peeling) an over-compressed glaze which, on cooling does not contract as much as the body, or major structural problems in the piece itself making it susceptible to cracking when exposed to thermal shock (or both).

Some of these structural problems might be thin wall or bottom sections with thickly pooled glaze, sharp-angled corners with different wall-section thickness, poorly sealed joints or rough-edged holes and openings, too wide and flat a base, too thick a glaze coating in general, and incompatible differing glazes inside and outside the same piece. If any or all of the above are present in conjunction with an already over-compressed low-expansion glaze, and above all, if the kiln cools too rapidly, then dunting is likely to occur.

Some solutions are as follows: as with peeling, lowering the temperature, and substituting higher expansion frit in the glaze might help; or better yet, reformulating the glaze to raise its general expansion by slightly increasing the proportion of higher-expansion frits and spars relative to the lower-expansion materials such as silica, clay and whiting. Slow and controlled firing, and cooling, of the kiln is also essential. Attention paid to even-walled construction of a piece, avoiding too-sharp angles and wide, thin bottoms, as well as even and not-too-thick glazing, can all help to avoid dunting. Large wide platters and bowls with or without feet, especially if made from dense smooth bodies, are more susceptible to dunting. I tend to fire these slightly raised on shards of tile, or low supports, to raise them off the kiln shelves and promote more even heating, and controlled cooling. To further minimise cooling stress, I try also to avoid leaving large unglazed areas on the bottoms of wide, shallow pieces, and make sturdy foot rings where possible, attaching them to as soft a shape as possible for best possible adherence.

4. White spots and pinholes

This is perhaps the most classic maiolica problem, and can occur for several reasons, of which the most common is insufficiently cleared bisque. If the clay body is not sufficiently cleared during bisquing it will continue to clear during the glaze firing. The organics burn out of clay at temperatures between 700°C and 900°C. It is imperative to go slow during this period and have enough free oxygen in the kiln to oxidise the carbon and sulphur. The recommended speed of firing during this phase (an increase of no more 100°C per hour is usually slow enough) will depend on how well-insulated the kiln is, whether there is a positive ventilation system, and how tightly the kiln is stacked. It also depends on how much impurity there is in the clay to be burned off. I've found that darker iron-bearing clay bodies require more attention in this regard than lighter ones.

If the bisque kiln is insufficiently cleared, gases will escape upward through the glaze during firing and where this might remain invisible in a transparent glaze, with tin glaze the more refractory on-surface layer of colour does not quite seal, and a small white spot remains. To allow the clay body to clear well, raise the bisque temperature a little, fire slowly, and/or prolong the bisque firing for up to an hour at its final temperature. Spy holes should be left open for good ventilation.

Rough surface is another cause of white spots. Often those clay bodies that are less fine, and contain a percentage of fire clay or grog, will be prone to white spots and pinholing, especially on trimmed surfaces where rough particles have been dragged away, exposing small holes. Here my solution is to trim fairly wet, and to seal the surface well with finger or rib after trimming. Sometimes a thin wash of clay slurry or white slip will serve to seal a rough surface.

Finally, white spots can disturb colour work in areas where two coats of glaze have overlapped during glazing. It may be that air trapped between the layers is escaping to the surface. I am usually careful to glaze without double-dipping and overlap marks, but if it is unavoidable, I try to relegate them to areas that will not be coloured. A pressured, dry rubbing down of the overlap glaze area with a finger tends to solve the problem.

5. Blistering

A mild case of too-rapid glaze firing and cooling can also cause white spots, but a severe case will manifest itself in larger blisters and craters. If the glaze has been fired too quickly towards the end of the cycle, and the kiln has a tendency to cool rapidly (as most smaller top-loading kilns do), then the over-active glaze does not have time to melt and even out, and small bubbles and craters stay frozen, so to speak. The answer here is to reach temperature slowly and to then soak the kiln for an hour or so at its final temperature, to allow the glaze to even out. Over-firing can also cause blistering and cratering, and that of course is solved by lowering the glaze temperature. Refiring can be an option here. Usually I prefer not to spend time making corrections on a piece, but if it already was very labour-intensive and has merit of character, then I sometimes will make a salvage effort. On one particular important piece, I sanded down literally over a hundred blisters and craters and filled them with thick, paste-like colour/frit mixtures (feeling very much like Georges Seurat, the *pointillist* painter). The piece was carefully refired at a slightly lower temperature, and emerged perfectly smooth, and with more character than before.

I also sometimes find blisters occurring in those areas where coloured stains are too thickly applied, or overlap, particularly at the end of a brush stroke. This can be due sometimes to an excessively refractory material (i.e., rutile) requiring a bit more frit to help it flux. I usually just cast an eye over a piece that has been heavily painted, and will lightly press down or smudge any spot that looks too thick. It is rarely a problem with those pieces where on-surface blending has been done with stiff-bristled brushes, and surface stains evenly distributed.

6. *Crawling*

The visible sign of crawling is glaze pulling away in patches after the firing, exposing areas of clay body. There are a number of reasons for glazes to crawl. I have encountered four. The first is standard: unclean bisque. If the bisque ware is dusty or greasy (you have unloaded the kiln after waxing, or eating a peanut butter sandwich) glaze will not adhere properly and will crawl later. The answer is to dust your bisque well, and handle it with clean hands.

The second reason is too-thick glazing. If the glaze on drying starts to crack, it is too thick and might also crawl. Cracks should be smoothed over, or the piece glazed a little more thinly. There are also binders that can be added to glazes to make them tougher and prevent the cracking that leads to crawling. A good way to improve this kind of glaze would be to add one to two percent of bentonite to it.

Thirdly, firing a damp-glazed and decorated piece too soon and too quickly can cause steam to escape which in turn can lift off the glaze and result in crawling. Work should be allowed to dry completely before firing, and pre-heated slowly.

The final reason for crawling that I have encountered has to do with over-fired bisque. Sometimes an over-saturated area of glaze has lifted after painting, like a shallow bubble, and gone unremarked. The too-hard bisque is unable to absorb water from brushwork, and the area will later not settle back down and adhere again, especially on a vertical surface, but will become a crawl mark. The solution here is to lightly rub and press the glaze back down when dry (if the colour work will allow), to keep the bisque temperature lower if possible, or to be extremely cautious in the use of water during brushwork if the bisque ware is not very porous.

7. *Dull surface colours*

I find that there are several reasons for colours appearing dull and lacking intensity after the fire. The main one has to do with the colour being applied to a piece not entirely dried after glazing. In the normal course of events, water from brushwork during painting is absorbed by the bisque below, allowing the colour to be deposited on top of the glaze with each stroke. If the clay body and glaze are still damp, then brushwork water is being repelled by the body, not absorbed, and the glaze is stirred up into the colour mixture. The opacifier in the glaze will then dim the colour. Overworking, and hence oversaturating, any one area will also have the same effect, as will too thin a coating of glaze. The solution is simply to let work dry overnight after glazing (or force-dry it), and to make sure that the glaze coating is thick enough to absorb water during brushwork. In tin glaze, in order to avoid later crazing, the bisque temperature is often fired higher than the final glaze temperature. This makes for a very non-porous bisque which will be slow to dry when glazed, and quick to repel water when being decorated. In this case water must be applied quickly and sparingly during painting, and each colour application must be allowed to dry before working over the same area again, making for a more lengthy decoration process in progressive stages. In my case, since I do a lot of spontaneous, layered wet-blending, I have instead chosen a clay body that when bisqued just less than one cone below glaze temperature still remains a little porous. When glaze-fired, it vitrifies just enough to avoid the crazing problem.

A further reason for dullness of colour can be the use of a dark terracotta body under a thin, under-opacified glaze. It's very much the difference between water-colour painting on brown or white paper – the whiter the ground, the brighter the colour. This could also be a particular aesthetic choice.

Yet another cause of colour dullness might be in the materials that comprise the glaze itself, and again, this could be a matter of choice, an attribute rather than a flaw. I have found, for example, when tin oxide is used extensively as the opacifier, the colours tend to be more in the opaque pastel range. A weak and watery colour mixture will also engender more subdued and transparent-appearing colours. This is usually due to inattention; colour mixtures tend to settle quickly, and should be frequently stirred while painting.

Finally, some colour stains have a very specific temperature range, and lose intensity the higher you fire. Some of the carbonate colours (i.e., cobalt and copper) are colour-stable right into the porcelain range. Reds and mauves, however tend to 'brown out', and become dull if over-fired. Here again, I might choose to sacrifice the clay-glaze durability provided by a higher temperature in exchange for a more brilliant lower-range palette of colour. I try to aim for both as much as possible.

8. Blurred surface colours

These are usually due to over-firing or a too-fluid glaze, and the consequent shift of colours on a glaze surface that was moved too much beneath the applied colour. It is best to conceive a glaze recipe that is not too heat-sensitive in general, and in particular, from one level of the kiln to the next. The answer here is a modified glaze recipe and/or better kiln control. Some oxides promote running – in this case, movement of the glaze itself, or of the medium the stain is mixed with. Making a glaze stiffer by adding alumina will stop the movement if enough is added. Take the glaze recipe and continue to add small increments of clay (kaolin and ball), up to about three percent, and test on vertical tiles with your usual colours until, when the blurring stops, you have the answer. Too much frit in the colour mixture can also cause blurring as the mixture becomes overfluxed.

9. Dry surface colours

As mentioned in Chapter Four, the colour-stain-to-frit ratio in a given mixture will determine surface gloss. Too little, or no frit can result in matt to dry surfaces, depending on that ratio (50:50, again, being my standard). Some stains require more frit, some less. Too thick an application of colour can also cause dryness (and blisters) and general under-firing of the kiln will result in matt or dry surfaces as well. Often a medium-dry thick wash of a frit-and-water mixture, applied over the too-dry fired surface, and then refired a third time, will save the piece.

10. Reglazing of bisque ware

As mentioned earlier, I rarely attempt to repair bungled work. However, sometimes the decoration on a well-made piece has not worked, and I want to reglaze the bisque. For some reason, I cannot simply scrub down the piece, dry it and reglaze. The glaze will not take the second time around, and looks pitted and wrinkled. The piece needs to be washed very thoroughly, dried and re-bisqued – and then it can be reglazed.

11. Waxing problems

I have found in some instances that waxing of wide, flat bottoms can be problematic. The wax appears to seep under the glaze, and after firing the glaze has pulled and curled away, leaving sharp edges. The problem is probably due to a too-thin mixture of wax spreading too widely on a very porous clay body. As mentioned in Chapter Three, I prefer scraping and wiping to waxing, for the extra glaze and water seal of the exposed clay body. For wax-decoration problems, see section 11 of Chapter 6.

Safety

There are two main concerns about health and safety in using ceramics materials.

The first is the risk to the maker of breathing or swallowing dangerous materials. Of these, the most hazardous are silica, followed by those light earthenware clays which contain very high proportions of free silica in the form of fine dust. If inhaled in sufficient quantity, these can cause serious lung damage. Also dangerous if ingested are most of the ceramic colour stains in powder form. I think most ceramists are probably a little bit cavalier about precautions and might consider the wearing of an industrial dust mask during any mixing and handling process as adequate. But beyond that, I think that habitual and regular cleaning is also important, since the perpetual fine dust under foot and floating about when masks are not worn can also cause damage, especially over years of exposure. For instance, I am probably more highly at risk in this regard, working in an almost hermetically sealed, dry space during the long Canadian winters. In more moderate climates, open windows and overall humidity will make the dust risk less problematic.

General precautions for reducing risk include wearing an industrial mask while doing any dust-generating work such as dry-clay work and general mixing of dry materials. Frequent washing or wiping of floors and work surfaces on which glaze or dust has spilled will also help to keep things under control. Avoid sweeping and vacuuming. Washing hands before eating, changing and washing work clothes often, and finally, keeping all dry materials in well-sealed containers will further help to minimise risks.

Good kiln ventilation is also important, especially with electric kilns, harmful fumes of which tend to linger in the room, rather than escape up the chimney as they would in a fuel-fired kiln. Some system should be provided to extract such emissions, such as a positive kiln vent or, at the very least, good cross-ventilation of the kiln area to the outside.

The second hazard to consider is that incurred by the consumer in using objects glazed with unsafe glazes. The toxicity of metals released from some kinds of glazes can make food-serving wares a risk, especially wares used to store acidic or alkaline foods, depending on the glaze deficiency. Higher-temperature glazes are more resistant to acid attack and metal release, but over-glaze enamels, and low-fire glazes (especially those, such as maiolica, with on-surface decoration) can be risky if certain materials are involved. Some of these materials are: cadmium- and antimony-based pigments, as well as zinc, nickel oxide, vanadium, chrome and lithium. Considered also unsafe are such glaze ingredients as unfritted and fritted lead, unfritted borax, and barium carbonate. In fact, the use of lead or cadmium in conjunction with food-serving glazes has been banned in North America and other countries. Copper compounds used in conjunction with lead glazes can be a problem, even if these glazes are to be used only on non-functional work. The copper and lead volatilise together in the firing and can contaminate any other glaze surfaces in the kiln. A protective option might be to give a light covering spray of non-toxic transparent glaze to the painted surface before glaze firing.

There are international guidelines and regulations governing metal release in glazes, and most commercial glazes for domestic tableware are designed to be safe. However, if there is any doubt about materials fired at a specific temperature and their subsequent use in serving food, advice from the ceramic supplier or a metal-release testing facility should be considered. Glazes with known toxins should be kept away from food-serving surfaces, and wares with such glazes should be permanently identified as unsuitable for serving food.

Conclusion

To conclude this chapter, I would have to say that good habits and systematic procedure are keynotes to the success of any work. There also needs to be the right working frame of mind, that even under occasional pressure, can direct the complex and skilful manipulations a particular process might demand. If operation is smooth and all things have been done attentively and correctly, most problems can be avoided.

However, problem-solving, sticky and unwelcome as it might be, has to be embraced. It has to do not only with technical resolution, but also with making aesthetic choices and juggling options. We are walking the fine line between crazing and shivering, over- and under-fired bisque, thick or thin glaze, bright or dim colours, higher or lower glaze temperature – all of these choices, hopefully, contributing to well-made and visually coherent work. I have said much earlier on that technical virtuosity for its own sake can leave me cold – I want to be talked to and engaged.

I feel that ideally the maker should not be at the mercy of her/his materials and processes, but have enough control to be able to make specific choices. At the same time, the necessity for the work to hold together as a permanent object with a specific function, be it practical or cerebral, should most certainly be respected. Neither should lack of technique nor of vision parade too boldly as 'free expression'. Real maturity and character are usually immediately visible in any given work, and imply a fair degree of technical control and well-resolved ideas.

A Final Word

The aspect of this profession that I find most satisfying is the balancing and integrating of diverse skills and states of mind into a coherent whole. I am not only referring to the ceramic product, but to a general sense of mental and spiritual well-being which flows from my practice of, and identification with, a time-honored tradition and community. I suspect that most people are not entirely happy with the work they do. Surely this must lead to a great deal of frustration, and uninspired or mediocre work. As a ceramist I find that despite any frustrations (and at times there are quite a few) the many varied making-skills and mental approaches that this job demands provide a simple kind of sanity that is constantly revitalising, and often helps to keep me on an even keel. I have always attempted to avoid water-tight compartments in my life, and have tried to allow events and learning experiences to interrelate and lead me forward. Lessons learned from the clay and its handling can be applied to other areas of life. As I get older, I look less for excitement and novelty and more for those kinds of learning experiences, and perhaps also a well-earned, more comfortable road.

Although the final products we make are important in terms of personal achievement, there is to me also something very important about the ritual and pleasure of gesture, which can soothe and gratify the maker, as well as contribute to a finished work. That gratification is no doubt why most of us are involved in this work. The bonus is that the final object can make known that intimacy of gesture and process, and there can be a further identification between maker and viewer on that level. Ceramics as a medium of expression is particularly revelatory in that regard: tightness, looseness, whimsy, serenity, rawness – all these attributes remain forever held in the fired clay, to reveal the maker and intrigue the viewer.

LANA'S GARDEN, IRELAND. MY HOME-AWAY-FROM-HOME

Photograph: Matthias Ostermann

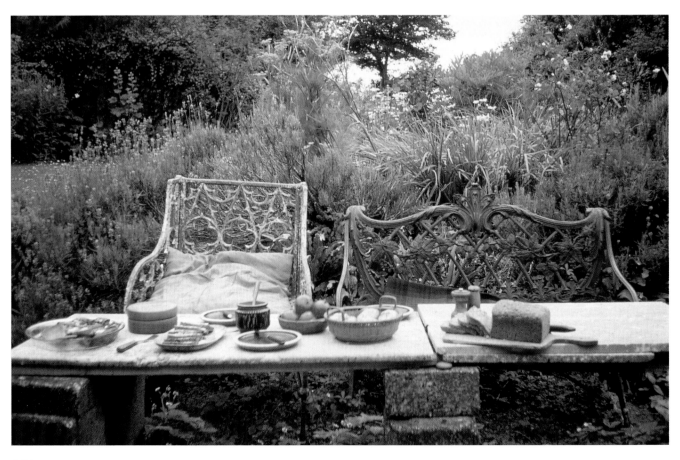

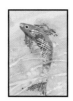

Recommended Reading

Historical and general

Caiger-Smith, Alan, *Lustre Pottery; Technique, Tradition and Innovation in Islam and the Western World* (Faber and Faber, 1985).

Caiger-Smith, Alan, *Tin Glaze Pottery in Europe and the Islamic World* (Faber and Faber, 1973).

Carnegy, Daphne, *Tin-Glazed Earthenware* (A & C Black; Chilton; Craftsman House, 1993).

Hess, Catherine, *Italian Maiolica* (Catalogue of the J. Paul Getty Museum collection, 1988)

Poole, Julia E, *Italian Maiolica* (Cambridge University Press, 1997).

Wilson, Timothy, *Ceramic Art of the Italian Renaissance* (British Museum Press, 1987).

Technical and practical

Constant, Christine and Steven Ogden, *The Potter's Pocket Palette* (Apple Press, 1996).

Fraser, Harry, *Ceramic Faults and Their Remedies* (A & C Black, 1986).

Gibson, John, *Pottery Decoration* (A & C Black; Overlook Press; Craftsman House, 1987).

Hamer, Frank and Janet Hamer, *The Potter's Dictionary of Materials and Techniques*, 4th edition (A & C Black; University of Pennsylvania Press; Craftsman House, 1999).

Hinchcliffe, John and Wendy Barber, *Ceramic Style: Making and Decorating Patterned Ceramic Ware* (Angus & Robertson, 1994).

Rhodes, Daniel, *Clay and Glazes for the Potter,* 2nd edition (A & C Black; Chilton,1973).

Philosophical and aesthetic

Flam, Jack D., *Matisse on Art* (E. P. Dutton, 1978).

Forestier, Sylvie and Meret Meyer, *Les céramiques de Chagall* (Michel Albin, 1990).

Itten, Johanes, *The Art of Colour* (Van Nostrand Reinhold, 1973).

Larson, Ronald, *A Potter's Companion* (Park Street Press, 1993).

Leach, Bernard, *Hamada, Potter* (Kodansha International, 1979).

Paz, Octavio, *Alternating Current* (Arcade Publishing, 1990).

Ramie, Georges, *Picasso's Ceramics* (Chartwell Books, 1974).

Theroux, Alexander, *The Primary Colours* (Papermac, 1996).

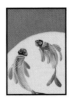

Appendix:
Technical Information on Glazes

Pottery glazes, like other kinds of glass, are formed by the cooling of a melt of earthy raw materials. The most important of these is silica, the material which forms the main body of the glaze. Other materials used include fluxes, materials such as soda and lime, which cause the mixture to melt by lowering its melting point. To make pottery glazes viscous, so that they stick to a surface rather than running off during firing, alumina must be present.

The components of the raw materials contribute to a glaze in the form of oxides, combinations of chemical elements with oxygen. It is important to distinguish between the raw materials, such as Whiting or Cornwall stone, which make up the glaze batch, and the oxides, derived from these raw materials, that are combined in the finished glaze. One raw material can yield several different oxides; and one oxide can be derived from several different raw materials.

A glaze recipe gives the relative dry weights of unfired, raw materials in a glaze.

A **glaze analysis** gives the relative weight of the various oxides found (typically, or specifically) as a percentage of the total weight of all the oxides combined in a fired glaze.

To calculate how much of some raw material to use as a substitute for another material listed in a recipe but not locally available, it is necessary to know **glaze formulae**, in which glaze composition is expressed in terms of the relative numbers of molecules of each oxide present in the fired glaze. The convention in ceramics is to use the **Seger molecular unity formula**, which requires that the numbers representing the relative quantities of molecules present be adjusted so that the sum of the numbers for those oxides that act as melters or fluxes in the finished glaze add up to one. In the tables below, such oxides are indicated by an asterisk. (These numbers are determined by first multiplying the percentage composition of each oxide in a glaze by that oxide's molecular weight, giving so-called molecular equivalent numbers for each oxide, and then dividing each such number by the sum of the molecular equivalents for the fluxes so that the resulting numbers for the fluxes will sum to one.)

The **ratio** of the number of molecules of silica (SiO_2) to the number of molecules of alumina (Al_2O) in a glaze formula predicts the nature of the glaze surface as follows: less than 5 – matt; 5 to 10 – semi-matt; greater than 10 – shiny or even transparent. (Added colours and opacifiers, and their effects, have been excluded in this prediction.) When fired, most solids lose some mass in the form of vapour. Clays, for example, become some 10% lighter. In the analyses that follow, such loss is accounted for in the loss on ignition (LOI).

For more detailed information on these matters, see the books by Frank and Janet Hamer and by Daniel Rhodes.

Typical analyses of clays and glaze materials

Ferro frit 3124

Oxides	%
SiO_2	56.8
CaO	14.5
B_2O_3	12.5
Al_2O_3	10.0
Na_2O	5.6
K_2O	0.6
Total	**100.0**

Ferro frit 3195

Oxides	%
SiO_2	47.4
B_2O_3	23.0
Al_2O_3	12.4
CaO	11.2
Na_2O	6.0
Total	**100.0**

Bell dark *(ball clay)*

Oxides	%
SiO_2	58.3
Al_2O_3	27.7
TiO_2	1.5
Fe_2O_3	1.0
K_2O	0.4
CaO	0.3
MgO	0.2
Na_2O	0.1
Subtotal	*89.5*
LOI	10.5
Total	**100.0**

EPK clay *(Edgar plastic kaolin)*

Oxides	%
SiO_2	45.35
Al_2O_3	36.87
Fe_2O_3	0.68
K_2O	0.39
TiO_2	0.30
CaO	0.13
MgO	0.12
P_2O_5	0.12
Na_2O	0.04
Subtotal	*84.00*
LOI	14.42
Total	**98.42**

Kona F4 feldspar *(a soda feldspar)*

Oxides	%
SiO_2	66.75
Al_2O_3	19.60
Na_2O	6.90
K_2O	4.80
CaO	1.70
Fe_2O_3	0.05
Subtotal	*99.80*
LOI	0.20
Total	**100.0**

Nepheline syenite

Oxides	%
SiO_2	60.70
Al_2O_3	23.30
Na_2O	9.80
K_2O	4.60
MgO	0.10
Fe_2O_3	0.07
CaO	0.07
Subtotal	*99.27*
LOI	0.70
Total	**99.97**

Nepheline syenite is similar to a soda feldspar but has a lower melting point. It is one of the few materials without free silica.

Whiting (*calcium carbonate*)

Oxides	%
CaO	55.10
SiO_2	0.20
Fe_2O_3	0.10
MgO	0.10
Subtotal	**55.65**
LOI	44.35
Total	**100.00**

Not all calcium carbonate is the same. Make sure you get an up-to-date analysis for the brand you are using from your supplier.

Formulae and analyses of glazes

Maiolica Glaze no.1 / Orton large cone 05 (1046°C)

Oxides	Relative numbers of molecules	% by weight
*CaO	.71	10.98
*MgO	.00	.04
*K_2O	.02	.48
*Na_2O	.27	4.52
Fe_2O_3	.00	.12
TiO_2	.01	.12
B_2O_3	.57	10.84
Al_2O_3	.42	11.66
SiO_2	3.27	53.85
P_2O_5	.00	.01
ZrO_2	.22	7.37

Ratio (SiO_2 : Al_2O_3) = 7.85
[Ratio (SiO_2 : Al_2O_3) excluding Zircopax = 7.28]

Maiolica Glaze no. 2 / Orton large cone 1-2 (1154°C -1162°C)

*Oxides	Relative numbers of molecules	%, by weight
*CaO	.73	10.85
*MgO	.00	.04
*K_2O	.02	.52
*Na_2O	.25	4.06
Fe_2O_3	.00	.17
TiO_2	.01	.17
B_2O_3	.48	8.81
Al_2O_3	.46	12.46
SiO_2	3.48	55.46
P_2O_5	.00	.01
ZrO_2	.23	7.45

Ratio (SiO_2 : Al_2O_3) = 7.57
[Ratio (SiO_2 : Al_2O_3) excluding Zircopax = 7.03]

Matt Maiolica Glaze no. 3 / Orton large 05 (1046°C)

Oxides	Relative numbers of molecules	%, by weight
*CaO	.69	11.11
*MgO	.00	.02
*K_2O	.03	.94
*Na_2O	.27	4.75
Fe_2O_3	.00	.06
TiO_2	.00	.02
B_2O_3	.43	8.45
Al_2O_3	.37	10.64
SiO_2	3.43	58.64
P_2O_5	.00	.01
ZrO_2	.15	5.37

Ratio (SiO_2 : Al_2O_3) = 9.37
[Ratio (SiO_2 : Al_2O_3) excluding Zircopax = 8.92]

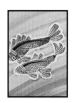

Index